THE DOCTOR'S WEALTH PROTECTION GUIDE

DAVID B. MANDELL, J.D., M.B.A.
ARNOLD S. GOLDSTEIN, LL.M., PH.D.
WITH
CHRISTOPHER R. JARVIS, M.B.A., R.I.A.

THE DOCTOR'S WEALTH PROTECTION GUIDE:
How To Shield Your Practice, Property and Savings From Lawsuits and Other Creditor Threats

*By David B. Mandell, J.D., M.B.A., Arnold S. Goldstein, J.D., LL.M., Ph.D.,
and Christopher R. Jarvis, M.B.A., R.I.A.*
© 1999 Guardian Publishing

Guardian Publishing LLC
269 S. Beverly Drive, Suite #810
Beverly Hills, CA 90212
Tel: (800) 554-7233   Fax: (310) 208-7506

All rights reserved. No parts of this publication may be reproduced or transmitted in any form or by any means, electronic or mechanical, including photocopy, recording or any information storage or retrieval system now known or to be invented without permission in writing from the publisher, except by a reviewer who wishes to quote brief passages in connection with a review for inclusion in a magazine, newspaper or broadcast. Requests for permission should be addressed to the publisher.

THIS PUBLICATION IS DESIGNED TO PROVIDE ACCURATE AND AUTHORITATIVE INFORMATION IN REGARD TO THE SUBJECT MATTER COVERED. IT IS SOLD WITH THE UNDERSTANDING THAT THE PUBLISHER IS NOT ENGAGED IN RENDERING LEGAL, ACCOUNTING, OR OTHER PROFESSIONAL SERVICES. IF LEGAL ADVICE OR OTHER EXPERT ASSISTANCE IS REQUIRED, THE SERVICE OF A COMPETENT PROFESSIONAL PERSON SHOULD BE SOUGHT.
—From a Declaration of Principles jointly adopted by a Committee of the American Bar Association and a Committee of Publishers.

ISBN: 1-890415-11-1
Library of Congress Catalog Number: 97-090452

Manufactured in the United States of America.

This book is dedicated to all of our families, for their endless love and support.

ABOUT THE AUTHORS

David B. Mandell, J.D., M.B.A. is an attorney, financial consultant, and renown authority in the fields of risk management, asset protection, and financial planning. As a writer, Mr. Mandell has also written <u>Risk Management for the Practicing Physician</u>, and the upcoming title <u>Offshore Done Right.</u> His articles have appeared in over thirty leading national publications, including The American Medical News and Journal of the American Society of Internal Medicine, and he is a featured expert on the "Money and Medicine" section of the medical website www.medscape.com. He is a principal of Jarvis & Mandell LLC, a firm specializing in asset protection, money management, and tax planning for physicians – with offices in Los Angeles and New York.

Mr. Mandell holds a bachelor's degree from Harvard University and a law degree from the UCLA School of Law, where he was awarded the American Jurisprudence Award for achievement in legal ethics. While at UCLA, Mr. Mandell also earned a M.B.A. from the Anderson Graduate School of Management. Mr. Mandell is a member of the California and New York bars and is a licensed insurance professional and registered investment advisor.

Arnold S. Goldstein, Ph.D. is a veteran attorney with 33 years experience in asset protection, tax resolution and debt restructuring to individuals and businesses nationwide. Dr. Goldstein has written more than 100 books on asset protection, offshore trusts and related subjects. His tax, financial and legal strategies have been featured in more than 350 magazines, journals and newspapers. Dr. Goldstein gives nationwide workshops and lectures on the aforementioned topics and he has appeared on numerous radio and television talk shows, including CNBC and The Today Show.

Dr. Goldstein is a graduate of Northeastern University (B.S., 1961) and Suffolk University (MBA, 1966, and LL.M., 1975), and he received his law degree from the New England School of Law (J.D., 1964) and a doctorate from Northeastern University (Ph.D. in business and economic policy, 1990). He is a member of the Massachusetts Bar only and has been admitted to practice before the Massachusetts State Courts, the Massachusetts District Court, the U.S. Court of Appeals, and the U.S. Supreme Court. He is also a member of various professional, academic and civic organizations. His academic career includes a professorship (now professor emeritus) at Boston's Northeastern University and research scholar on offshore trusts at the London School of Economics. He also has taught law, finance and management at several other colleges and universities.

Christopher R. Jarvis, M.B.A. is a financial consultant and expert in the fields of personal finance, tax planning and investments. Jarvis is a financial expert on the physician website Medscape's "Money and Medicine" section and has authored articles in numerous periodicals including Anesthesiology News and Orthopaedic Special Edition. A frequent speaker to medical groups nationally, Mr. Jarvis is also a coauthor of <u>The Doctor's Investing Guide</u>, to be released early in 2000.

He is a principal of Jarvis & Mandell LLC, a firm specializing in asset protection, money management, and tax planning for physicians – with offices in Los Angeles and New York. His prior experience includes being: an actuary, insurance executive and business consultant. Mr. Jarvis holds an honor's degree, in applied mathematics, from the University of Rhode Island. He also earned an M.B.A. in finance from the Anderson School at UCLA where he was awarded the Ken Kennedy Fellowship. Mr. Jarvis is featured in Lexington's "Who's Who in Finance."

Authors' Note: To preserve confidentiality and privacy, the names and locations of individuals used in the case studies portrayed in this book have been changed. The case studies are used for illustrative purposes only. The author cannot guarantee identical outcomes under similar circumstances.

Publisher's Note: While a great deal of care has been taken to provide accurate and current information, the law changes constantly, as new statutes are enacted and the latest court decisions are announced. The reader is thus urged to consult legal counsel regarding any points of law – this publication should not be used as a substitute for competent legal advice.

TABLE OF CONTENTS

1. Why you must protect your assets...right now! 1
2. Anatomy of a lawsuit 15
3. Asset protection planning 27
4. Building a totally legal financial fortress 39
5. Using existing laws to protect assets 51
6. Co-ownership can protect or threaten you 63
7. Corporations as important protective tools 77
8. Family limited partnerships 93
9. Limited liability companies 117
10. Using trusts to protect your wealth 133
11. Foreign asset protection planning & other offshore strategies 149
12. Advanced protection for professionals and business owners 173
13. Legally shield your assets from the I.R.S. 191
14. Safeguarding assets against divorce 205
15. Pre-bankruptcy planning 219
16. Asset protection and Medicaid 233
17. The typical physician's asset protection plan 247

SPECIAL BONUS: Financial risks every doctor must avoid 253

Appendices A-1

Bibliography B-1

Glossary of terms and definitions C-1

Index D-1

FOREWORD

On behalf of coauthors Arnold Goldstein and Christopher Jarvis, I would like to thank you for purchasing this book. We would also like to offer our congratulations. You have started the journey toward financial security. You have made the choice to understand the many financial and legal threats you face in your professional and personal life every day — threats which endanger your practice, savings, and property. More importantly, you have taken the first step in learning what asset protection is and how it can shield your personal and professional wealth. Before reading this book, you may have asked yourself, "How can I ensure that I and my family will keep everything I have earned .. so that we can enjoy it through retirement?" This book will give you that answer ... and it is written only for you, the practicing doctor.

After you read this book, you will be able to analyze how **you and your family** are vulnerable to financial, legal, and other creditors risks — from medical malpractice lawsuits and claims by employees against you, your partners, or your practice ... to lawsuits against you personally from outside businesses or investments ... to stock market downturns ... to improper estate planning, and more.

You will learn from the **dozens of case studies** involving doctors and their real-life lawsuit problems. From their experiences, you will be able to see how you too can get into trouble in ways you may have not yet considered. Regardless of your medical specialty, these case studies will be extremely valuable ... and they may even be fun to read.

But this book will do more than simply point out the ways your practice and personal savings are threatened. Its main mission, in fact, is to provide you solutions — practical, workable financial and legal strategies for achieving your central goal: total financial security. After reading this book, you will understand which investment or insurance products to look for and which legal entities are best for running your medical practice. In addition, you'll know how to use trusts, limited partnerships, corporations, and limited liability companies to own your personal wealth — so that you protect your savings from lawsuits and other threats and save taxes as well.

The advice in this book would surely cost you many thousands of dollars from an attorney or financial advisor billing you by the hour. Now, when you do speak to such a professional, you'll be an educated client — saving yourself aggravation, time, and money. Even more, the money you save by discouraging one lawsuit or avoiding one key financial pitfall will pay for this book a hundred times over.

Before you begin reading the first chapter, I should briefly make some comments about the case studies, about the necessity of using a professional, and about the book's structure.

First, a **comment about the case studies**. The case studies are designed to illustrate concepts and strategies — do not take them for real cases. Many of them are based on real-life situations of the authors' clients. Others are based on the facts of published cases. In either situation, all names and identities have been changed and any similarities to actual persons is wholly coincidental.

Regarding **the necessity of consulting a professional** — please understand that this book is designed to illustrate general financial and legal principles and strategies. When you need to create a financial plan or implement an actual asset protection plan, or get advice on a particular legal issue, please call a professional, either a financial consultant or an attorney. Learn from this book, but recognize that it cannot substitute for a consultation with a financial professional or an attorney licensed to practice law. We authors are interested in speaking with readers and deal with clients on an nationwide basis. Certainly, you may contact us at (800) 554-7233 if you are interested.

Finally, an outline of the structure of the book:

The first chapter is where we begin the business of legal asset protection planning. In the **first and second chapters,** we outline the reasons why asset protection is so crucial today — why you face a host of lawsuit risks and why our legal system makes a lawsuit a losing process for any defendant, even if he or she "wins" the case in the end.

Chapter 3 outlines the basics of what asset protection is all about — what it means, what the goals and objectives of asset protection are, how asset protection has emerged as a legal specialty, what you can expect from an asset protection lawyer and more.

Chapter 4 discusses the laws which dictate what type of asset protection planning is legal and which is illegal. These laws are called "fraudulent transfer" laws, and you will learn, in this chapter, why everything I recommend in this book is 100% legal and how to make sure your plan is completely effective and unquestionably lawful and legitimate.

In **chapters 5 through 11**, we explain the various tools asset protection experts use to create asset protection plans around their clients' wealth. **Chapter 5** begins with state and federal laws which automatically protect you — but which you may not be taking advantage of presently. **Chapter 6** discusses the protective qualities, and dangerous risks, of owning property through co-ownership, such as joint ownership.

Chapter 7 begins the discussion of legal entities which can be used as powerful protectors of your medical practice and business interests, as well as of your personal wealth and savings. Chapter 8 reviews corporations and **Chapter 8** continues with limited partnerships and the pitfalls of general partnerships. **Chapter 9** outlines limited liability companies, **Chapter 10** covers trusts established here in the U.S., and **Chapter 11** discusses foreign asset protection planning.

The next phase of the book handles asset protection strategies in particular situations. **Chapter 12** reviews advanced strategies for shielding a business or medical practice from lawsuits and creditor claims, including detailed examples of how best to structure all types of medical practices. **Chapter 13** continues with tactics for protecting wealth from the clutches of the IRS. **Chapter 14** covers asset protection and divorce, **Chapter 15** discusses proper pre-bankruptcy planning, and **Chapter 16** handles the topic of asset protection and Medicaid planning.

Chapter 17 is a short one. It sets out *our typical physician client's asset protection plan* — what we implement, with individual variances, of course, for many of our doctor clients throughout the country.

Finally, **the last chapter is a Special Bonus** on the *9 top financial risks facing today's physician*. This chapter is written primarily by Mr. Jarvis with input from me. We included this special chapter because we have seen so many asset protection clients ignore financial issues that, in the end, were more damaging than any lawsuit. We tell our clients: "Why protect your savings from legal hazards and not shield them from poor financial planning?"

The concluding section of the book contains the appendices, the glossary/bibliography and the index. While the glossary, bibliography, and index are fairly self-explanatory, we should make some comments on the appendices.

The appendices give further treatment to issues which are briefly described in the text. For example, if you are a landlord and want to learn more about landlord liability, you would read Appendix A. Other topics in the appendices include liability for corporate officers and directors, estate tax-saving strategies, and all about living trusts. Appendix H is the **Financial Assessment Worksheets**.

The worksheets, consisting of the "Lawsuit Risk Factor Analysis" and the "Asset Checklist," are designed for you to complete with your personal financial information. In doing so, you will understand (1) the exact types of lawsuits to which you are most vulnerable and (2) which of your properties or other assets are likely to create the most liability problems. With this knowledge, you'll be well-equipped to begin your road to financial security.

Of course, to begin this road, you must first turn the page and begin learning. We sincerely hope you will enjoy the contents as much as you will learn from them.

Sincerely,

David B. Mandell, J.D., M.B.A.

CHAPTER 1:

WHY YOU MUST PROTECT YOUR ASSETS... RIGHT NOW!

The lawsuit has become a serious threat to every doctor's long-term financial security. The explosion of lawyers and the changing attitudes of our society have created a litigation juggernaut—directed especially against "Deep Pockets," like physicians. Insurance does not necessarily protect you from the many types of lawsuit and creditor risks that exist today. As a physician, you are at risk. That's why we say...you must protect your assets today!

THE LAWSUIT EXPLOSION

The number of *civil lawsuits* in this country has skyrocketed in the past few decades, with no sign of slowing. *Forty million new lawsuits* will be filed this year alone—triple the number filed thirty years ago. One new lawsuit is filed every 1.3 seconds. You may be the next target.

■ Your Odds of Becoming a Lawsuit Victim

The lawsuit explosion translates into one fact—the odds are 1 in 4 that you will be sued this year. Statistically, *you have nearly a 100 percent chance of being hit with a lawsuit within the next four years*. Are you under 40? Expect at least 4 lawsuits against you in your lifetime. Add the dangers of professional suits against you as a doctor, and you can understand why doctors are considered such high-risk targets.

■ Everyone Wants Your Money

Why are there so many more lawsuits today? Because today *the lawsuit is a way to "get rich quick," not a method to achieve justice*. We now believe that whenever something goes wrong, someone should pay, regardless of fault. Unfortunately, juries routinely adopt this idea and often disregard the facts of the case. Through emotion and bias, they give away large sums of money in the process....your money...whether or not you are at fault.

You read about these cases in your daily newspaper. A woman receives $2.6 million because her coffee was too hot; a homeowner pays thousands of dollars to a trespasser injured while burglarizing the homeowner's property. People see these same awards and ask, "Why not me?" They also want to win the lawsuit lottery. Their first step is to spot a target and manufacture a reason to sue. It is only a matter of time until that target is you.

■ Too Many Lawyers

Too many lawyers in this country helps feed the lawsuit fire. A questionable lawsuit can always find a hungry lawyer ready and willing to file the suit. Open your local yellow pages. Watch daytime television. Notice the many legal advertisements of those anxious to sue you. Even if your patient cannot pay the lawyer a dime, the lawyer can usually harass a *defendant* to settle or take a chance on a legal lottery at trial. How he can get the most fees controls his strategy.

Lawyering has grown tremendously in the last 20 years. Lawyers need to make a living, and the lawsuit is a fast source of instant income—whether in defending or prosecuting a suit. With just too many lawyers, each attorney must drum up business, finding any client willing to sue, whether or not his suit is legitimate.

Why You Must Protect Your Assets...Right Now!

FACT: *One Chicago law firm proudly announces to its many clients and prospects that it obtained the LARGEST VERDICT EVER FOR AN ARM AMPUTATION: $7.8 MILLION. [U.S. News and World Report, January 30, 1995].*

■ People Abuse the Legal System

Another factor adds to the lawsuit explosion: Many people simply abuse the legal system for their personal gain. This trend is so severe in California that their legislature recently passed a law: the *Vexatious Litigant Act,* a list of people who routinely abuse the legal system by filing too many frivolous lawsuits. Of course, these same individuals cannot be denied their "constitutional right" to sue; but, they cannot file suits without attorneys, unless with a judge's permission. This list is available to every lawyer in the state.

Who is on this list? People who, in a judge's opinion, have repeatedly filed meritless lawsuits without attorneys or engage in other frivolous tactics. Two awful examples:

1. One Los Angeles claimant filed over 200 lawsuits in seven years. Very few were successful.

2. A court clerk recommended certain individuals for this list. These individuals made the clerk a lawsuit target and has since been sued 11 times in two years—unsuccessfully. The clerk's reaction: "I do not exaggerate when I say I am extremely frightened by these people." (*The Sacramento Bee*, November 26, 1995)

With such a law, Californians demonstrate that they are fed up with lawsuit abuse. Their law, however, is not effective. A person on the list can still frequently sue, as long as he has an attorney. Unfortunately, he will find one—no matter how ridiculous his case. In fact, the California law helps lawyers get more clients by preventing suits without a lawyer. Remember, many legislators who voted for the law are themselves lawyers!

ENORMOUS AWARDS FOR NEGLIGIBLE DAMAGES

An auditor wins over $2.5 million when fired from a $52,000 a year job after employed by the company for 2 1/2 months.

A college student is awarded $75,000 for a broken arm suffered at a friend's house.

An accounting firm settles a harassment case for $800,000.

A mugger shot by the police wins $4.5 million from New York City claiming excessive force.

Such awards were once the exception, but now are commonplace. Juries today routinely dole out millions of dollars, frequently even more than the plaintiff demands.

FACT: In a study of over 23,000 Illinois jury trials, the Institute for Civil Justice found that the average **punitive damages** award increased, in inflation-adjusted dollars from $43,000 in 1965-1969 to $729,000 in 1980-1984. Those figures are higher today!

Large damages awards motivate more and more people to file lawsuits. It also means that if you are hit with one suit, the judgment can be enormous. Do not take a chance that you will not be sued. You have too much to lose if you come out on the wrong end of an enormous award.

YOU ARE AN OBVIOUS TARGET

The facing page shows a list of today's popular targets for lawsuits. How often are you mentioned? Whether the claim is negligence, malpractice, or products liability, these are the **Most Vulnerable Targets to the Lawsuit.**

<u>Professionals</u> are an exceptionally high risk because the public perceives them to be able to fix any problem in their field. When a surgery is not completely successful, a trial is lost, or a consultant's client loses money, the patient or client concludes that the professional must be to blame. Because the outcome was not favorable, they sue the professional. These potential plaintiffs swiftly find a lawyer ready and willing to take the case. A quick survey of the local yellow pages is all that is required. Whether or not the suit has merit, the professional/defendant can count on either a jury who feels for the "injured" plaintiff or a hefty settlement proposal. Either way, the professional pays.

NOTE: A survey of medical malpractice claims filed in New York found that more than 80% of the claims were without merit. [U.S. News and World Report, January 30, 1995].

Vulnerable Targets for Lawsuits

- **Parents of Teenage drivers**
- **Real Estate owners— especially rental real estate**
- **Small business owners**
- **Employers**
- **Doctors and Dentists**
- **Chiropractors**
- **Attorneys**
- **Accountants and other business advisors**
- **Stockbrokers**
- **Architects and Engineers**
- **Corporate officers and directors**
- **Directors of charitable organizations**
- **Partners in a general partnership**
- **Manufacturers, wholesalers and retailers**
- **Police officers**
- **Real estate developers**
- **Celebrities, sports figures and the conspicuously wealthy**

This frightening case demonstrates the potential liability of a landlord, architect, or builder:

■ Case Study:
Tina Tenant's Slip and Fall

Tina Tenant descends the outdoor stairwell of her apartment building one cold winter evening. Heavy snow makes the stairs icy. Tina slips and falls, severely injuring her face and head.

Tina's attorney searches for a Deep Pocket defendant— someone with money. Without such a Deep Pocket why pursue this case? There is no payoff even if Tina wins. Because Tina's lawyer is on a contingency fee, he will only be paid if Tina wins money damages.

In this case, Tina may sue a number of people. These include:

1. Landlord — for not maintaining a safe stairwell. Did the landlord recently inspect the stairwell? Did she hire someone to shovel the stairs? Were there adequate lighting, handrails, etc.?? Some states make the landlord liable even if she acted completely reasonably and responsibly.

2. Snow Shoveling/Maintenance Company — When a shoveling service and its owner is a Deep Pocket, you may also sue that company? The theory: the company negligently failed to promptly clean the stairway or didn't do it properly.

3. Building Contractor/Subcontractor — If the stairs were improperly built or designed, these potential wealthy defendants can also be sued, even many years after completing their work.

4. Manufacturer — Did the lights or stairs or railing fail? Perhaps the manufacturer of the product can be held responsible.

Tina's attorney will search for a payment source and only then design a theory of responsibility around these Deep Pocket defendant(s). If you are involved in such an accident, the injured party's lawyer will investigate whether it makes financial sense to sue you!

Professionals, builders, manufacturers, etc., are common targets; but, they are not alone. There are more obvious victims. As a doctor, you are already one of the most attractive Deep Pockets for lawsuits. However, you may also encounter other lawsuit dangers through personal or financial roles. Some examples:

- **Corporate officers and directors** can be sued for anything from securities law violations to improper loans to conflicts of interest to environmental or discrimination violations of their corporation. So can directors of charitable organizations. Chapter 7 and the Appendix details the many ways officers and directors can get into trouble.

- **Partners in a general partnership** are liable for the debts of the partnership, as well as for the wrongful acts of their partners. This is also true with general partners in a limited partnership. One architect, for example, was forced into bankruptcy when his partnership was successfully sued for millions because of building defects. Six partners were liable for the partnership debt, including our friend, who was not involved in the defective project.

- **Small business owners, like doctors,** are perhaps most vulnerable. They have a dangerous triple liability threat. They face the same lawsuit risks as any landowner or car-owner, such as personal injuries at their place of business or involving their cars. They face business-oriented lawsuits, such as breach of contract, employment discrimination, sexual discrimination, or defaulted bank loans. Finally, they may be responsible for the acts of their employees or partners. And, they often are personally liable for lawsuits involving their business. Hundreds of thousands of small business owners gamble their personal and family security on the hope that their business will never be sued, as do doctors who face many of the same problems.

SPECIAL NOTE:
Do not believe that the lawsuit can arise only from professional malpractice. This is a terrible mistake! Today's practicing professional is also a small business owner, who faces the "triple threat" of liability from your place of business, from your employees, and for your employees' behavior. You may also face liability as a corporate director, as a general partner, or as a trustee of a pension plan. Finally, if you own businesses or rental real estate outside your professional practice, you encounter all the risks associated with these ventures as well.

7 UNAVOIDABLE RISKS

The last section outlines how specific individuals, including doctors, are especially vulnerable to losing assets in a lawsuit. In addition to professional dangers, everyone is vulnerable to the following risks. When combined with some unfortunate turn of events, they could leave you with a devastating lawsuit or unmanageable liability.

- Unforeseen general economic downturn
- Well-financed and newer competitors (HMO or medical group)
- Government reimbursement cuts
- Natural disasters (earthquakes, floods, fire, riots, hurricanes)
- Personal hardships which effect your income
- Catastrophic illness to you or a member of your family
- Heavy tax assessed from an audit

These are even more dangerous to your financial health when you have loans to pay. Business loans, home mortgages, personal credit loans, student loans, car loans, credit cards, or other debts, fall behind in payments. Soon, you have a major financial crisis on your hands. Your **creditors** won't tolerate missed payments. Eventually, you will be sued and your house or car may be foreclosed upon or repossessed.

Bankruptcy may then be a real option. *Over one million personal bankruptcies are filed annually.* And, the numbers are climbing. Bankruptcy filers did not always have chronic debt and cash flow problems. Rather, one unavoidable financial event may start a downward financial spiral which left them insolvent. We have heard the same true but unfortunate scenario from many of such filers, which is why we stress the following point so strongly:

No matter how strong your present financial state is, or how carefully you plan, no one has the ability to foresee all the things that can go wrong. The best strategy: be adequately protected before any unfortunate event occurs.

6 REASONS WHY YOU CAN'T RELY ON INSURANCE

You may think: "But I have medical malpractice insurance, and homeowners insurance, and an umbrella policy to protect me against lawsuits." But, you are wrong. Insurance provides some protection, but it is never adequate. Consider:

1. The many exclusions

In many cases, you wouldn't know about these exclusions until it is too late; and you are looking to your insurance carrier to take you off the hook. Only then are you are told that you are not covered because of some fine-print exclusion.

Case Study:

Orthopedist Alan was sued for over $150,000 when his teenage daughter was involved in a car accident, using his car. Alan was certain that his insurance policy covered his daughter. Only then did his insurance agent tell Alan that the policy no longer covered his daughter, since she had recently moved out of the house. Alan alone faced a lawsuit which cost him over $150,000.

The list of reasons you can be sued is limitless. New theories of liability are created every day by inventive lawyers and accepted by juries and judges. Insurance on your significant assets (home, cars, boats) cannot truly safeguard against the threat of a lawsuit. Your malpractice policy may not cover you for harassment, discrimination, or wrongful termination suits by your employees, as only a few of many examples.

2. The policy has inadequate limits

Even if your insurance policy does cover you on a particular lawsuit, the policy coverage may be well below what a jury will award. You must pay any excess above the coverage out of your own pocket. Juries routinely hand out awards in excess of traditional $1 million /$3 million coverage. If you were hit by a large judgment, would your policy cover you completely?

3. Your insurer no longer exists

There is no guarantee that your insurance company will exist when you finally get sued. Insurance companies are not invincible. Like other businesses, some go bankrupt or out of business for other reasons, and leave you without coverage when you most need it. This is exactly what happened to a large physician-owned malpractice carrier in California. Now, the physicians are being forced to pay the outstanding debts of their former insurer.

4. Insurance forces you to lose control of the defense

Even if your insurance policy covers against a specific claim—consider the consequences. You have lost negotiating power, because your insurance company will dictate whether the case is settled, and for how much. While this may not matter with a personal injury car accident lawsuit, a malpractice case against you professionally is another matter. Here you may not want to admit liability and settle, while your insurance company does.

On the other hand, if the claim involves your professional reputation, you may want to settle the case out of court and away from the public view. There is no guarantee that your insurer will see things the same way. In these situations, if you rely solely on insurance, you lose all ability to negotiate effectively.

5. Lawsuits bring ever-higher premiums

An additional consequence of relying solely on insurance to protect you from lawsuits is that once sued, your premiums rise. Given the dismal statistics, you will probably endure many lawsuits over your life—your cost of insurance will rise with every suit, even if you are winning. Consider the following solution for a cardiac surgeon who, before protecting his assets, relied solely on malpractice insurance. After his insurance company defended four unsuccessful lawsuits against him, three of which went through trial, his insurance premiums rose to over $70,000 per year. Insurance cost him more over the next five years than any one lawsuit. This is not an extreme example. The point is clear. With your insurance company, the lawsuit has cost you dearly, even if you win.

6. New risks are unprotected

As a doctor, you may still think, "My malpractice insurance protects me adequately from lawsuits, so why should I care?" Remind yourself of all the ways you can be sued in your practice which do not constitute malpractice. Just as important are the changes going on in the medical marketplace today—changes which put medical professionals under more lawsuit risk.

Under many emerging HMO contracts, a medical professional must indemnify the HMO for any malpractice payouts from lawsuits against him. This means that if the HMO will not approve a diagnostic test and the patient later sues you for not administering the test, you will end up paying for the lawsuit. Even though the lawsuit will likely name you and the HMO jointly, and even though the HMO will pay the judgment initially, the HMO will look to you for reimbursement for the judgment amount. While it seems grossly unfair to make you liable when the HMO, in fact, tied your hands regarding the testing, the situation may be even worse.

Various medical insurance experts have explained that it is possible that a professional malpractice policy would not cover the above scenario. This is because, according to some policies' fine print, the business decision of the HMO not to order a test would not be considered "malpractice" of the insured professional. *Because it is not considered "medical malpractice," the policy would not apply, and the professional would have to reimburse the HMO out of his own pocket!* Although this controversy is presently unresolved, the possibility exists that HMOs may force additional personal liability on medical professionals.

DIVORCE, LONG-TERM MEDICAL CARE & DEATH TAXES: THREE UNIVERSAL THREATS

The simple fact is that nobody can foresee the future. Today, we may be healthy and have good marriages, but in the future? For many Americans, a divorce or a need for long-term medical care can be financially devastating. Far worse financially can be dying without a tax-avoiding estate plan. Your survivors then lose their inheritances to pay enormous estate tax bills. Unfortunately, nobody is immune from these three powerful threats. Consider:

■ Divorce

Nearly 50% of first marriages in this country end in divorce. So, the odds are 50/50 that you will get divorced, if you are presently married. For a second marriage, the divorce rate increases to 75%. What does a divorce mean in terms of that financial security? Unless you protect yourself against this potential eventuality, you will lose much of your savings and property in a divorce.

A divorce may be equally destructive for children who have an interest in family-owned businesses or investments—unless, of course, you have already protected yourself against this situation. Unprotected, your ex-daughter-in-law or son-in-law may claim part of your family property or business. Unfortunately, we commonly see this avoidable scenario rip families apart. Fortunately, you can make the appropriate plan to keep family property within the family ... always.

Why You Must Protect Your Assets...Right Now!

■ Long-Term Medical Care

As a doctor, you know all too well how likely it is that an individual will someday suffer an illness which eventually requires long-term care, whether in a hospital or nursing home. You also understand how costly this care can be. Elderly, infirmed middle class Americans forfeit their entire life savings to pay for medical care before Medicaid takes over. While this may not be a near-term risk for you, someone in your family may consider this risk as much more ominous.

Avoiding old age and sickness is impossible. However, good planning strategies available allow someone to save more of his/her wealth, while still qualifying for government medical benefits. These strategies are later described.

■ Death Taxes

When you die, your survivors will have to pay taxes on your estate—everything you owned at death. After the exempt amount, the tax starts at 37% and quickly rises to 55%—often resulting in a huge tax bill which rapidly eats-up inheritances. Why make Uncle Sam the principal beneficiary of your hard-earned savings? That money should go to your children, friends, charities, or anyone else you designate! Do not make the same mistake as Elvis "The King" Presley:

> Elvis Presley died in 1977, leaving an estate valued at approximately $12 million. Unfortunately, Elvis did not draft a smart estate plan, adopting the strategies we outline to reduce his taxable estate. The result: his family paid over $8.5 million in estate taxes and probate fees. Only 20% of Elvis' life savings went to his loved ones—the rest went to the government and lawyers. Elvis is still probably singing the blues!

Fortunately, you can legally avoid estate taxes while protecting your savings during your life. As you will soon learn, many strategies used to protect property feature the added benefit of also saving estate taxes. And these savings can be quite significant—often tens or hundreds of thousands of dollars.

"WHAT ASSETS?" — YES, YOU OWN MORE THAN YOU THINK

Many people believe that asset protection benefits only the extremely wealthy. They think you need millions of dollars to justify an asset protection plan. Yet, middle income Americans are most at risk because of the many legal liabilities they incur. The same is true for assets which need protection. Like multi-million dollar investment portfolios and real estate holdings, the cash value of your family home, IRAs or Keogh retirement accounts, vacation condos, or college funds also need protection. Even your life insurance policy should be safeguarded—your family will rely on it and it is vulnerable if left exposed. This is why you may be a "Deep Pocket"—someone worth suing.

You need asset protection if you own:

- Automobiles, motorcycles, boats, or recreational vehicles
- Certificates of deposit or savings accounts
- Stocks in public companies, mutual funds, savings bonds
- Family home or condominium
- Vacation home or condominium
- Rental real estate of any kind
- IRA, Keogh, pension or other retirement plan
- Interest in any closely-held corporation, partnership or other business entity
- Notes or mortgages receivable
- Life insurance
- Investment art, coins or other collectibles

While we could continue this list, the idea is clear. Practically every individual has assets which need protecting. Asset protection is not only for the rich. *If you own a valuable asset and if you can lose that asset to a lawsuit, creditor, the IRS, or others—you need asset protection. It is as simple as that.*

YOU ARE MORE LIKELY TO BE SUED THAN TO . . .

1. . . Be Injured in a Car Accident
Almost 40 million new lawsuits will be filed this year; yet, only 5.7 million injuries and deaths will result from car accidents. Thus, you are seven times as likely to be sued than to be injured or killed in a car accident. If you think going without car insurance is foolish, you are twice as foolish to ignore lawsuit protection.

2. . . Lose Your Home to Fire
The number of new civil lawsuits filed this year will be nearly 80 times the number of residential fires nationwide. You surely have insurance to protect your home against fire loss and even floods. But, have you taken the simple steps to safeguard your home from lawsuits and creditors? We hope that after reading this book, you will.

Our point: Being sued is more likely than many of the losses we typically protect ourselves against. Yet, protecting our valuable savings and possessions from lawsuits and other creditor problems is possible. And it need not be overly expensive, especially when the protection is established early on.

DO NOT DELAY

These are the three most important words in this book. Timing is the key to successful asset protection. Protect your assets *before* trouble arises. Courts look down on transfers of assets that take place after a liability has arisen. Because you have purchased this book, you already recognize the many dangers to your financial security. Perhaps you heard the many horror stories of people who lose their life savings, their homes, or their practices. After reading this chapter, you may accept your own vulnerability. Do Not Procrastinate. The Procrastinator, hit with a liability while totally exposed, loses everything. The Opportunist acts *before* a threatening liability, and lives with the peace of mind that he and his family are protected, no matter what happens.

Make a commitment, today, to yourself and your family. Protect what you've earned. Read this book. Become familiar with asset protection strategies and techniques. Commit yourself to talk to an asset protection specialist. This is the one promise you must make to safeguard your assets, and enjoy the peace of mind that comes from the knowledge that you and your family are protected.

SUMMARY

- Lawsuits are exploding in this country. The odds are 1 in 8 that you will be sued this year; even higher if you are worth more than $100,000.
- In today's lawsuit-crazy society, you must not ask, "will I be sued," but rather, "when will I be sued?"
- Enormous jury awards can be extremely costly.
- Doctors are especially at risk. They face the triple-threat which all business owners face; plus, they are obvious targets.
- As everyone is subject to many unavoidable risks, anyone can lose hard-earned assets.
- Insurance will not give you the security you need. It may fail to cover you altogether, or cost you dearly if you rely on it too heavily.
- Three financially devastating risks we all face: Divorce, Long-Term Medical Care, and Death Taxes.
- Asset protection is not only for the rich. You have more wealth exposed than you think—wealth you must protect.
- You are more likely to be sued than to be injured in a car accident or to lose your home to fire. Protect yourself from this odds-on risk.
- Commit to learn about asset protection—and to act!

CHAPTER 2:

ANATOMY OF A LAWSUIT

The lawsuit is the most serious and common threat to your financial security. Now, you will learn about the extraordinary rights other people have to find out about your wealth and to seize it through a lawsuit. You will see how frustrating it is to defend against a lawsuit—spending so much time and money on lawyers that, even if you win, you lose due to the emotional strain on you and your family.

5 Key Litigation Terms

Before reading on, review and understand some basic terms. The glossary at the end can help you with other less common terms.

- **Civil Lawsuit**: A lawsuit between private parties, *plaintiff* and *defendant*, usually for money.

- **Award:** The sum the plaintiff is entitled to from the defendant because of the lawsuit. Also called *recovery*.

- **Judgment**: A court finding that determines the outcome of a civil lawsuit, usually declaring that a sum of money (the *award*) is owed.

- **Judgment Creditor**: The person that is owed the money, the amount of which has been decided in court in the form of a judgment. This person "won" the lawsuit.

- **Judgment Debtor**: Person who owes the judgment creditor the money. This person "lost" the lawsuit.

ECONOMIC CONTROL: "ARE YOU WORTH SUING?"

Before anyone sues you, he and his attorney will make an economic analysis of their case against you. This analysis weighs the costs of suing you against the likelihood of success against you and the amount of probable recovery. In short, no one will sue you unless it is "worth it."

In order to determine whether or not you are worth suing, the plaintiff's counsel will make a thorough financial investigation of your assets and income. This is especially important to the *contingency fee* lawyers, with personal injury suits. Contingency fee lawyers dislike working on a case against a defendant who cannot pay a recovery— if the defendant cannot pay, the lawyer gets no fee.

How will the plaintiff's attorney investigate your ability to pay? By hiring a private investigation firm. Many exist in your area. These private investigators can quickly and easily discover much of what you own and earn. Consider:

- Investigators check the county records for real estate you may own. This information is public and easily obtainable, especially in computerized counties. They can learn the date of purchase, its value at that time, and the amount of loans or mortgages on the property. The investigator thus knows how much *equity* you have in your home, as well as any other real estate in the county.

- Your credit reports will also be examined. Through credit reporting agencies, investigators gain access to your reports and their valuable information, including your payment history and possibly the name of your bank. It may even include a financial statement revealing your assets and liabilities, if you have filled one out for the credit agency.

From the investigator's findings, the plaintiff and his lawyer decide whether or not it makes economic sense to sue you. If you have the ability to pay a judgment the lawyer will push forward. You will be served a summons and the lawsuit nightmare will begin...again!

Case Study:
Rick's assets are found

Rick, a dermatologist, was sued by a former medical assistant. He had been forced to discharge the assistant because his revenues were down after a competitor opened a clinic down the street. The former assistant brought an age discrimination claim against Rick, alleging that she was fired because of her age.

The medical assistant's lawyer hired an investigator. Within one week, the investigation revealed that Rick had about $140,000 of equity in his house, an investment property with another $150,000 equity and a savings account with $10,000. The decision: Sue Rick!

THE LAWSUIT PROCESS

Once a lawsuit is filed against you, your options are to settle (and pay) or defend. Defending a lawsuit is time-consuming, expensive, and emotionally draining. To defend a suit will also subject you to these burdens:

■ Pre-Judgment Remedies

Depending on the specific case and the laws of your state, a party suing you may be able to lien on your real estate, attach your personal property, or even seize your property before proving their case at trial! While these remedies are not widely known, lawyers throughout the country commonly use devices such as Attachment, Injunction, Lis Pendens, Replevin, and Receivership.

1. **Attachment:** Allows the plaintiff to get the court to direct the sheriff to seize your property, whether in your or someone else's possession. While the plaintiff must show that she can expect to win the suit at trial, under state law, she may ask for such a seizure without notice to you. New York, for example, allows attachments in certain cases; but, it can be granted before you even know you are being sued.

2. **Injunction:** A court order which directs action or prevents action. Again, although the plaintiff must comply with specific requirements, the preliminary injunction is often available before you are given notice of the lawsuit.

3. **Lis Pendens:** Also called a *notice of pendency*, it is a lien the plaintiff can file against real estate which you own in the county where the lawsuit occurs. This notice informs potential buyers or lenders that another lien may be coming as a result of the lawsuit. This makes the property virtually unmarketable.

   A plaintiff can usually file the lien before you even realize you are being sued. And, the plaintiff will not ask the court for permission.

4. **Replevin:** This is available for a plaintiff suing to recover possession of an asset. Similar to attachment, the plaintiff asks the court to direct the sheriff to seize the property in dispute. Like the other remedies, there are specific requirements that the plaintiff must fulfill to use this remedy.

5. **Receivership:** A receiver is appointed by the court to manage property or money during a lawsuit. A plaintiff can ask the court to appoint a receiver to take over your savings or property and

manage it while she sues you. Again, the court requires the plaintiff to show good cause before it makes such an appointment. In New York, this is one remedy which cannot be granted until you are served with a summons (notified that you are being sued). Other states have similar laws which allow others to tie up your property and possessions before they have actually won in court.

■ Discovery

With the lawsuit started, the discovery phase begins. Discovery is the process by which each side probes the other side for facts which may be helpful to them at trial. Discovery usually takes the form of depositions (oral questioning under oath), interrogatories (written questions answered under oath), and requests for production (of documents or other "things").

Over 80% of the time and cost of a typical lawsuit involves discovery. Why? Because the more powerful party often tries to intimidate the opposition by piling on the discovery requests. While the official rules of discovery prohibit using discovery as a tactical weapon, lawyers do violate the rule.

FACT: *A recent survey of a lawyer's bar association disclosed that 77% of litigators had used discovery as an economic weapon against their opponents.*

Discovery becomes so expensive because answering each deposition or interrogatory involves lawyers to guide you through the process and defend against unwarranted questions. Even worse, though, are requests for documents, especially in lawsuits involving businesses. Such requests are easily made, while the cost of responding is severe, involving the time to find and produce the materials, attorney's fees for reviewing the materials, and the physical copying and recording costs.

FACT: *In one antitrust case, the discovery process lasted almost a decade! The plaintiff's final pre-trial statement, over 100,000 pages long, referred to approximately 250,000 pages of documents, all produced through discovery. Imagine what this cost the defendant in legal fees, and the trial still had not started!*

■ Trial

The trial may take years, and you will have spent many thousands of dollars. Also, no matter how strong your case, you may still lose a large judgment at trial because the jury often disregards the facts and votes with emotion. This is called *jury nullification*. Any observer of today's trial knows it is foolish to risk trial and play the "legal lottery." Consider these actual cases and judgments. Then, ask yourself, "How can I defend myself when juries are making these decisions?"

1. A Philadelphia jury awarded a soothsayer $1 million after she allegedly lost her psychic powers following a CAT scan.

2. A Roanoke, Virginia jury gave a former railroad brakeman $2.6 million because the noise of the trains left him with a hearing problem that supposedly drove him crazy.

3. A San Francisco cab driver rescued a 24-year-old Japanese woman who was being mugged. After he saw the perpetrator take her purse and shove her to the ground, he set off in pursuit and pinned the assailant against the wall until the police arrived. The perpetrator was convicted of a felony and sentenced to 10 years in prison, but the cabbie was not treated as a hero. Instead, the mugger sued the cabbie and won, paying over $24,000 to the mugger for using excessive force.

One point we make repeatedly throughout this book is that you should *always* try to avoid the need to defend a lawsuit. Lawyers, law school professors, and even judges recognize this. Now, you understand why. *Protect your assets. It is less likely that you will be sued and more likely that you can settle before trial, if you are sued.*

EXPECT HEFTY LEGAL FEES

Whether you win a case at trial, or lose, you can expect a large legal bill. The U.S., in fact, is one of the few countries in which a successful defendant must pay his own legal fees and costs. In England and other countries with similar legal systems, the losing party pays the victor's legal fees. But, in the United States, each party pays his own fees and costs, unless a contract between the parties expressed otherwise. *You may "win," yet still owe tens of thousands of dollars in legal fees and costs. Not much of a victory!*

Legal fees will likely be significant. Legal fees have increased by 57% in the last five years. More disturbing is the common practice of overbilling, now alarmingly rampant. An auditor who investigates attorney bills reports that 90% of the cases he examined contained overcharges between 25% to 50%. While the auditor only works on already suspicious bills, consider some outrageous examples:

- A bankruptcy firm charged its bankrupt client over $177,000, simply to prepare their bill.

- An attorney drafted one legal motion which applied to thousands of separate cases that his client insurance company faced in asbestos litigation. The attorney billed the client 3,000 separate times for the same 12 minutes spent on the motion.

- A lawyer billed 62 hours in a single day.

Bill-padding is no laughing matter, especially when you must pay the bill. Nonetheless, it reminded us of this joke: A lawyer appeared at the gates of heaven and loudly protested that he was only 42, and much too young to die. "That's funny," St. Peter replied. "According to the hours you've billed clients, we figured you were 93."

YOU MAY OWE MORE THAN JUST THE JUDGMENT

If you lose the lawsuit and become a judgment debtor, you may owe more than the amount the judge or jury awards the plaintiff. You will also owe interest on the award, which starts from when the lawsuit was filed with the court. In many civil cases, the trial begins 2-3 years after the lawsuit was filed, and in larger cities, 4-5 years! You will then likely owe between 2 and 5 years interest on the award, plus the award amount. The interest rate? Depends on the state, but ranges between 5% and 18% annually.

Example: If you are in a state with a 12% interest rate—about average for all states—and found liable for a $50,000 award to the plaintiff and live where there is a five year backlog of cases, you will owe $38,117.07 in interest for a total over $88,000! Check with a local attorney for the statutory interest rate is in your state.

THE JOINT & SEVERAL LIABILITY TRAP

Joint and several liability applies when two or more parties jointly cause injuries or damage to the victim. The victim can then sue any one of the defendants for the full damages, even if the defendant was only partially at fault. Consider this example:

> Valerie Victim was injured when Driver Dave, Driver Dan, and you were all involved in a car accident. The jury finds that Valerie's injuries warranted $100,000 in damages. The jury also finds that Dave was 45% at fault, Dan was 35% at fault, and you were 20% at fault. Even though you were only 20% at fault, joint and several liability allows Valerie to sue you for the full $100,000. Of course, you can then sue Dave and Dan for reimbursement, but again, this costs time and money.

While each state has different limitations on when joint and several liability applies, it is available in many types of cases. For example, partners of a general partnership have joint and several liability for the debts and liabilities of the partnership. The key point to realize: You may have to pay for another's fault.

Between expensive legal fees, outrageous awards, severe interest, and joint and several liability, you can see how any lawsuit can become a financial disaster.

THE POST-JUDGMENT SEARCH FOR YOUR ASSETS

A plaintiff who wins a judgment against you becomes a judgment creditor. The judgment creditor can then commence a thorough investigation of your assets and income or *debtors' examination*. (You may appeal the judgment before the debtor's exam, but this may involve posting a bond, paying more legal fees and costs, and it is as risky as the trial).

In the debtor's examination, the judgment creditor and his attorney have the authority of the court behind them. They can use depositions, interrogatories, requests for production of documents, subpoenas, and possibly even in-court questioning, to force you to reveal information regarding your finances. In most states, your spouse can also be compelled to reveal financial information. The creditor may use of all these tools, or any combination. You and your spouse must make good faith, reasonable efforts to respond to such requests.

Anatomy of a Lawsuit

Your judgment creditor will minimally want to know:

- Your/your spouse's current employment and full compensation, if any
- Your/your spouse's part-time employment, if any
- Any other sources of income
- Occupations or business interests held by you/your spouse during the last five years
- Bank accounts, savings accounts, checking accounts, CDs, and securities in your/your spouse's name
- Safe deposit boxes in your/your spouse's name
- Real estate owned in your/your spouse's name
- Whether or not you/your spouse own any life insurance with cash value, or annuity insurance
- Whether or not you/your spouse own any automobiles, boats, RVs, trucks, etc., and what the equity in such items is
- Whether or not you/your spouse own any jewelry, collectibles, antiques, and what the equity of such items is
- Whether or not you/your spouse own any patents, trademarks, or copyrights, and whether or not any rights to them are assigned
- Whether or not you/your spouse has transferred any property within the last five years
- Whether or not you/your spouse made any gifts of property within the last five years
- The extent to which you/your spouse has other liabilities
- Whether or not you have filed for bankruptcy
- Whether or not there is anyone holding property on your behalf

Remember, answers to the judgment creditor's questions and requests are under oath. A false response to these questions is the same as lying on the witness stand. It is perjury: a felony punishable by imprisonment. If you ignore a creditor's requests to appear in court or at a deposition, or fail to respond to interrogatories or requests for production, the creditor can obtain a court order to compel you to comply. Failure to respond to a court order will put you in contempt of court, which can bring fines and even jail.

TIP #1: Answer questions at depositions, in-court examination, or in interrogatories, directly and briefly, without offering additional information. In daily conversation, we often feel the need to explain our responses. Do not do so here. Make the creditor's job as difficult as possible by answering the question and no more. But remember, never lie under oath.

TIP #2: Dress down when attending any examination or deposition. The appearance of wealth only makes your opponent more determined to take your assets.

HOW JUDGMENT CREDITORS SEIZE ASSETS

Once a judgment is entered against you, the judgment creditor can seize your assets or *execute on a judgment*. Although the process varies by state, typically:

- For real property, the creditor must file a summary of judgment in the county recorder where your real property is located. This "liens" the property for the amount of the judgment. This lien is valid against any real property you own in that county at the time, as well as future real estate you acquire. Once liened, you cannot sell or refinance the property(ies) without satisfying the judgment. This effectively ties up your real estate until the judgment is paid!

- Personal property is seized through a levy. The Sheriff or Marshall who enforces the levy can physically take property named in the levy. They can seize property directly from you or someone else. This can include money in a bank account, items in a safe deposit box, automobiles, jewelry, antiques, collectibles, equipment and other unprotected physical assets (see chapter 5 for these assets). If the item seized is not cash, the sheriff will convert the property into cash through a *sheriff's sale,* at public auction.

- Wages are also seized by a levy or *garnishments*. The creditor, through a levy, can order your employer to send your pay to him, except for legally protected amounts (see chapter 5).

HOW TO STOP SEIZURE OF YOUR ASSETS

If a creditor is in the process of taking your assets or garnishing your wages, there are three possible steps to protect yourself:

- File a claim of exemption to protect exempt assets. Each state lists assets which a creditor cannot take. Generally, this includes tools of the trade, household items, and a specified amount of other personal property. Federal law provides further exemptions. Often, you must file a claim of exemption to properly shield your property; protection is not automatic. We will more fully discuss state and federal exemptions in a later chapter.

- Offer to pay the judgment amount voluntarily, perhaps over time. Negotiating payment saves the creditor the hassles of foreclosure and allows you to keep your property.

- File for bankruptcy under chapter 7, 11, or 13 *before* the auction sale. While filing bankruptcy has serious consequences, it stops any forced sale of your assets. If you plan bankruptcy anyway, do so before seizure and sale, thereby saving your assets. A later chapter more fully discusses pre-bankruptcy planning.

CONCLUSION: AVOID LAWSUITS

This is obvious—and, you probably tried this before you bought this book. However, now you know exactly how expensive, time-consuming, stressful, and risky defending a lawsuit can be. So, how will you avoid a lawsuit?

We could tell you to always act reasonably, foresee behavior that might get you in trouble, pay debts when due, pay your taxes, avoid marriage, and never start a business. But this would be ridiculous. *We do not want you to surrender to the threat of a lawsuit—we want you to beat the threat itself!*

The key to avoiding lawsuits is to protect yourself against them. Your property, possessions, and savings must all be shielded from the lawsuit. *Only when you are properly protected can you partake in all of life's various activities and not worry about being sued and losing what you have worked so hard to build.*

SUMMARY

- Potential plaintiffs and their lawyers can, and will, discover what you own before deciding whether or not to sue you.
- Defending a lawsuit is time-consuming, extremely expensive, and an emotionally draining experience.
- Plaintiffs can possibly get at your assets before they even begin their lawsuit against you through pre-judgment remedies.
- Even when you supposedly "win" a lawsuit, you lose.
- To defend against a lawsuit at trial, you play a "legal lottery" where the payouts come out of your pockets.
- Through joint and several liability, you can be forced to pay damages you did not cause.
- Lose a lawsuit and expect a thorough investigation of all your income and assets.
- The plaintiff has powerful legal tools to find and take your property, possessions, and even your income.
- Use last-second tactics to protect your savings and property from being seized.
- Avoid lawsuits by protecting your savings, possessions, and property—you discourage lawsuits and negotiate from a position of strength.

CHAPTER 3:

ASSET PROTECTION PLANNING

This chapter covers the basics of asset protection planning, beginning with a clear definition of "asset protection" and ending with the six key rules of proper protection planning. You will learn that asset protection is 100% legal and extraordinarily effective in protecting wealth from lawsuits as well as in encouraging cheap settlements quickly.

THE DEFINITION, GOALS, AND OBJECTIVES OF ASSET PROTECTION

To understand asset protection is to learn its definition, its overall goal, and specific objectives that lead to that goal.

Asset Protection: Means holding your savings, property, and practice in a way that shields them from lawsuits, business risks, and claims of creditors of all types.

Or: Asset protection prevents adversaries from taking your wealth.

Goal of Asset Protection: To provide the ultimate security for you and your family, so you keep what you own, notwithstanding financial or legal problems.

Objectives of Asset Protection: To discourage lawsuits against you by showing potential plaintiffs that they cannot reach your savings, property, or practice; and to reach favorable settlements when you choose to settle, by allowing you to negotiate from a position of strength.

As you can see, asset protection concerns safeguarding everything you now own, and will own in the future, from outside threats. The goal of asset protection planning is to provide you and your family with a powerful well-deserved sense of security. To reach that goal, and live up to its definition, asset protection's primary objective is to keep people from suing you.

■ Discourage Lawsuits

By preventing lawsuits against you, asset protection planning shields you from the devastating costs of defending a lawsuit. After all, discouraging suits against you is much better than defending a suit and winning—you still spend money, time, and energy when you "win" while discouraging suits at the outset costs you nothing. *The money you save, discouraging even one lawsuit, will pay your asset protection costs many times over.*

■ Negotiate Inexpensive Settlements

Despite solid asset protection, some people will be foolish or stubborn and sue you, even though they cannot "get" anything. You may also face people who won't sue if you give them a quick, small settlement. A quick "pennies on the dollar" settlement may be just what you want. Everyone feels they have won. You pay a fraction of what it would cost to defend the claim, and you have the matter behind you quickly and cleanly. Asset protection's

Asset Protection Planning

secondary objective, therefore, puts you in the position to negotiate pennies on the dollar settlements with any creditor. *Negotiate from the position of strength, knowing that you truly "have nothing to lose."*

ASSET PROTECTION PREVENTS LAWSUITS

As mentioned in the previous chapter, before a potential plaintiff sues you, he and his lawyers must make an economic analysis of the case against you, regardless of whether the idea to sue you arose because of some action or inaction on your part or because of a debt that you failed to pay. They must weigh the costs of suing you against the likely benefits from suing you (what they might get if they win). In other words, using the following formula, the attorney and client must decide: "Are you worth suing?"

Sue when:

(Cost of suing you) is less than	(Likelihood of success against you) times (amount of probable recovery)

This formula suggests that a plaintiff will not sue you unless he or his lawyer think that they will recover more money from you than they will spend suing you. However, even when a case fails this formula, a lawsuit may still result because lawyers also know that even a faulty suit has an ascertainable "settlement value." Lawyers know you will pay to "make it go away," because of privacy concerns, because it is a nuisance, or because it would cost more to defend. You may consider this coercion and dislike lawyers because of it, but it is reality today. Thus, lawyers also follow this formula:

Also sue when:

(Cost of suing you) is less than	(Likelihood of settling) times (amount of probable settlement)

This formula means that even if it costs more for the plaintiff to sue you then she will likely get at trial (i.e., she would lose money on the deal), she may still sue you if the cost of continuing the case against you is less than what you will probably pay to settle the case out of court.

Proper asset protection planning effects both formulas by reducing the "amount of probable recovery/settlement." After you properly protect your assets, the plaintiff cannot touch your possession, property, or savings. Therefore, "the probable recovery" is reduced to virtually $0.

Also, to make an out of court settlement, you negotiate from a position of strength. You know that you have little, if anything, to lose, so you can settle on your terms. Protect your assets and *give potential plaintiffs the answer to their question: "Are you worth suing?" "NO!"*

Case Study:
How "Protected Howard" settles malpractice claims for pennies

Howard, a gynecologist, is well-respected in his community. Nevertheless, he had endured a number of costly malpractice suits in the last five years. Although he never lost a suit, he faced years of depositions and court appearances and spent thousands of dollars in legal fees. Also, despite winning or settling the cases, his malpractice insurance premiums increased dramatically. Tired of the expense and aggravation of being "defensive," Howard protected his assets.

Howard was advised to trim his liability coverage and to set-up an asset protection plan which involved transferring his significant assets to a family limited partnership and an offshore trust (discussed later). When Howard was later threatened with lawsuits, his first move was to inform the plaintiff's counsel how his assets were held, and about his low malpractice coverage.

Howard later successfully settled six cases for a tiny fraction of what the plaintiffs demanded. His total payout in all these cases about equalled the legal fees he paid defending one suit before he was protected. Most importantly, Howard no longer worried about the malpractice sword hanging above his head. Instead, Howard now feels secure, knowing that his most important assets are safe from all creditors, and that he is no longer at the mercy of the lawsuit and the legal system.

FACT: A recent study by a leading insurance company showed that medical malpractice awards were significantly less when the doctor carried less insurance coverage.

ASSET PROTECTION ALLOWS YOU TO KEEP YOUR WEALTH BEFORE AND AFTER TRIAL

Despite the most thorough asset protection, you may still be sued by plaintiffs who are irrational or who are motivated purely by emotion. Or, they may refuse to accept that you are lawsuit-proof. Whatever their motive, by protecting your assets, you ensure that even if you are sued, the plaintiff cannot seize your assets before or after trial.

In the last chapter, you learned how a plaintiffs' lawyers can tie-up your cash, property, and possessions even before trial—through "pre-judgment remedies." With your assets tied-up by these remedies, you may not be able to financially survive the lawsuit. This allows the plaintiff to force you into an unfavorable settlement. Similarly, if the plaintiff successfully wins a judgment, your real estate and bank accounts will be effectively frozen.

A sound asset protection plan prevents plaintiffs from tying-up your property, savings, and possessions in these ways. As you will discover in later chapters, an asset protection plan includes the transfer of key assets out of your name and into such legal entities as limited partnerships, corporations, or trusts, which you still control, but are no longer in your name. Plaintiffs cannot then tie them up with pre-judgment remedies or post-judgment seizures.

ASSET PROTECTION NEVER RELIES UPON SECRECY

Many people believe asset protection involves hiding what you own so no one can find it. That is not so! Asset protection is not asset concealment. *You protect what you own, you don't hide it.*

The primary objective of asset protection planning is to discourage lawsuits. We tell prospective asset protection clients that, after their asset protection plan is in place, they can be upfront with people contemplating suing them. These clients openly disclose their assets and possessions and how they are owned and protected. The contingency fee lawyers drop the case before you can say, "fully protected."

While asset protection does not require secrecy, asset protection can achieve privacy, as well as security. What you own and earn is easily discoverable by anyone with an interest in your financial affairs. Rather than allow this intrusion into their private financial affairs, many people welcome the privacy gained by using trusts, corporations, and limited partnerships. However, when questioned under oath about their assets, they must answer fully and truthfully.

That does not mean that you should flaunt your wealth and how it is protected to anger creditors. Should anyone challenge your protective maneuvers, you may want additional non-protection reasons for setting-up the trusts, partnerships, transfers, corporations, etc. These reasons can include tax planning, estate planning, even investment reasons. Use common sense. Only tell people who must know about your asset protection planning, shooing threats away like flies.

PROPER ASSET PROTECTION IS 100% LEGAL

We make this perfectly clear—*everything we advise in this book and all that we tell potential clients is perfectly legal.* The simple fact is that we do not need to do anything illegal to achieve our goals. All 50 states, plus the federal government, have laws which recognize asset protection as a perfectly legitimate activity. These laws separate the permissible from the impermissible. We use these laws to design strategies which protect you fully and stand up under any challenges.

Think of proper asset protection as proper tax planning—you use the laws to achieve your goal, whether to pay as little tax as possible, or to protect yourself from lawsuits. Improper asset protection, on the other hand—like tax evasion—is illegal, unjustified, and has no place in your life.

Yes, some disregard our advice and try to perform asset protection on their own—making haphazard fraudulent transfers to family and friends, or even commit illegal acts and perjury in their attempt to hide what they own. Concealing assets, committing bankruptcy fraud, or issuing false statements is foolish because you may get caught and go to jail. It is also completely unnecessary.

A good asset protection specialist can help you achieve total protection in a way that is 100% legitimate and legal. While your expert will set up your plan, you must also make the commitment to act lawfully. That means being honest and open with your attorney when disclosing your assets, and when answering all questions put to you under oath, whether in court, deposition, or in financial disclosure forms.

LAWYERS PROTECT THEIR ASSETS

Some of our friends and family found this was the most convincing reason to start an asset protection plan. Alec, a good example, confessed, "If the lawyers are using asset protection, I should too. They know about lawsuits and whether or not this stuff really protects you." Alec makes sense, don't you think?

Next, consider two articles published over the last year. The first appeared in the American Bar Association (ABA) Journal, the largest U.S. magazine for lawyers. "PROTECT ASSETS BEFORE LAWSUIT ARISES" (January 1996, page 89). The author explains to over 300,000 ABA lawyer members how important asset protection is for them. The author outlines the very same reasons to protect assets that we explain—expanding theories of legal liability, juries and judges who decide with emotion, unpredictable awards, inadequate insurance, etc. Obviously, lawyers realize that lawsuits threaten them as well, and are now protecting themselves. As one lawyer interviewed in the article admitted, *"I do not want people doing to me what I do to people all day in court."*

The second article, from The Wall Street Journal (page A14, March 1, 1996), in direct response to the ABA Journal article, makes a convincing point that if the lawyers know the legal system is out of control, then they should change the system, not protect themselves against it. While you might agree with this author, the fact remains that the legal system has not yet been reformed, and probably never will be. The lawsuit threat won't disappear. Join the lawyers who use the law to protect themselves. Then, reform the legal system, if you choose. Fully protected, you will have nothing to lose.

ASSET PROTECTION ... NEEDED BY EVERYONE

This may be the first time you have heard the term "asset protection." You may ask yourself, "if this is so important, why haven't I heard about it before?" A fair question. The answer is that, until recently, only the country's wealthiest families and their sophisticated lawyers used asset protection techniques. They were the ones most worried about being sued—because they were "deep pocket" targets and because they had real wealth to lose.

Throughout this century, families like the Rockefellers and Kennedys have used partnerships, trusts, and family corporations to protect their vast holdings and to keep them private, although they never referred to it as asset protection.

■ Asset Protection, Now Needed By Nearly Every Middle-American

The Rockefellers are no longer the only lawsuit targets. Today, middle-income Americans need to protect their wealth from lawsuits. With the growing lawsuit threat, more lawyers are protecting their clients' wealth. Often, the clients ask their lawyers how to legally protect themselves from lawsuits.

■ More Attorneys Are Learning Asset Protection Strategies

Over the past five years, a number of professional asset protection manuals emerged, specifically for lawyers—also an Asset Protection Journal began publication, aimed at professionals performing asset protection planning. While these manuals and journals cover different practice issues, the fact remains that there is more asset protection planning today than ever before, a trend likely to continue for as long as lawsuits remain a dangerous threat to financial security.

More and more legal practitioners are sending their message. A quick survey of the nation's leading newspapers and magazines reveal an increasing number of articles on asset protection. A small sample: *"Protecting Assets Is Not Only For The Wealthy"* (Los Angeles Times, June 6, 1993); *"How To Protect Assets and Sleep At Night"* (Los Angeles Times, June 20, 1993); *"Cover Your Assets,"* (The Economist, April 8, 1989); *"An Offshore Trust Can Be the Ultimate Insurance Policy for Your Assets"* (Barrons, August 7, 1995); *"Litigious World Forces Investors to Rely on Asset-Protection Trusts"* (Money, June 26, 1995); *"Seven Ways You Can Protect Your Assets From Lawsuits"* (Investor's Business Daily, July 24, 1995). The bibliography contains a list of articles in medical magazines and newsletters.

■ Find An Expert

While more lawyers now practice asset protection, does more ensure better protection for you? Not necessarily. Asset protection is an extremely difficult legal specialty merging a knowledge of property law, pension law, corporate law, wills and trusts, tax law, law of partnerships, bankruptcy law, contract law, creditor and debtor rights, and even laws of foreign countries. Combine this complexity with the importance of the asset protection goal—financial security—and it becomes clear that you want an expert. You would no more entrust important surgery to a inexperienced resident than you would want a lawyer just learning about asset protection to protect you.

SEVEN ESSENTIALS YOUR ASSET PROTECTION PLAN MUST HAVE

1. A Sound Legal Foundation
An illegal or fraudulent asset protection plan is no plan. Your plan needs an expert who knows the law and how to use it. You can safely disclose your entire financial situation, knowing that you and your family will remain safe.

2. Discourages Lawsuits
This is the primary objective of asset protection. The money you will save by discouraging one lawsuit will pay for itself many times over. A plan that does not discourage potential plaintiffs and lawyers does not work.

3. Encourages Favorable Settlements
A secondary, but equally important, objective of your asset protection plan. If you are a lawsuit target, trouble may arise even after your plan is in place. But, you can negotiate "pennies on the dollar" settlements, because you have little wealth exposed.

4. Little Loss of Control
Protecting your assets may involve some loss of control because certain assets may be titled with legal entities such as trusts, limited partnerships, limited liability companies, or corporations. However, a first-rate asset protection plan offers you practically as much control as when the assets are in your own name.

5. Easy to Operate
Your asset protection plan should be easy and convenient to set-up and continue to maintain. Much of this depends on the skill of the attorney who handles your plan.

6. Consistent With Your Estate Plan
If you have an existing estate plan, such as a will or a living trust, the plan should be consistent with these arrangements. The top-notch asset protection plan may help you to revise your estate plan, supply you with superior documents (living trust rather than a will) and furnish tactics to save on estate taxes and probate fees so more of what you have earned goes to your loved ones.

7. Protects Your Wealth from All Threats

This is the ultimate test of our asset protection plan—to protect your hard-earned wealth from those who want to take it from you. A first-rate plan provides total protection—your entire wealth is safeguarded against any and all creditors, whether they be business or personal, government or private citizens. Only with this ultimate protection can you and your family rest easy and enjoy the peace of mind you deserve.

SIX KEY RULES TO ASSET PROTECTION PLANNING

1. PLAN AHEAD: Protecting your savings, property, and possessions before you are sued. It is the smartest thing you can do. As you learn in the next chapter, courts frown upon transfers made after a lawsuit threat. Only if you are fully protected before a lawsuit or other claim arises, can you be completely secure.

2. FIND AN EXPERT: Proper asset protection planning requires an expert. This should become clearer to you as you read about the specific asset protection strategies. It makes sense to find an expert, even if he is not local. With the phone, fax, and FedEx, the expert can handle your case much more effectively than can a local lawyer with little or no experience. Often, the expert will work with your local lawyer, accountant, or financial planner, for a coordinated approach.

3. INVOLVE YOUR FAMILY: Because much of asset protection involves changing ownership of assets and using estate planning devices like wills and trusts, your close family members' cooperation can be extremely valuable. Let them know what you are planning early on, so that when you put your strategy to work, they are willing and able to assist you.

4. COMPROMISE: The most effective asset protection program calls for you to personally own no assets. The least effective program titles assets in your own name. Somewhere in between lies your best program. You do not want to necessarily overdo it by owning nothing. It is often better to compromise. Throw creditors "a bone," while protecting most of your wealth.

5. REVIEW YOUR PLAN REGULARLY: No asset protection plan is set in stone. Rather, it must be flexible and adaptable to changes in your life. If you take on new risks, or purchase new property, or get divorced or re-married, your asset protection plan should be altered to these changes.

6. BEGIN TODAY: Repeat the first key rule. The most effective protection is one that is set-up *before* any threat to your security arises. Overcome the apathy, laziness, and resistance to new ideas that plague so many of us. You are ahead of most because you are at least reading this book. Do not stop half-way. Continue to read and to learn about how you can achieve ultimate protection. But, it is only one step on the path to gaining the financial security that you and your family so richly deserve.

SUMMARY

- Asset Protection means titling your savings, property, and possessions in a way that shields them from lawsuits, business risks, and claims of all creditors.
- The goal of asset protection is to provide ultimate security for you and your family—ensuring that you keep everything you own.
- Asset protection is not about secrecy or hiding assets—it is about showing potential creditors that they cannot reach your wealth.
- Asset protection discourages lawsuits and allows you to negotiate from a position of strength.
- Proper asset protection planning is 100% legal—there is no place for concealing assets, committing perjury, or other illegalities.
- Lawyers consider it wise to protect assets—they now protect themselves.
- Asset protection is a growing trend—join it!
- Every asset protection plan must have a solid legal foundation, discourage lawsuits, encourage favorable settlements, bring little loss of control, be easy to use, be consistent with your estate plan, and protect your assets from all threats.
- Follow the six key rules for proper asset protection planning: Plan Ahead, Find an Expert, Involve Your Family, Be Prepared to Compromise, Review Your Plan Regularly, and Begin Today.

CHAPTER 4:

BUILDING A TOTALLY LEGAL FINANCIAL FORTRESS

A carefully created asset protection plan can become your financial fortress, if it is built to withstand fraudulent transfer claims—especially important if there already exists a lawsuit, overdue debt, or any other present liability.

Asset protection planning is a vaccine, not a cure. To avoid fraudulent transfers, your asset protection plan must be in place before trouble arises. Once a lawsuit is threatened, many protective strategies can no longer be used—just as a vaccine is not effective once you are afflicted with a disease. Proper asset protection is always preventative planning.

This chapter explains the "ins and outs" of fraudulent transfer laws—what they are, how they work, and how you can avoid violating them in your asset protection plan. Later chapters discuss the legal tools that can protect you—bricks in your financial fortress, if you will. But, before you learn these strategies, you must first gain a basic understanding of fraudulent transfers. Regardless of which protective tools you use, always keep fraudulent transfer laws in mind. In this way, your asset protection plan will stand against any challenge.

WHY YOU MUST AVOID FRAUDULENT TRANSFER LAWS

Every state has laws against fraudulent transfers, either in the form of the *Uniform Fraudulent Conveyances Act (UFCA)* or the *Uniform Fraudulent Transfers Act (UFTA)*. Throughout this chapter and in later chapters, we use the terms *fraudulent transfer* or *fraudulent conveyance* as virtually interchangeable. Transfers include both sales and gifts.

Fraudulent transfer laws give creditors the right to undo certain transfers that debtors have made so that the transferred property can be seized by creditors (including judgment creditors). In other words, *under certain circumstances, the courts invalidate sales or gifts by debtors. Whatever the debtor sold or gave away is transferred back to the debtor, allowing the creditor to seize the property, using the tools described earlier (lien, levy, seizure).* These laws have been enacted so that debtors cannot transfer property to defraud their creditors.

Fraudulent transfer laws are important because they may partially, or totally, destroy your asset protection plan. Asset protection is achieved by titling your wealth beyond the reach of creditors. Fraudulent transfers laws are obstacles to that goal, because they allow a creditor to get at your assets even when you no longer own them in your name. This is extremely important—*fraudulent transfer laws separate valid legal asset protection from illegally disposing of assets.*

When creditors come after your assets with a lawsuit—or when judgment creditors attempt to seize your wealth or wages—they will use fraudulent transfer laws to reach assets you may have transferred out of your name to a spouse, a family member, a friend, a corporation, a partnership, a trust. . . or any other third party. Whether or not the creditor succeeds will depend on whether or not you can convince the court that the transfer was not a last-ditch effort intended to defraud your creditor(s).

If your asset protection plan was undertaken with a good asset protection specialist, you will convince the court, and prevent your creditors from recovering previously-transferred assets. If not, you lose the protection which your plan was supposed to provide. A fraudulent transfer challenge, then, often becomes the true test of your asset protection plan.

WHEN A TRANSFER IS "FRAUDULENT"

Under the two laws (the UFTA and the UFCA), courts find two types of fraudulent transfers, each explained separately:

1) Fraud in fact — or "actual fraud"
2) Fraud in law — or "constructive fraud"

1) Actual Fraud

For actual fraud, *your creditors must prove that you actually intended to hinder, delay, or defraud your creditors.* This may be every difficult to prove directly, as they must prove your state of mind, or get you to confess fraudulent intent. To assist creditors, the courts recognize signs of fraud or "badges of fraud" which, if proved, can allow the court to infer fraudulent intent.

BADGES OF FRAUD

- The transfer was made to a close family member or friend.
- The transfer was made secretly.
- The transfer was for less than fair value.
- The debtor continued to use or possess the property after the transfer.
- The debtor disappeared.
- The debtor had been sued or threatened with suit before the transfer.
- The debtor concealed assets.
- The transfer was around the same time the debtor incurred a large debt.
- The transfer left the debtor with no property.
- The transfer left the debtor insolvent (unable to pay debts as they came due).

Even if a creditor proves these "badges," it does not always mean that the judge will automatically find the transfer to be fraudulent and allow the creditor to recover the property. These badges only "infer" fraudulent intent; that is, they are evidence which can allow the judge to conclude that you had fraudulent intent when not confessed to. They do not create a presumption of fraud. Your creditor still has the burden of proof to demonstrate that you intended to defraud. The court, therefore, can still uphold any challenged transfer as proper, even if certain "badges" are shown. This becomes even more likely when we can explain transfers as achieving legitimate business, investment, or estate planning objectives.

2) Constructive Fraud

Because actual fraud is so difficult to prove, even when certain "badges of fraud" exist, creditors more often rely on constructive fraud to undo transfers by debtors. Constructive fraud occurs when there is *a gift or sale of the debtor's property*:

    a) **for less than fair value** (also called *fair consideration*)
    b) **in the face of a known liability**
    c) **which leaves the debtor insolvent**

In this way, under the constructive fraud theory, your transfer can be deemed fraudulent, even though you acted completely innocently, without any intent to hinder your creditors; as long as the above factors are proved. But, someone challenging your transfers must show all three factors. We now analyze each of these factors:

■ Factor A: "For Less than Fair Value"

Creditors must first show if they want to prove *constructive fraud* that the transfer was for less than fair value. While this is not a problem when the debtor makes a gift, proving an actual sale was for less than fair value is more difficult for the creditor, because of the way a court defines fair consideration.

Fair consideration is a price which a reasonably prudent seller would obtain using commercially reasonable means. This may not mean the fair market value; it depends on what type of item or property is involved. For stocks or bonds of publicly-traded corporations or commodities, fair value does mean fair market value. Exact value of the stock/bond/commodity can easily be determined by looking from the quotes of the day of the transfer. If the debtor transferred the stock/etc. for less than its price that day, then the sale would be for less than fair value and might be a fraudulent transfer.

For items that are more difficult to value precisely, like real estate, stock in a privately held business, antiques, vehicles, and others, fair consideration may be much less than fair market value because reasonable minds differ about the exact value of a piece of real estate, or a painting, or a business. Also, as the debtor, you may not have the luxury to wait through a series of negotiations or for the right buyer willing to pay full fair market value price. You may want to settle for less than optimum price fast cash. For these reasons, courts typically conclude that real estate which is over 70% of fair market value satisfies fair consideration. For other items, like jewelry or closely-held businesses, courts will look at all the facts—especially certified appraisals—for whether the payment was in the ballpark.

Case Study: *Your House*

Your house is an easy example. Suppose your neighbor Ned recently sold his house, which is quite similar to yours, for $200,000. The sale finally closed after two years on the market, because Ned was in no rush to sell and was willing to wait for the right buyer. Now, you try to sell your house over the next few months, because you need money to keep your struggling business afloat. After two months, you sell your house for $170,000. As this is over 70% of the fair market value, you received *fair consideration*.

If you transfer property for something other than money, such as other property or services (i.e. exchange your home for a boat), the same rules apply. Courts examine the property or services you receive to determine whether or not they satisfy the *fair value* requirement when compared to the asset you transferred. Only past services rendered constitute fair value -- no "future services" are allowed.

■ Factor B: "In the Face of a Known Liability"

Even if a creditor attacking a transfer shows that it was a sale for less than fair value or a gift, he must still show that you made the transfer "in the face of a known liability." What does this phrase mean? Courts define it to mean that you cannot transfer assets to protect against future *probable liabilities*, but you can make a transfer to protect yourself against future *possible liabilities*. Again, it is difficult to precisely define the difference between *probable liabilities* and *possible liabilities*. The courts look at the facts of each case, focus on the timing of when the act creating the liability occurred and when you realized that you may be liable for that act.

Understandably, there is much gray area in determining whether or not a liability was probable or possible at any given point in time. You want the best legal talent to position you in the best light. Consider the following example:

Case Study: *Doctor Dave and Patient Pete*

Doctor Dave always knows that malpractice liability is possible and transfers assets to protect against possible future malpractice suits. However, if Dave clearly botched an operation on patient

Pete, realizing he made a mistake, it would be likely that Pete would eventually sue. Pete's malpractice suit, therefore, would be a *probable liability* from the moment of the operation.

Assume, instead, that it was unclear whether or not Dave operated negligently. If Dave transferred his wealth, not foreseeing any lawsuit by Pete, it would be arguable whether or not the liability to Pete was *probable* or *possible*. It would be up to the courts.

Consider the following Florida case, *Hurlbert v. Shackleton*. A physician, Shackleton, lost his malpractice coverage and divested himself of his assets to protect them in case he was someday sued again for malpractice. When Dr. Shackleton was later sued for malpractice, the plaintiff attempted to get his asset transfers undone as fraudulent. While the doctor won at trial, the determined plaintiff appealed. The appellate court sent the case back to the trial court with instructions to the trial court judge that the transfer could only be deemed fraudulent if, at the time of the transfer, Dr. Shackleton had the actual intent to defraud a specific creditor. As the plaintiff Hurlbert had not even seen Dr. Shackleton when the doctor made the asset transfers, how could the doctor have intended to defraud him? These instructions effectively dismantled Hurlbert's case. The lesson from this case: Protect assets *before* the threat arises and your transfers will be upheld.

■ Factor C: "Which leaves the debtor insolvent"

Even if a creditor attacking your transfer can show it was for less than fair value, and even if they can show you made the transfer when a probable liability existed, the court will not undo the transfer, unless it left you *insolvent*. *Insolvent* means the market value of all of your assets is less the amount needed to pay your existing debts as they come due. In other words, you are left in the position where you cannot pay your debts.

To summarize: You cannot safely transfer your property for less than fair value, when a probable liability exists, and when your remaining wealth cannot cover your debts as they are due.

WHAT A CREDITOR CAN DO WHEN YOUR TRANSFER IS "FRAUDULENT"

A creditor who believes your transfer is fraudulent has powerful remedies to recover the transferred property. These remedies can be against you and the person to whom you transferred the property—the *transferee*. The creditor's specific rights depend on whether or not the creditor has already been awarded a judgment against you for the underlying liability.

1. Judgment Creditors

If the creditor has already won a judgment against you (a *judgment creditor*) and suspects a particular transfer by you was fraudulent, then the creditor can ask the court to:

- Freeze the asset—while the court determines whether or not the transfer was fraudulent. Meanwhile, the transferee cannot transfer it again or "use it up" (cash), or take a loan against its value.
- Appoint a receiver to manage the asset while the court decides whether or not the transfer was fraudulent.
- Undo the transfer—if the transfer is judged fraudulent. This restores title of the transferred property to you, so the creditor can then seize it from you and force you to return the sale proceeds, if any, to the transferee. Thus, each party is again in the same position as prior to the transfer.
- Recover the proceeds from you if you previously sold the asset.

2. Non-judgment Creditors

If there is no present judgment against you, the creditor will have more difficulty in asking the court to interfere with your transfer. The creditor must show the following before the court grant the remedies listed above:

- A reasonable expectation of winning a judgment against you for the underlying liability.
- That you have no other assets available from which you could pay the creditor's judgment; and,
- A reasonable expectation that the transfer will be later judged fraudulent.

A FRAUDULENT TRANSFER IS USUALLY NOT A CRIME

A fraudulent transfer is usually not a crime. *Fraudulent transfer* is a civil term which divides safe, allowable transfers from those that can be undone by the courts. Neither the transferor nor transferee becomes subject to criminal penalties in the vast majority of cases. In most cases, there is considerable gray area in which the attorney can argue that the transfer at issue was not fraudulent, for all of the reasons noted previously. In these cases, the most severe action a court can take is to grant the noted remedies—essentially, to undo the transfer. Only when the parties clearly acted in bad faith—with the intent to defraud or delay creditors—can it be a criminal misdemeanor, in the few states that make it so.

Under no circumstances should an attorney allow clients to make transfers which could bring criminal sanctions. Instead, he should design transfers which, even in the most extreme cases, can be justified as non-fraudulent using all of the factors explained above. The next three sections outline ways to structure asset transfers, not only to avoid criminal sanctions, but to also stand up to fraudulent transfer challenges as well.

DEFENSES TO FRAUDULENT TRANSFER

The previous sections uncovered the factors a creditor must show for the court to hold that a transfer was fraudulent under either "actual" or "constructive" fraud theories. When defending a client's transfers, an attorney need only prove one of these factors, and the court cannot find the transfer fraudulent under either theory. He may show that there was no fraudulent intent, that the client received fair value, that there was no probable liability at the time of the transfer, or that the transfer did not leave the client insolvent. Always document that the transfer was not made exclusively for asset protection purposes, but also for other reasons.

In addition, another defense is available. The statute of limitations—a time period within which a plaintiff must bring a case. For example, a plaintiff in state X may have to file a lawsuit based on contract law within 3 years of the alleged breach. A later lawsuit cannot be started.

Under the UFCA, claims of fraudulent transfer laws must be brought either four years after the challenged transfer was made, or the liability incurred, or one year after the transfer was discovered, or reasonably could have been discovered by the creditor, whichever event occurs last. While this sentence is typically confusing "lawyerese," have your asset protection lawyer decide whether a transfer is beyond challenge because of your state's statute of limitations.

HOW TO AVOID FRAUDULENT TRANSFER CLAIMS

These are more common ways to structure asset transfers to insure that they will not be judged to be fraudulent:

1) Transfer before the liability arises.

Simply put, there cannot be a fraudulent transfer if you make the transfer *before* a probable liability arises, underscoring why it is so important to set up your asset protection plan sooner rather than later.

2) Show that the transfer was for purposes other than asset protection.

Support your transfer with adequate correspondence and documentation that the transfer was part of an estate or investment plan. Often we put language in the legal documents—or *preliminary recitals*—which confirm that the transfer was for purposes other than creditor protection alone.

3) Document what you receive in the transaction— higher is better.

This is especially important if the transfer was made for past services. Be prepared to prove that the value you received satisfies the fair value requirement. If you received property, obtain favorable appraisals.

4) Document the value of the property you transferred—lower is better.

For the same reasons, shop around to document the lowest appraisal of transferee property. Emphasize defects or damage to the appraiser to help insure a low value.

5) Utilize overlapping asset protection techniques.

Good attorneys use *overlap* techniques to protect certain assets. For example, in addition to transferring rental property to a family limited partnership, the attorney might also recommend a mortgage on the property to an uncle for the $15,000 owed an uncle. Now, a creditor must attack the transfer to the partnership, and also the mortgage.

6) Continue your regular gifts and donations.

Even if you gifted property when a liability existed, it may not be fraudulent if it was part of an established pattern of gifting. For example, if you always paid your children's college tuition, you can probably continue without incurring sanctions.

WHY EXPERT ASSET PROTECTION IS SO IMPORTANT

Laws against fraudulent transfers are complex. They create a tremendous gray area—as most challenged transfers are neither clearly fraudulent nor clearly legitimate. An asset protection specialist will understand the complexity and the nuances of fraudulent transfer laws. The specialist understands how transfers can be justified. *Further, a specialist knows how to structure a transfer so that the very documents which create the transfer, any claim of a possible fraudulent intent is eliminated.*

An asset protection plan's ultimate test is often a fraudulent transfer claim by a frustrated creditor. An experienced asset protection specialist can ensure that your plan will survive such a fraudulent transfer attack.

SUMMARY

- Fraudulent transfer laws allow creditors to undo certain debtor transfers.
- A successful fraudulent transfer challenge can destroy the protection an asset protection plan was designed to establish.
- A transfer can be fraudulent because of either actual fraud or constructive fraud on the part of the debtor.
- Actual fraud involves the intent to frustrate creditors, while constructive fraud can exist even if you acted completely innocently.
- There is considerable gray area in what will be deemed fraudulent—which invites many convincing defenses to a fraudulent transfer attack.
- There are steps to take to insure that your transfer will be upheld. The most effective: *Protect yourself now*, before trouble arises.
- Using an asset protection specialist is crucial to successfully avoiding fraudulent transfers.

CHAPTER 5:

USING EXISTING LAWS TO PROTECT ASSETS

You understand how the lawsuit has become a dangerous threat to your financial future. You also know the powerful rights creditors have against you before, during, and after a lawsuit. Finally, you now understand the general goals and objectives of an asset protection plan, and the restrictions fraudulent transfer laws impose on such a plan. Essentially, you understand the problem that faces all of us—the threat of losing our savings and property to a lawsuit—and a strategy for solving that problem. Now, we show you how to solve the problem itself.

This and later chapters show the tools that asset protection specialists use to create a financial fortress. You may think of these "tools" as the "building blocks" to construct a legal wall around you and your family—to protect your possessions and savings from any outside threats. This chapter examines the first "tool" or "building block"—state and federal laws which already exist, but which the vast majority of Americans do not advantageously use. With this chapter, you learn how to maximize your protection under these laws.

Whether it be homestead laws, wage or pension exemptions, bankruptcy exemptions or other protective laws, the government helps to protect particular assets. That is why we organize this chapter asset-by-asset, beginning with your home. The government's aid is completely inconsistent. These laws can be extremely valuable or virtually meaningless, depending on the creditor we are protecting against and the state in which you live. As with all asset protection, maximizing protection under these laws can be tricky business, best left to an experienced expert.

SAFEGUARDING YOUR HOME USING HOMESTEAD LAWS

Many Americans consider their homes their most valuable asset. In fact, you may have already thought you knew about the laws which protect your home. *Perhaps you have previously heard the term "homestead," and assumed that you could never lose your home to bad debts or other liabilities because of homestead protection. You would be wrong.* Homestead laws are hot and cold—some give you total protection, while others, are no shield whatsoever. We discovered that the best way to understand these laws and their protective power is through a series of questions and answers.

1. What are homestead laws?

Homestead laws are state **statutes** which protect the home from certain creditors. Forty-five states have such laws. *And, each state declares a certain amount of equity (value) of the homestead protected against particular types of creditors.* To understand whether or not these laws protect you, it is necessary to understand what the term *homestead* means.

2. What is a "homestead"?

This can be very tricky, for not everything you might consider to be a "home" qualifies for "homestead" status. *Homestead exemption only applies to real estate which is your primary residence and which you own and occupy.* Beyond this, whether or not a certain piece of real estate can be considered your homestead depends completely on your state statute.

For example, many states extend homestead protection to condominiums, but some do not. Also, certain state statutes cover only single-family homes, not duplexes, triplexes, or larger structures. Some states even shield mobile homes, in the right circumstances; while others offer them no homestead exemption.

3. How much of the homestead's value do these laws protect?

This answer also depends on your state, but in most cases the answer is "not enough." Most states only protect between $10,000 and $60,000 of the homestead's equity, while some states, like New Jersey, provide no protection. Given today's real estate values and the equity many people have in their home, most state homestead exemptions provide inadequate protection.

Using Existing Laws To Protect Assets

On the other hand, if you to live in Texas or Florida, your homestead is protected up to an unlimited value. In Florida or Texas, you could keep a debt-free multi-million dollar home, even when you file for bankruptcy!

Remember, *to determine how well a homestead law protects your home, compare the protected value to the equity*. First, subtract the value of any mortgages from the fair market value of your home. For example, if you live in a home with a $300,000 fair market value and a $150,000 mortgage, then your equity is $150,000. If your state protects only $20,000 through it homestead law, then you still have $130,000 equity vulnerable to lawsuits and other creditors.

4. Is homestead protection automatic?

Usually not. Each state has specific requirements for claiming homestead status. In some states, you must file a declaration of homestead in a public office. Others set a time requirement for residency before homestead protection is granted. *Never assume your home is protected and do nothing— you may be wrong*. Your asset protection attorney can show you how to comply with the state law formalities.

5. Who can claim homestead protection?

Certain states allow only the head of household to make the homestead declaration. Others allow either spouse to do so. Beware: if both spouses file a declaration, they could cancel each other out (in some states). Once again, have your asset protection attorney investigate who can determine who can file the declaration.

6. Who does homestead protect against?

While it will again depend on your state's statute, the general rule is that homestead will protect your home from all debts (including judgments) that arose after the homestead status attached. Some states provide protection from debts incurred even before homestead status attached.

Homestead laws won't protect your home from certain types of creditor claims. *The following creditors can ignore homestead laws and take action against your home:*

- The IRS and other federal agencies—if you owe federal taxes or are sued by the SEC or the EPA, you can lose your home, no matter what state you live in. If you owe state taxes, homestead may protect you, depending on the state.

53

- Spouses in a divorce action and family members challenging inheritances.
- Plaintiffs with intentional tort claims; libel, fraud, deceit, and others.
- Creditors to whom you voluntarily gave interests in your home, such as mortgages or deeds of trust.

6. Is there any downside to making a homestead declaration?

Yes, there are downsides. You may have to endure legal complications if you try to sell or refinance your home after making the declaration. The bank or buyer may need you to temporarily lift the homestead exemption while the transaction closes. While this is not too burdensome, it can be inconvenient and time-consuming.

The most significant downside, however, is that you will be lulled into an illusory sense of security. For example, today you may have $30,000 worth of equity in your home. If you live in a state with a $30,000 homestead exemption, your home is fully protected today. But, what about in your future? Lulled into a false sense of security, you believe your house is still fully protected. Yet, as the years move on, you build up more equity in your home. When you are eventually sued 5, 7, 10 years down the road, all the additional equity you have built in your home could be lost. *Asset protection clients never suffer this mistake. Their advisors analyze how homestead protects them today, and how it will continue to do so in the future—using other tools to protect their savings wherever homestead comes up short.*

3 WAYS TO MAXIMIZE HOMESTEAD PROTECTION

Your asset protection lawyer should not have you file a homestead declaration until he/she has considered all of your financial circumstances. The goal is to determine whether homestead protection can be the strongest "building block" of your financial fortress. To maximize homestead protection:

- The *spouse who is more vulnerable to lawsuits should file the declaration,* so the protection can shield against claims facing that spouse.

- If you have multiple homes, have her *file the homestead declaration for the home with the most equity exposed.* This can be tricky because the person declaring homestead must show that he lives at that dwelling with the intent to make it his permanent domicile. If your homestead status is challenged, be prepared to answer:

Using Existing Laws To Protect Assets

- Where you filed your federal tax returns.
- Where your mail is received.
- Where you are registered to vote.
- Where you spend most of your time.

■ *Move to a state where the homestead exemption is unlimited—Florida or Texas.* This is part of the more general asset protection tactic: convert wealth held in ***non-exempt assets*** into wealth held in ***exempt assets***. Consider the extreme case following:

Case Study:
Ron Moves to Florida

Ron, a St. Louis radiologist, invested heavily in commercial real estate. Involved in a major condominium project, he personally guaranteed a note of over $1 million. Ron did not think he could lose his home, because he had heard that homestead laws protected it. Early on in the project, Ron worried that the project would lose money because of a downturn in the economy. But, what could he do to better protect himself in case the project went failed?

Ron met with an asset protection attorney and was surprised to learn that his house was only protected up to $8,000. After a series of consultations, the attorney set out Ron's asset protection plan. Since Ron had thought about moving to the warmer weather, now was his time.

Ron liquidated his major non-exempt assets (stocks, bonds, his home, his boat) and used the entire sale proceeds to buy a home in Palm Beach, Florida. For two years, Ron considered Florida his home, paying taxes in Florida, filing a affidavit of domicile and a declaration of homestead, and spending weekends and vacations there as well.

Meanwhile, he rented a house in St. Louis to continue his part-time radiology work at a clinic and to finish the real estate project. As it turned out, the project incurred losses and the bank sued Ron on the guarantee. Almost three years after buying the house in Florida, Ron filed for bankruptcy under Chapter 7.

While the debt was large, the St. Louis banker did not even bother to send a representative to Florida to challenge Ron's bankruptcy filing. The debt to the bank was completely discharged and Ron's Florida home was fully protected by Florida's generous homestead laws. Free and clear, Ron could now move back to Missouri—if he could only leave the golf course.

Ron's case may be an extreme example, but you get the point—a real master of asset protection strategies does not simply know the laws that can work for you. Rather, the specialist uses the laws that are the best tools for the job.

LAWS WHICH PROTECT YOUR WAGES

Creditors who win a judgment against you can seize your paycheck through a *wage garnishment*. A creditor's right to take your paycheck is limited. Both federal and state laws partially protect wages.

Like the homestead laws, each state's protection for wages differs. Texas and Florida are again the most friendly to debtors and exempt 100% of wages from creditor garnishment. The remaining states protect a certain percentage of one's wages and allow the creditor to take the rest.

Even if your state offers only limited protection of your wages, the federal *Consumer Credit Protection Act (CCPA)* sets a limit on the amount a creditor can take from your wages. Because it is a federal law, the CCPA trumps any state law which offers less wage protection. Thus, if your wages are threatened by a creditor, you will be protected at least by the limits of CCPA and possibly more, depending on your state's law. The CCPA limits the amount of wages a creditor can take to the lesser of:

a) 25% of your disposable income per week (*disposable income* means your paycheck after federal and state withholding taxes have been taken out), or
b) the amount by which your weekly disposable income for the week exceeds 30 times the federal minimum hourly wage then in effect.

LIFE INSURANCE—CAN PROTECT YOU IN MANY WAYS

Life insurance, like homes, are protected solely by state law. Today, all 50 states have laws protecting life insurance, but they all protect differing amounts. Some general trends:

Using Existing Laws To Protect Assets

- Most states shield the entire policy proceeds from the creditors of the policyholder. Some also protect against the beneficiaries' creditors.
- States which do not protect the entire policy proceeds set amounts above which the creditor can take proceeds. For example, Arizona exempts the first $20,000 of proceeds.
- Many states protect the policy proceeds only if the policy beneficiaries are the policyholder's spouse, children, or other dependents.
- Most states also exempt term and group life policies.
- Some states protect a policy's cash surrender value in addition to the policy proceeds. If you have substantial cash value in a life insurance policy(ies), be sure to consult your state exemptions to determine how well protected you are.
- No state can protect life insurance from the IRS—they can take your insurance proceeds and cash value. If you already have an IRS problem or anticipate owing more taxes than you can pay.
- If the policy is purchased as part of a fraudulent transfer, a court can undue the policy, like any other fraudulent transfer.

MAXIMIZING LIFE INSURANCE PROTECTION

An important part of any asset protection plan is the irrevocable life insurance trust. If the beneficiaries have creditor concerns, the policy has cash value, the IRS is a potential creditor, or if you live in a state with minimal protection, such a trust is essential. As you see later in more detail, a properly drafted irrevocable life insurance trust provides maximum protection for your policy proceeds and its cash value—shielding them entirely from all creditors of the policyholder and the beneficiaries, including the IRS. It also may provide you significant tax benefits.

TIP: *Never assign your life insurance policy to a bank or other creditor. Even if your policy was originally exempt, you could lose the exemption if you made such an assignment.*

ANNUITIES—AN ASSET-PROTECTED INVESTMENT IN MANY STATES

An annuity is a investment contract where the investor pays a certain amount of money up-front, and the seller then pays the investor back at a certain interest rate in fixed installments. Most states do not protect annuities from creditor claims. However, in the states that do exempt annuities, annuities are an ideal tool to safeguard wealth. Depending on the state exemption, there may be a limit on the value of the annuities to be protected.

As part of asset protection planning, also review your investment objectives. By investing in life insurance and annuities, you may achieve both your investment goals and asset protection..

RETIREMENT PLANS: A MIXED BAG OF PROTECTION

Along with the family home, an individual's retirement savings is often the most important asset he owns. In terms of asset protection, retirement plans next must be divided into: 1) ERISA-qualified pension plans and 2) all other retirement plans, such as *Individual Retirement Accounts (IRAs)* and Keogh plans.

1. ERISA-Qualified Pension Plans

ERISA-qualified means the pension meets the requirements of the *Employee Retirement Income Security Act of 1974 (ERISA)*. ERISA was enacted specifically to protect the rights of employees enrolled in benefit plans sponsored by their employers or unions. A key requirement of ERISA is that the pension plan must be a spendthrift trust—one that prohibits the beneficiary from in any way giving away the plan's principal or income.

A 1992 U.S. Supreme Court decision solidified the protection for ERISA-qualified pension plans. *The Court clearly concluded that ERISA-qualified plans cannot be taken by creditors, whether in bankruptcy, by lawsuit, or through other means.* This decision applies to all ERISA-qualified pension plans. Public pensions (those funded by state or federal government) have always been exempt from creditor claims.

Is your pension ERISA-qualified? If both owners and employees are covered by the plan, most likely it is ERISA-qualified. To be sure, contact your asset protection lawyer to review the pension documents themselves.

2. Keogh Plans

If you participate in a Keogh plan that has multiple participants, the same principles that apply to ERISA-qualified pensions will apply to your Keogh plan. Most likely, the plan will be safe, whether attacked by one creditor in a lawsuit or a host of creditors in a bankruptcy. A sole-participant Keogh plan, however, is considerably more vulnerable.

State courts routinely allow creditors to seize sole-participant Keogh funds, on the theory that the beneficiary/debtor is able to withdraw the funds at will; and, because the beneficiary/debtor is his own trustee.

3. IRAs

IRAs are less secure than ERISA-qualified plans and Keoghs. An IRA is basically a custodial account set aside for the owner, who can withdraw the funds at any time. As there is no "spendthrift" provision and no trustee, there is no federal protection for IRAs. Also, because the owner can always reach the IRA funds by incurring a tax penalty, courts have held that creditors should have the same right to get at the funds. Nevertheless, many states exempt all retirement funds, including IRAs, from creditors.

Because protection of IRAs can only come from the states, federal government creditors like the IRS, the EPA, or the SEC can take your IRA. Although it is often last on their list of assets to seize, the IRS can and will eventually take your IRA funds if you owe back taxes. We will later cover strategies of how to protect those funds if you owe back taxes.

TIP: *If you need last-second asset protection because a creditor is about to seize assets, it may make sense to liquidate your IRA and transfer the funds into an exempt asset, or to pay other debts. While you will incur and early withdrawal penalty, that is preferable to losing the entire amount to a creditor seizure.*

Case Study:
An Avoidable Mistake

Jim, a physician, made a terrible asset protection blunder about three years ago. Frustrated with what he saw as excessive costs involved with the administration of his partnership's pension plan, Jim thought he could achieve better overall returns if he withdrew his money out of the pension plan and managed the funds himself, using an IRA. That is exactly what Jim did.

Jim never realized that his pension plan was fully protected against all attackers while his new IRA account was shielded by neither federal nor state law. Jim was later sued after an outside business deal collapsed, and his IRA funds were completely vulnerable in the lawsuit. Jim finally settled the lawsuit for much more than he would have, had he left his retirement savings in the safe pension.

Jim's mistake could have been avoided if Jim had understood the asset protection benefits of his pension plan versus money to an IRA. Jim might have realized that the protection of the pension plan outweighed the additional administrative costs.

ASSET PROTECTION TACTIC: TURN NON-EXEMPT WEALTH INTO EXEMPT WEALTH

As with the earlier example of Ron in St. Louis, an important tactic in asset protection strategy is to convert non-exempt assets into exempt assets—those protected from creditors under law. This general tactic can be put to use in hundreds of different ways, depending only on the creativity of the asset protection advisor and the client, considering viable alternatives. Here are a few of the many ways individuals have successfully used this general tactic:

- A doctor obtained a second mortgage on the family's non-homestead vacation home to reduce the mortgage on the primary homestead home.

- Foreseeing creditor problems, a woman converted her vulnerable mutual funds into annuities and investment life insurance.

- Before engaging in a risky business venture, a chiropractor added her brother as co-trustee to her sole-participant Keogh plan, thus immunizing it from lawsuits.

- A New York businessman had to sell his homestead-protected home for financial reasons, just as another creditor threatened to sue. He transferred the sale proceeds directly into exempt assets—in his case, annuities. Thus, a corollary tactic: when selling exempt assets, direct funds into another exempt asset.

- Starting out in his own medical practice, a Massachusetts heart doctor moved his IRA account to a bank in a state that protects such accounts from creditors.

SUMMARY

- Homestead laws are state laws which protect your primary residence from certain types of creditors.
- Each state protects a different amount of equity in its homestead exemption, but none can protect the home from the IRS, child support, and certain other claims.
- Homestead laws can lull some people into a false sense of security. Do not let that be you!
- Wages are given some protection by Federal law, but your state may provide even more.
- Life insurance can be an ideal protection tool for the policy proceeds and the cash value.
- State laws differ regarding the amount and type of life insurance which is protected, but no state can exempt it from the IRS and other federal claims.
- Annuities can provide investment returns and asset protection in many states.
- Pensions which are ERISA-qualified are fully protected from creditors other than the IRS.
- Keogh plans are likely protected, if they are multiple-participant. Sole-participant plans are more vulnerable.
- IRAs are not protected by federal law, but they may be by your state. Again, this asset protection is not good against federal creditors like the IRS.
- The asset protection tactic—turn non-exempt wealth into exempt wealth—utilizes these laws for your maximum protection.

CHAPTER 6:

CO-OWNERSHIP CAN PROTECT OR THREATEN YOU

Wealth can be protected from creditors and lawsuits by using co-ownership. Co-ownership simply means owning something with another person—you each co-own the item or property in question. This chapter explains the three types of co-ownership, as well as the basics about community property.

Asset protection uses the legal system for your protection, like a shield. With this imagery in mind, think of co-ownership as the sword you would hold along with your shield when defending your castle. This co-ownership sword is "dangerous" and "double-edged" because co-ownership often causes more problems than it solves. It can frustrate your desired estate plan, cost you excessive taxes, and even subject you to more liability than if you owned property in your own name!

Despite these significant dangers, co-ownership is an effective asset protection tool in certain situations. This chapter explains the dangers to avoid when owning property with another person, as well as the ways to wisely use co-ownership.

THE THREE TYPES OF CO-OWNERSHIP

To understand the risks and benefits of each type co-ownership, learn how each is defined, created, and works. Remember that, unless otherwise noted, these ownership arrangements can apply to personal property (bank accounts, stocks and bonds, motor vehicles, copyrights, partnership interests, etc.) or real property (land, a home, a condominium, a building, etc.). Also, do not be confused by the fact that these ownerships use the word *tenancy*. This does not mean that they only apply to leases and tenants. These ownerships apply to outright ownership as well as leases of property.

1. Tenancy in Common:
- Each co-owner owns a fractional interest in the property. (i.e. if there are three co-owners, each owns 1/3 share).
- Each co-owner can transfer or mortgage his or her share of the property without the consent of the other co-owners.
- When a co-owner dies, she can pass down her share of ownership as she chooses.
- Tenancy in common is the *default tenancy* for non-married co-owners—meaning that if you do not specifically designate another type of ownership in the title or transfer documents, the law will assume that the rules for tenancy in common apply.
- **EXAMPLE:** Two roommates sign a lease for an apartment, or when two business partners buy an empty lot in their names. If they do not state otherwise, they will own their lease/lot as tenants in common.

2. Joint Tenancy:
- Each co-owner owns an undivided interest in the property (i.e. if there are three co-owners, each has an undivided share of the whole property).
- Any co-owner can transfer his interest without the consent of the others. If he transfers his interest, this severs the joint tenancy and the new owner becomes a tenant in common with the previous joint owners.
    > Example: Assume three owners in joint tenancy—A, B, and C—each owning an undivided 1/3 share. If joint tenant A sells to Buyer, Buyer then owns as a tenant in common with joint tenants B and C. B and C still own as joint tenants between themselves.
- When a joint tenant dies, her share automatically passes to the surviving joint tenants. She cannot pass the ownership share through inheritance. This is called the joint tenant's *right of survivorship*.

Using the previous example, if C later died, B would automatically take C's 1/3. B would then own 2/3 of the property, as tenant in common with Buyer, who owns 1/3.

- Most states require joint tenancy to be created by a written agreement, using the words *joint tenancy, jointly, jointly with the right of survivorship,* or similar wording. Some states do not presume that joint tenancy carries the right of survivorship, so include it in the documents if you want this right.
- **EXAMPLE:** If two people own a joint bank account or purchase a house with the proper "joint" wording in the documents, a joint tenancy is established. The right of survivorship will usually apply.

3. Tenancy by the Entirety:

- This ownership form is available in only 31 states. Even within those states, only husband and wife can use tenancy by the entirety ownership. (For a list of the states which have tenancy by the entirety—see the Appendices.)
- Tenancy by the entirety is essentially a special type joint tenancy for married couples. As a joint tenancy, it carries with it the right of survivorship—the surviving spouse automatically takes the deceased spouse's share.
- Neither husband nor wife can transfer or mortgage the property without the other's consent.
- The tenancy by the entirety remains in tact until both spouses agree to change the ownership type, until divorce, or until one of the spouses dies.
- Some of the states that allow tenancy by the entirety restrict its use for real estate, such as the marital home. Others allow all types of personal property and real estate to be owned in tenancy by the entirety. (See Appendix).
- **EXAMPLE:** Husband and wife in Pennsylvania purchase a home. In the deed, they write the home is owned by them, as husband and wife, by tenancy by the entirety.

THE RISKS OF TENANCY IN COMMON OWNERSHIP

Because each co-owner in a tenancy in common (also called a *tenant in common*) owns a divided fractional share of the property in question, this arrangement has serious ramifications for lawsuit and creditor protection. As we explore the risks of co-ownerships, keep the following example in mind:

The Building You and Frank Own
You and your friend Frank are each tenants in common owners of a residential apartment building—each of you can sell, give away, or mortgage your 1/2 share of the building without the consent of the other. You are partners in the business of renting the apartments, collecting the rents, maintaining the premises, etc., and plan to use the building to provide you both with an income. You both agree that, given the right market conditions, you should sell the building, for a hefty profit.

Because each tenant in common has a separate ownership share, distinct from the other tenants in common, her creditors cannot get to the shares owned by the other tenants in common. To use the above example, if Frank is sued for a reason unrelated to the building, Frank's creditors can only come after his half of the building. Your half is safe from Frank's creditors. While this arrangement may seem like an asset protection advantage, if you are the *safe* co-owner, it is not.

The risk of tenancy in common ownership is that your co-owner(s) creditors can ask the court to sell the entire property, including your share, to satisfy the outstanding debt. This is called *forced liquidation*. The legal theory is that because your co-tenant can transfer her share of tenancy in common property without your consent, her creditor can "step into her shoes" and force the transfer of her share as well. While you can buy the liquidated share to avoid the sale of the entire property, this is not always practical, as you may not have the money to do so. If not, the court can sell the entire property on the open market. You lose your share of the property, but you get to keep your share of the proceeds.

If the co-tenant's creditors do not want the entire property sold to get cash, they may simply take the debtor co-tenant's share of the property. Now, you have a new partner. Returning to the above example, Frank's financial problems could cause any number of problems for you, even though you are supposedly *safe*. Consider these:

- Frank's creditors force a sale of the entire building during a terrible market for sellers. They know even a rock-bottom price will pay off their debt, so they do not care. Because you cannot come up with the cash to buy Frank's share, the building is sold well below its fair market value. Frank's creditors are paid, and you get half of the proceeds. However, you lose a building which provided you a steady cash flow, and which you know is worth much more than its selling price.

- Frank's creditors like the apartment building. They decide they would rather keep the building themselves than sell it. Now, you have a new partner—someone (or likely something, like a bank or credit union) you do not know, trust, or understand. Not an ideal partner for a business venture going forward.

- Frank's creditors like the apartment building. They take Frank's half share. When the market turns into a strong seller's market you want to sell the building and make your profit. However, Frank's creditors, now your partners, disagree. You end up selling your half, which gets much less on the market than half of the whole building would yield. It turns out that a few others also want to accept Frank's creditors as their partners.

While the list could continue further, the point is clear—owning property with others by tenancy in common is risky. If your co-tenant(s) develop financial problems, you can lose control of your ownership share and lose significant amounts of money. Avoid this trap. Future chapters will show you ownership forms superior to tenancy in common which can be used in a variety of settings, including the above example of the apartment building with Frank. If you must use tenancy in common ownership, make sure that your co-tenants are financially secure. Otherwise, you risk a forced sale, a new co-owner, and losing all control of your investment.

WHY JOINT TENANCY IS SO DANGEROUS

Joint tenancy is the most popular form of ownership in the United States for stocks, bonds, real estate, and bank accounts. As explained above, when one joint tenant dies, property owned in joint tenancy automatically passes to the surviving joint tenant(s). In this way, jointly owned property passes outside of a will and avoids the expense of probate. Because it avoids probate, many financial and legal advisors recommend joint tenancy as a form of ownership. But what these advisors do not tell you are the ways you can be burned by owning assets in joint tenancy. As you will see, using joint tenancy as an ownership form is almost always a big mistake. Joint tenancy subjects you to lawsuit and creditor risks. It can frustrate your true estate plan, and there are better ways to avoid probate. We examine each of these pitfalls individually.

1. Joint Tenancy Creates Lawsuit and Creditor Risks

If you own property (personal property or real estate) jointly, you face the same lawsuit and creditor risks explained for tenancy in common ownership, plus you have additional exposure. To review, you will have tenancy in common protection—only your creditors can take your share of tenancy in common property. You will also have tenancy in common risks—that your co-owner(s) develops financial problems and her creditors either take her share of the property and become your co-tenant in common, or force a sale of the entire property to pay the debt.

In addition, joint ownership puts you in a "winner take all" game, where you are gambling that you survive longer than your fellow joint tenants. Because jointly owned property automatically passes to the surviving joint tenant(s), if the safe tenant dies before the debtor tenant, the whole property becomes the debtor's, and can be taken by debtor's creditors. Returning to the previous example, if you and Frank owned the building in joint tenancy and you died before Frank, Frank would own the building outright. Frank's creditors could then come in and lien, levy, or seize the entire building. Your family would have no rights whatsoever.

The other outcome of the "winner take all" game is that the safe co-owner (assume: you) survives longer than the debtor co-owner (assume: Frank). Does this mean that you take the building free and clear of Frank's creditor problems? In most cases, yes. This is the one asset protection aspect of joint tenancy—winning the "winner take all" game. This victory, however, is not absolute. In the following situations, even if you survive and take the entire building, Frank's one-half share may still be vulnerable:

1) Frank owed federal or state taxes.
2) Frank declared bankruptcy—the bankruptcy trustee can sell any property Frank owned, even if he is now dead. You must then claim a share of the sale proceeds.
3) The situation occurs in a limited number of states which allow a dead joint tenant's creditors to come after the surviving joint tenants' property.

2. Joint Tenancy Can Ruin Your Estate Plan

Recall that in a previous chapter you learned that your plan to give away your property at your death to your friends and "heirs" is called your "estate plan." This plan is usually set out in a will, although as you will soon realize, no one should have a will without a living trust.

Joint tenancy threatens to ruin your estate plan because any property you own jointly will pass automatically by the right of survivorship to the surviving joint tenant(s). This automatic transfer takes effect, in the eyes of the law, the very instant you die, before any will or living trust can dispose of your property. In this way, your will or living trust will have no effect on jointly held property. If you designated certain beneficiaries in a will or trust to receive your share of jointly held property, they will be "disinherited"—the surviving joint tenant(s) will take it. This avoidable tragedy occurs everyday in this country; because people do not realize the dangers of joint ownership and because their advisors are not giving them adequate information. Consider these stories:

1. William, a man in his late 60's, marries for the second time. Shortly after the wedding, he puts all of his significant property—his main home, his winter vacation condominium, and his stock portfolio—into joint tenancy with his new wife. Within six months, William dies. The home, the condo, and the stocks all go to William's new wife. His three children and eight grandchildren inherit virtually nothing, even though William had made ample provisions for them in his will.

2. Susan's will left her property equally to her son and daughter. Because her son lives near her and he pays her bills, Susan puts her house, her safe deposit box, and her bank account in joint tenancy with him. When she dies, Susan's son will get all of the money in the bank account and deposit box, as well as the house, regardless of the will provisions. Unless the son is extremely generous, the daughter will get close to nothing. Do you want to rely on your children's generosity to carry out your estate plan?

3. Assume the same situation as in #2, but add to the facts that the son has serious creditor problems. Overdue on $15,000 in credit card debts and a defaulted loan, the son's creditors can come after the bank account, the safe deposit box contents, and likely the house, the instant Susan dies. The only real beneficiaries of Susan's estate may be banks and finance companies.

4. Cecilia, a single mother in her thirties, is trying to build a college fund for her eight-year old daughter, Debbie. Cecilia has invested some of her excess income to buy old residential multi-family homes, which she and her partner then fix-up and rent to tenants. While her relationship with her partner has been strained at times, Cecilia thinks nothing of taking title to the investment properties in joint tenancy with her partner, never realizing that if she dies before they resell the properties, her partner will take them all, leaving nothing for Debbie.

Why do well-intentioned people get stuck in these predicaments? Because they do not know any better, and their advisors are not doing their jobs. Sometimes, owners may not even realize what type of ownership they have chosen. In other cases, people consciously decide to use joint ownership because they know it will avoid probate. But, this is never a reason to use joint tenancy.

3. Never Use Joint Tenancy to Avoid Probate — Use a Living Trust

Assets titled in joint tenancy and assets titled into a living trust both avoid probate. At your death, your interest in these assets will pass outside the probate process—the process by which the court validates your will and distributes your wealth under the will provisions. Why would you want to avoid probate using joint ownership or a living trust? Because of the many pitfalls of probate.

WHY YOU MUST AVOID PROBATE

- **TIME:** Probate often takes between a year and two years to complete. Your beneficiaries must wait for their inheritance.

- **MONEY:** Probate costs vary between 3-8% of your "probate estate;" the value of all your property passing under the will. This pays the courts, the lawyers, appraisers, and your executor (the person in charge of handling your affairs during this process), among others. In some states, these probate fees are paid on your gross estate—not taking into account any mortgages on your assets! In these states, if you die owning $1 million worth of assets, but which have mortgages of $800,000, your estate will pay probate fees on the $1 million, or around $50,000—money which could have gone to your beneficiaries, rather than to courts and lawyers.

- **PRIVACY:** Probate is a public process. Anyone interested in your estate can find out details about who inherits under your will and how much, the beneficiaries' addresses, and more. While you may not be famous and worry about the newspapers exploiting this information, think of your beneficiaries; your surviving family members. They certainly will not appreciate the many financial advisors calling them with "hot tips" on investments. These salespeople find beneficiaries by examining probate records. They know who they are and how much "found money" they have to invest.

Co-Ownership Can Protect or Threaten You

- **CONTROL:** In probate, the courts control the timing and final say-so on whether or not your will—and your wishes expressed in the will—are followed. Your family must follow the court orders, and pay for the process as well. This can be extremely frustrating.

You are probably thinking, "How can anyone use a will, when probate is this unappealing?" It is hard to believe. We are continually astonished by how many families endure the time and expense of probate, when it is completely avoidable. You will now learn why, to avoid probate, using a living trust is far superior to using joint tenancy. (As bad as probating a will is, there is an even worse alternative—not having a will and not using joint tenancy. If you die under this scenario, you have the pitfalls of probate plus the court decides who to give your property to—see the Appendices).

HOW A LIVING TRUST CAN BENEFIT YOU

A living trust, also called a *loving trust,* is a legal document which creates a trust to which you can transfer assets during your life. It is revocable, meaning you can change it at any time. During your life, the assets transferred to the trust are managed and controlled by you. When you die, these trust assets pass to whomever you designate in the trust automatically, outside of the probate process. For further information, see the Appendices, which describes this in more detail. A short list of the benefits that a Living Trust provides:

- Avoids the unintentional disinheriting risked by joint tenancy.
- Prevents court control of assets if you become incapacitated.
- Can reduce or eliminate estate taxes.
- Can be changed at any time prior to your incapacity or death.
- Can protect dependents with special needs.

Considering these and other benefits a Living Trust provides over joint tenancy, and given all of the downsides associated with probate, it is amazing that so few people pass their inheritance using a living trust. Only a minority of Americans have a living trust today. Everyone should have a living trust. Without one you are simply throwing away time, money, privacy, and control.

HOW TENANCY BY THE ENTIRETY CAN PROTECT YOU

Tenancy by the entirety is a special form of joint tenancy available only in some states, and only for husbands and wives. In most of the states that have it, the creditor protection is the same as that provided by joint tenancy—very little. However, in certain states, tenancy by the entirety provides very strong protection from creditors and lawsuits.

In these states, a creditor of either spouse alone cannot touch any property owned by the married couple as tenancy by the entirety property. Only creditors of both spouses together can come after tenancy by the entirety property. For example, if both husband and wife guaranteed a bank note, that bank could come after any property owned as tenancy by the entirety. But, if one spouse is being sued, then property owned in tenancy by the entirety is completed protected. This type of protection is extremely valuable.

Check the Appendices to see your state laws on tenancy by the entirety. If this type of protection makes sense for you, you will need an attorney to draft transfers (and new deeds for real estate), identifying the property as tenancy by the entirety. For certain personal property, you can change registrations yourself. Nevertheless, consult with an attorney to make certain that the courts in your state treat tenancy by the entirety differently than joint tenancy. Otherwise, there is little reason to go through the expense of changing titles.

SHIELDING COMMUNITY PROPERTY

Nine states have community property ownership: Arizona, California, Idaho, Louisiana, Nevada, New Mexico, Texas, Washington, and Wisconsin. Although these states all have community property laws, there are important differences among them. If you live in one of these states, make sure that you review with your attorney exactly how the system in your state works. This is especially important in regard to what rights creditors have against community property.

IMPORTANT: COMMUNITY PROPERTY LAWS CAN BE QUITE COMPLEX: WHAT FOLLOWS IS A BASIC SUMMARY—THERE MAY BE EXCEPTIONS TO THESE RULES IN YOUR STATE—CONSULT AN ATTORNEY FAMILIAR WITH YOUR STATE LAWS IF YOU HAVE QUESTIONS.

Community Property Basics

Under community property principles, each spouse has an equal one-half interest in all community property. Community property is any property (including personal property) acquired by either spouse during marriage, except inheritances or gifts to one spouse. Property acquired by one spouse before the marriage began or after divorce (or, *permanent separation*, depending on the state) is that spouse's separate property. Similarly, debts which are incurred before or after the marriage are separate debts, while those incurred during the marriage are community debts if they benefit the couple, which they most often do. This is true even if the debt is in one spouse's name.

For example, Harry Husband and Wife Wilma married in 1985 and divorced in 1995. Harry's boat, which he owned since 1980, remained his separate property, as did his inheritance from his father, which he received in 1989. The debt on Harry's boat dating back to 1980 also remained his separate debt. All the money Harry made as an accountant during their marriage was community property, as was the car he held in his name, but which he bought in 1987.

NOTE: There are ways for couples, using marital agreements, to legally convert community property into separate property and vica versa. However, these agreements must be carefully drafted according to state law and closely followed by the couple. As they rely so heavily on state law, we will not address them here.

Creditor Rights Against Community Property

A creditor's right to levy, lien, and seize property in a community property state will depend on the type of debt he is enforcing—community or separate—and, the type of property he is coming after—community or separate. Often, however, it is quite difficult to make these determinations. This means you often end up defending your side with lawyers, gambling on a jury's decision at trial. Nevertheless, consider these general principles:

1. Generally, creditors of one spouse's separate debt can go after that spouse's separate property in all cases. In most cases, they can also attack community property. They can even come after the separate property of the other spouse in certain cases when the debt was to pay for necessities—food, shelter, clothing, utilities, etc.

2. Creditors of community debt can come after community property and either spouse's separate property, in many situations.

3. Consider this excerpt from a summary of California community property law: "Most community property states, including California, employ a system that is most favorable to creditors. Creditors under this system may satisfy their debts out of property over which the debtor spouse has management and control. In California, this means that generally a creditor may reach the separate property of the debtor spouse and all community property, since the spouses have equal management and control of the community property."

You Must Protect Community Property

As you have probably realized, the safety of community and separate property is often times unclear. In many situations, both are clearly vulnerable. The bottom line: If you live in one of these states, you are no different than citizens of the other states—you must protect yourself as well. What you learn about in this book can protect you and your family just as effectively as anyone else. Be sure that when you are setting up your plan, you call on the advice of an attorney who understands your state's community property laws.

DO NOT HOLD ASSETS IN YOUR OWN NAME

If you hold property in your name, you have absolutely no title protection against your creditors, or against lawsuits. Unless homestead or other state or federal exemptions protect the asset, an asset held in your name is wide-open for attack. While owning assets in your own name does provide you with maximum flexibility, unless your asset is otherwise protected, such flexibility is too minor an advantage to justify exposing your wealth to all of the lawsuit and creditor risks. This is especially true, as you will learn, when trusts and partnerships provide you with flexibility, while also protecting your assets.

INVESTIGATE HOW YOU HOLD YOUR ASSETS

This previews the *Typical Physician's Asset Protection Plan* in the second-to-last chapter—exactly what you can do today to begin the road to total financial security. Before you approach an asset protection lawyer, understand the ownership form for all your assets. List, on the *Financial Assessment Worksheets*, all the property you own, from the most significant to the least, and write down how you own the asset. Remember, if you have not titled an asset specifically, the law assumes you own it a certain way. This exercise will accomplish the following:

- Show you how vulnerable you are. Chances are you have much of the "unintentional disinheriting" and lawsuit risks caused by joint tenancy.

- Show you how much you really own. As mentioned in the first chapter; you are likely much wealthier than you think and need to protect yourself more than you think.

- Show you the many assets you have which could create liability— through injury, property damage, or other forms of debt.

SUMMARY

- Co-ownerships are a double-edged sword, creating as many problems as they solve.
- There are three types of co-ownership: tenancy in common, joint tenancy, and tenancy by the entirety.
- If you own property by tenancy in common, you risk losing the property by forced sale, taking on an unwanted partner, and losing control of your investment in the property—all because of the financial problems of your co-owners.
- Joint tenancy can subject you to lawsuit and creditor risks and ruin your estate plan; and while it avoids probate, a living trust is far superior for probate avoidance.
- Probate is an avoidable process which costs your family time, money, privacy and control.
- The Living Trust is an ideal tool for passing property at death. However, it does not protect assets.
- Community property is an ownership form in nine states. Although each state has slightly distinct rules, community property is not safe and should be protected.
- You should not own assets in your own name, unless they are otherwise protected.
- Find out how you now own your assets. It is an important step on the road to financial security.

CHAPTER 7:

CORPORATIONS AS IMPORTANT PROTECTIVE TOOLS

This and the next four chapters discuss more important tools used in asset protection planning. Our discussion here covers corporations. Family limited partnerships (FLPs), limited liability companies (LLCs), domestic trusts, and offshore vehicles are covered in later chapters.

Asset protection planning is like building a financial fortress around your savings, possessions, and property. One of the most important building blocks in creating such a fortress is the corporation. This chapter highlights the asset protection benefits of the corporation, helping you to understand the differences between the "S" corporation and the "C" corporation, and why the professional corporation is often a strong asset-protector. In essence, you will learn how the corporation can play an important role in any asset protection plan.

DEFINITIONS

Generally, there are four ways a business can be organized: as a sole proprietorship, as a partnership (limited or general), as a corporation, or as a limited liability entity (company or partnership). Now, examine these arrangements, leaving the limited partnership and the limited liability entities for the next two chapters.

1. Sole Proprietorship

- A proprietorship exists when an individual operates a business without registering it as a formal legal entity, like a corporation or LLC. The proprietor may have employees, but no partners.
- There is no separation under the law between the proprietor and the business.
- The sole proprietor assumes personal liability for all business debts.
- Most small businesses in the U.S. are sole proprietorships.
- 4 out of 5 new businesses fail within the first five years—thus the proprietor is making a terrible gamble of his and his family's financial security on his venture. If the business fails, he will likely be in financial ruin.
- Bear in mind this common example:

Case Study:
Elizabeth Falls into the Proprietorship Trap

Elizabeth, the wife of a successful podiatrist, opened La Trattoria, a trendy Italian restaurant, about three years ago. She did not think she needed to incorporate, and thus ran the business as a proprietorship. While the restaurant did fairly well for three years, Elizabeth ended up declaring bankruptcy. Why? Because one night, one of her two delivery people was at fault in a serious car accident. While Elizabeth had some insurance, the policy limit was well below the $650,000 the victim was awarded in his personal injury suit. Because she ran the restaurant as a proprietorship, Elizabeth was personally liable for the $400,000 difference between her policy and the award. As she did not have the resources to pay the judgment, she was forced to declare bankruptcy under Chapter 7.

2. Partnerships

- A partnership exists when two or more people run a business together without a corporation.
- In a general partnership, all partners are liable for the partnership debts. In a limited partnership, only the general partners are liable for such debts.

3. Corporations
- A corporation is a legal entity owned by shareholders. The shareholders elect a board of directors who set policies for the corporation, allowing their selected officers (president, secretary, etc.) to run the corporation day-to-day.
- There can be as few as one shareholder who owns the corporation and elects a board, consisting of one director. In this way, one person can be a corporation's sole shareholder, sole director, and serve as every officer (president, vice-president, secretary, and treasurer).
- Corporations can be "C" or "S" corporations; the letter stands for a section of the tax code which controls that type corporation. C corporations dominate the market (all public corporations are Cs) and will be discussed here simply as *corporations*. S corporations are only for closely-held businesses and will be treated in a separate section of this chapter.

6 KEY CHARACTERISTICS OF A CORPORATION

The most important aspects of a corporation for asset protection purposes are:

■ Created by State Law
Each state has a statute which sets the requirements for establishing and maintaining a corporation. Some state laws are more corporate-friendly than others.

■ Distinct Legal Entity: Like Another Person
A corporation is a separate legal entity, distinct from its shareholders. The law, in fact, treats the corporation as a separate person in many circumstances. For example, the corporation has constitutional rights, such as the right to Due Process under the 5th and 14th amendments and the right to be free of unreasonable searches and seizures under the 4th amendment, among others. Thus, if an asset is titled in a corporation, that corporation owns the asset, not the corporate shareholders.

■ Limited Liability of Shareholders
This is the key attribute of a corporation for protecting the assets of a individual from her business debts (like Elizabeth's situation above). Because a corporation is a legal entity distinct from its shareholders, its shareholders are not generally liable for the debts of the corporation. In other words, the shareholders can

only lose their investment in the corporation (what they paid for their shares) if the corporation cannot pay its debts.

■ Unlimited Existence

Unless the corporation states otherwise in its Articles of Declaration, it lasts forever.

■ Centralized Management

Shareholders do not manage the corporation, even though they are its owners. The board of directors, elected by the shareholders, sets the overriding corporate policy and approves major deals. The daily operations are run by the corporate officers, who are chosen by the board.

■ Double Taxation

C corporations are taxpaying entities, subject to double taxation. The corporation is taxed on its income and the shareholders are taxed on the dividend income, which the corporation distributes to them. Thus, if you set up a corporation as a shareholder, the income will be taxed twice, first at the corporate level, and then when it comes to you. S corporations are not taxed twice in this way.

THE 2 WAYS TO USE CORPORATIONS AS ASSET PROTECTORS

1) If you have a business or practice—the corporation can be used to protect you from any and all claims against your business. This *outside protection* protects your wealth which exists outside of the corporation, from any creditors of the business. In other words, it isolates business debts to within the walls of the corporation. This protection will be covered in the first sections of this chapter.

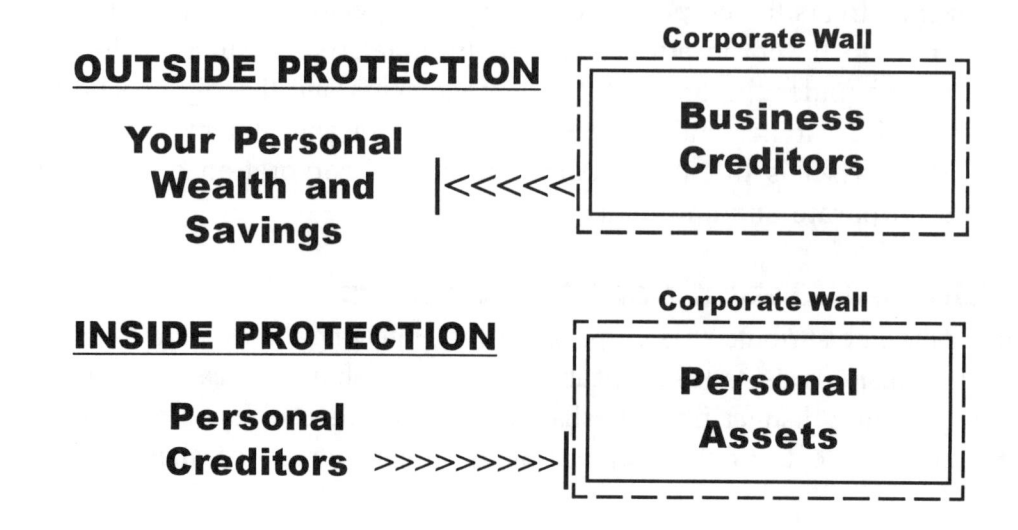

OUTSIDE PROTECTION

Your Personal Wealth and Savings |<<<<< [Corporate Wall | **Business Creditors**]

INSIDE PROTECTION

Personal Creditors >>>>>>>>> [Corporate Wall | **Personal Assets**]

2) Whether or not you have a business, the corporation can also be used to protect your personal assets. This corporation(s) is set up as your personal or family company—you pour your assets into the corporation, own the shares, and then enjoy protection from your creditors. This *inside protection* protects assets inside the corporation from your personal creditors, who exist outside the corporation. This protection is discussed in the final sections.

INCORPORATING YOUR BUSINESS: SHIELDING YOURSELF FROM BUSINESS CREDITORS

Incorporating your business is an absolute must (your only other option should be an LLC). While it may not provide 100% protection from business creditors, incorporation is an important first step.

■ Incorporating Protects You From Tort Claims and Business Debts

You can shield your personal wealth from many of the most popular forms of lawsuits by incorporating your business. These claims are based on negligence (slip and falls, car accidents, etc.), or arise out of the employer-employee relationship (being held responsible for the acts or omissions of your employees, employment discrimination). You are also protected from debts which the corporation owes, provided you did not personally guarantee the debt.

■ Incorporating Protects You From Claims of Your Customers

By incorporating, you can usually protect yourself from claims arising from the goods or services you provide to your clients or customers. These lawsuits for product liability claims, negligence, breach of warranty, and even malpractice—often bring outstanding jury awards.

■ Incorporation Does Not Protect You on Personal Guaranteed Debts

Often someone doing business with a corporation will require an officer (i.e. president, vice-president, etc.) to sign a personal guarantee backing up the corporation's debt. For example, your landlord may ask you to guarantee your corporation's lease for the business premises. If the corporation breaches the lease and cannot make the payments, the landlord can sue you personally on the guarantee. In this way, any debt that you guarantee for your corporation overrides any corporate protection.

■ Incorporation Does Not Protect You When You Cause the Harm

If you are the one who personally caused the harm for which someone is suing, you are not protected by the corporate shield. For example, if you are driving the corporate car and cause a car accident, the victim can sue both the corporation and you personally, as you were personally negligent.

6 TYPES OF BUSINESSES THAT ESPECIALLY NEED INCORPORATION

Since incorporation may and may not protect your personal wealth, the following businesses that would be well-suited for the corporate form. Is your business on this list? Incorporate immediately!

1. Your business or profession has employees.

2. Your business or profession often interacts with clients, patients, or other businesses.

3. You are involved in joint ventures with others, where you may be held liable for their mishaps.

4. Your business involves potentially hazardous materials or situations (contractors, builders, businesses using chemicals or toxic substances, etc.)

5. You are a professional who shares office space with another professional and outsiders might think you are partners.

6. You employ independent contractors in situations where outsiders might reasonably believe the contractors are actually your employees.

SPECIAL CONSIDERATIONS FOR PROFESSIONALS

Many physicians, dentists, accountants, lawyers, architects, and other professionals use professional corporations (PCs) or professional associations (PAs) to structure their practices. Most of these professionals originally set up their entities for tax reasons, without regard to their corporation's asset protection attributes. Nevertheless, there are important asset protection characteristics of a professional corporation. The most important are:

- **Professional corporations cannot protect the professional from his acts of negligence.** For example, if you as a doctor negligently mistreat a patient, you cannot avoid personal liability in a malpractice action.

- **Professional corporations can protect the professional from the acts or omissions of subordinates and associates.** For instance, a doctor can protect him or herself from the acts or omissions of nurses or other doctors, as can other professionals.

    To take advantage of this type of protection, professionals often combine a PC with a partnership entity—the various professionals working together each set up a PC. These PCs then become the partners in the partnership. The professionals then protect themselves from the lawsuits caused by anyone but themselves, but still get the benefit of working as a partnership.

- **Professional corporations can protect the professional from other types of claims which do not involve the act or omission of the professional** (car accidents using the corporate car, slip and falls at the place of business, etc.).

In sum, the professional corporation can protect the professional from lawsuits arising from the behavior of others, but not from their own behavior.

REQUIREMENTS FOR CORPORATE PROTECTION

You will not enjoy the limited liability associated with corporations simply by setting up the corporation and paying the registration fees. Whether you are using a corporation to structure your business or practice, or to work as a personal holding company, you must strictly adhere to "corporate formalities" to enjoy corporate asset protection. Observe these procedural formalities:

■ **Do not commingle cash or other assets:** You cannot commingle corporate funds with personal funds. Use separate bank accounts. If you loan money to the corporation or vice versa, make certain the loan is well-documented. The same prohibition against commingling applies to other assets, like accounts receivable or inventory.

■ **Always sign corporate documents with your corporate title:** Documents signed on behalf of the corporation should state your position in the corporation. Correct: "President of XYZ Corp., John Doe" or "John Doe, as President of XYZ Corp." Incorrect: "John Doe." This is true for invoices, contracts, checks, orders, etc.

■ **Identify the corporation:** Have the word *incorporation* or *Inc.* on all letters, signs, bills, checks, etc. Creditors and others then know that the business is a corporation—this in itself will discourage lawsuits.

■ **Keep adequate corporate records:** Maintain records of the articles of incorporation, the corporate bylaws, minutes of board meetings, and pay the annual registration or franchise fees.

■ **Keep the corporation sufficiently capitalized:** Check with a corporate attorney to determine the proper capitalization for your type business, with a given amount of debts. Certain states require predetermined minimal capitalization.

■ **Maintain other indicators of a legitimate corporation:** This can be as simple as listing a phone under the corporate name, transacting business with non-interested third parties, and obtaining a business license under the corporate name, among others. Set up the corporation with the formalities of a Fortune 500 corporation, on a tiny scale.

If you do not follow these formalities, then the court may not recognize the corporation as a legitimate stand-alone entity. Instead, the court will decide that the corporation is a sham entity and your alter-ego. If the court makes this decision, it may then pierce the *corporate veil*—ignoring the protection the corporation gives to its shareholders. Rather than limit your liability limited to your investment for the corporate shares, the court will allow your personal wealth to be seized by the creditors of the corporation. *When the corporate*

Corporations as Important Protective Tools

veil is pierced in this way, you are as vulnerable as when operating a proprietorship.

How strictly you must adhere to the required formalities is difficult to say. Certainly, if you are missing minutes of one director's meeting, or failed to use the word "Inc." in certain letterheads, this alone will not be enough to lose corporate protection. However, there are cases where an officer/shareholder lost corporate protection for certain contracts where she forgot to sign using her corporate title. Safest strategy: Learn and adhere to the corporate rules as diligently as you can.

ADVANCED PROTECTION FOR YOUR INCORPORATED BUSINESS OR PRACTICE

If you own a business or have a professional practice, your goal should not be simply to protect your personal wealth from your business' or practice's creditors. While this is certainly a mandatory first step, you must do more. You should also have a second and equally important goal—to make your business or practice itself invulnerable to creditor attacks. In other words, set-up your business like your personal financial situation; as an impenetrable fortress. It only makes sense. You have probably invested much of your personal wealth into your business or practice, why would you then want to protect only your personal assets, while leaving your business or practice completely vulnerable?

To protect your business or practice, we often use multiple corporations in conjunction with trusts and partnerships, "friendly" mortgages, and even personal ownership. These techniques and others are found in the chapter, *Advanced Protection for Business Owners and Professionals*— must reading for anyone with a business. Here, we outline two advanced strategies: *Using Multiple Corporations* and *Isolating Dangerous Assets from Safe Assets*— because they apply also when we use limited liability companies, limited partnerships, and trusts, all discussed in upcoming chapters.

1. Using Multiple Corporations to Protect Your Business/Practice

Using multiple corporations (or limited liability companies, limited partnerships, or trusts) to structure your business/practice can put a limit on any potentially devastating lawsuit or damaging debt. Rather than have all business assets available to the creditors or plaintiffs of the entire business/

practice, split ownership of the business assets—so any one creditor or plaintiff can claim only a portion of the entire business. The rest is completely safe. Consider the example:

Case Study:
Ted's Nightclubs: Each Its Own Corporation

Ted, a retired osteopathic physician, owned three nightclubs around Los Angeles. Justifiably concerned about all of the lawsuits nightclubs were facing these days from disgruntled employees, injured customers, and even angry neighbors, Ted wanted to set-up a corporation to own all three nightclubs, so that his personal finances were protected.

We advised Ted to set-up three distinct corporations; one for each nightclub. Now, any lawsuit from nightclub #1 is no threat to nightclubs #2 or #3, and vice versa. Ted has not only successfully eliminated his personal exposure, but also limited his business' exposure by one-third. It would now take three distinct lawsuits against each of the three nightclubs to wipe him out. If all three nightclubs were owned by one corporation, all three could be lost in one lawsuit.

When does multiple incorporation make sense? Not only in circumstances where there are multiple stand-alone businesses, as with Ted. Chapter 12 shows how we use multiple corporations to protect any business, even if it has only one place of business and one central operation.

NOTE: *To take advantage of multiple corporation protection, you must operate each corporation separately, as a distinct entity. Commingling of funds or ignoring formalities could jeopardize the very strategy of using multiple corporations.*

2. Isolate Dangerous Assets from Safe Assets

When setting up multiple corporations (or multiple limited liability companies, limited partnerships, or trusts) it is crucial to isolate dangerous assets from safe assets. What are dangerous assets? Assets that have a high probability of causing liability problems. Examples of dangerous assets are: rental real estate, cars or boats, airplanes, business premises, business vehicles,

Corporations as Important Protective Tools

leases, or anything else that can foreseeably lead to a lawsuit. The corporation (or LLC, limited partnership, or trust) which owns these dangerous assets should not own safe assets.

Safe assets have a low likelihood of creating liability: stocks, bonds, other passive investments, savings accounts, CDs, inventory, non-dangerous equipment, trade names, accounts receivable. Because these assets will likely not create liability, we do not want them owned by the entity which owns dangerous assets—why subject safe assets to claims created by unsafe assets? Isolate safe assets to ensure that no creditor can claim them.

S CORPORATIONS: A SPECIAL BREED

The S corporation is a special type corporation, available only to closely-held businesses. The S corporation allowed since the 1950's, has been quite popular for tax reasons, although it will be likely be replaced by the LLC. Chapter 9 shows the LLC has many of the benefits of the S corporation, but is more flexible and easier to operate. The key attributes of the S corporation are:

■ The S corporation has *pass-through* taxation— meaning the profits of the corporation are only taxed once, when they are "passed through" to the shareholders. In this way, the S corporation is like a partnership—the entity is not taxed, its owners are.

■ The S corporation may only be owned by natural persons; not corporations, partnerships, or other legal entities, with few exceptions.

■ The S corporation may have at most 69 shareholders. All must be U.S. citizens or residents.

■ The S corporation must be organized under U.S. law, may only have one class of stock, and may not own 80 percent or more of another corporation's stock.

■ When to use an S corporation: A closely-held business, like a family business. Even then, an LLC or a limited partnership may be better as we will discuss further in later chapters.

87

DANGERS FACING DIRECTORS AND OFFICERS

Corporate officership or directorship is risky business, as is being a director of a charitable organization. Not only are you responsible for managing these organizations, but, whenever your organization is sued, you are usually sued personally as well. Lawsuits can come from disgruntled employees and former employees, disappointed shareholders, or even government agencies. Almost every major decision by a corporate or charitable board, in fact, can be a source of a potential lawsuit.

The law imposes a heavy duty on officers and directors. They must demonstrate an undivided, unselfish loyalty to the corporation at all times. They must take special precautions to never profit personally at the corporation's expense. They cannot personally take advantage of an opportunity in which the corporation may be interested. And, most importantly, they must manage the organization with prudence and reasonable judgment.

Using these guidelines, judges and juries find more and more directors and officers individually liable for their behavior. The following lists some reasons why officers and directors are sued:

- Inadequate investigation of facts before taking corporate action.
- Acts beyond the corporate powers.
- Granting improper dividends.
- Allowing the corporation to violate discrimination laws.
- Allowing the corporation to violate environmental laws.
- Allowing securities laws violations—especially for false or misleading information contained in the prospectus.
- Improper loans to officers, directors, or other "insiders."
- Profiting from inside information.
- Transactions with other entities where the director or officer has a direct interest.
- Patent, copyright, or trademark infringement.
- Willful wrongdoing.
- Unpaid withholding taxes—when the IRS can show directors controlled the funds, they will be responsible, along with the corporate officers.

Corporations as Important Protective Tools

What can the corporate or charitable officers and directors do to combat these lawsuit threats? The Appendices list *10 Blunders You Must Avoid* and *2 Ways Officers and Directors Can Protect Themselves*.

YOUR CORPORATION CAN PROTECT PERSONAL ASSETS

This chapter primarily discussed the outside protection which a corporation provides for someone with an active business. Now, we explain how you can set- up your own passive corporation to safeguard assets inside the corporation. This is *inside protection*.

To use a corporation for inside protection, you must transfer your personal wealth into the corporation. With the transfer, you no longer own the boat, car, paintings, etc.—the corporation does. Any personal creditor cannot claim assets owned by the corporation, but they can seize your corporate shares. If you own more than 50% of the corporation, your creditor then gains control of the corporation and, indirectly, the corporation's assets. You must then use corporation with other asset protection tools, to protect the corporate assets while still allowing you to maintain control. You have three options:

1. **If you are married, transfer most of the corporate shares to the less vulnerable spouse who then controls the corporation.** Your creditor would not be able to touch the spouse's shares or control the corporation and its assets. This solution, however, prevents you from having equal control of the corporation in a family dispute.

2. **Transfer the shares to a family limited partnership (FLP).** Husband and Wife may be the two general partners—and control anything owned by the partnership. The limited partners can be any beneficiaries—children, friends, charities, etc. or the husband and wife. This way, Husband and Wife *control* the partnership which controls the corporation which owns the assets. So, indirectly the Husband and Wife *still control* the assets. But, since they do not *personally own* the assets, the assets themselves cannot be taken by creditors. Chapter 8 shows how to use FLPs in this manner.

3. **Transfer the corporate shares to a trust set up for your children, or other expected beneficiaries.** The Husband and Wife could be

co-trustees and maintain control of the trust which controls the corporation. Thus, they control the corporate assets, without directly owning the corporation shares. Again, this prevents their creditors from seizing the corporate assets.

NOTE: *Scenarios 2 and 3 are strategies which are explained clearly and completely in later chapters. For now, understand that to use a personal corporation to protect assets, you cannot simply own the shares outright—you need an extra layer of protection which trusts and limited partnerships provide.*

Remember, if inside protection is the goal, then your personal corporation must remain passive. Should the corporation engage in business activity, it may incur liabilities. Assets owned by the corporation would then be at risk to these business liabilities. For the corporate assets to remain safe, the corporation should not conduct any business whatsoever.

Also, note that using corporations in this manner has serious tax implications. C corporations are subject to double taxation. S corporations are only taxed once, but they cannot be owned by a trust or partnership. Also, IRS taxes passive income of holding corporations at higher rates. Thus, the use of the corporation for inside protection in this way must be reviewed carefully for tax implications. Usually, it is preferable to use a limited partnership or limited liability company, as we explain next.

WHERE TO INCORPORATE?

Corporations are governed by state law. Because state laws differ, there are advantages and disadvantages of incorporating in a particular state. In deciding where to incorporate, consider:

- If the corporation is to run an active business operating in only one state, incorporate in the state in which you will do business. Otherwise, your out-of-state corporation will have to file a declaration of foreign corporation in your home state. This then subjects the corporation to your home state laws anyway, nullifying any advantage of incorporating in another state.

- If the corporation is not to actively operate a business (passive corporation), or if you have flexibility in choosing a state of incorporation, Delaware can be a desirable state. Many of the nations' largest corporations, in fact, are incorporated in Delaware.

Why? Because the Delaware corporate laws take a very protective view of directors, officers, shareholders, and the corporate entities themselves. If director or shareholder liability is important for you, and you can take advantage of the Delaware laws, seriously consider incorporating in Delaware.

- Incorporating in Nevada may also be desirable. Nevada, like Delaware, has extremely protective laws regarding corporations and their officers, directors, and shareholders. Additionally, Nevada has these advantages:

1. Nevada has no corporate franchise tax, corporate income tax, estate or inheritance taxes, gift taxes, or inventory taxes. It also is the only state which does not automatically exchange tax information with the IRS.

2. Shareholder names are not a public record (No one knows who owns the corporation).

3. Only one director is required, no matter how many shareholders there are (Only one person is "on the hook" if the corporate veil is pierced).

SUMMARY

- The three major types of business forms are proprietorships, partnerships, and corporations. Proprietorships and general partnerships are not recommended for lawsuit protection—you are completely vulnerable.
- Corporations are legal entities which have centralized management, double taxation, and shield their owners (shareholders) from liability for the debts of the corporation.
- Corporations can provide either *outside protection* shielding personal assets from your business debts, or *inside protection*, safeguarding personal assets from personal liabilities.
- Incorporation does protect you personally from torts committed by the corporation, from corporate debts, and from claims of customers.
- Incorporation does not protect you personally if you personally caused the harm or guaranteed a corporate debt.
- Professionals can protect themselves from the acts or omissions of their partners and associates by using Professional Corporations, but not from claims arising from their own negligence.
- Corporate protection is not automatic—you must comply with the reporting and other formalities.
- The S corporation does not have the double-taxation disadvantage, but there are many restrictions on when S status can be used.
- Corporate directors and officers face numerous liabilities for their acts and decisions.
- You can use a corporation for inside protection, if the corporation is passive and you share ownership of the shares with another person, limited partnership, or trust.
- If your corporation engages in an active business in only one state, incorporate in your home state. Delaware and Nevada are very corporate-friendly states and good choices for your corporation.

CHAPTER 8:

FAMILY LIMITED PARTNERSHIPS

The family limited partnership plays a fundamental role in asset protection. Because it features favorable pass-through tax treatment, strong creditor protection, two-tiered management structure, and estate tax benefits, the family limited partnership (FLP) is a powerful asset protection and estate planning tool.

This chapter covers the basics of the limited partnership and compares it to a general partnership. Exposing the hidden dangers of general partnerships, it then shows you how useful FLPs are in asset protection planning—for both business and personal assets. Next, we discuss the valuable estate tax advantages you can enjoy by using FLPs. Finally, are the requirements you must follow to enjoy the protections of the FLP.

> **CONTROL VS. OWNERSHIP: A Key Difference**
>
> In this and the next few chapters, you must understand the difference between *control* and *ownership*. Often we think of they are virtually the same—but, they are quite different. If you own a bicycle, for example, you completely control it. You decide where to store it, who can ride it, whether or not to sell it, etc.
>
> However, if you own stock in a public corporation, you own part of the company. The only right to control the corporation is to vote for the board of directors. Officers, chosen by your elected board members, control the corporation's day-to-day activities. While you own the corporation, you have very little direct control over it.
>
> The effectiveness of the asset protection tools come essentially from this distinction—between ownership and control. You will see this exemplified here with limited partnerships and in later chapters, with limited liability companies and domestic and foreign trusts.

THE TWO TYPES OF PARTNERSHIPS

Any partnership must have at least two partners. Also, all partnerships enjoy single income tax treatment, as opposed to corporations which are ordinarily subject to double income-tax. Single taxation is also called a *pass-through* tax because the partnership itself does not pay income tax, the tax liability is *passed through* to the partners in proportion to their ownership.

Beyond these two common characteristics, there are fundamental differences between a general partnership and a limited partnership.

■ General Partnerships

With general partnership, two or more people join together to run a business or venture for profit without registering the business as a corporation, limited partnership, or other legal entity. The law assumes that any business involving more than one person is a general partnership, unless the partners prove otherwise. Similarly, the law assumes that a business run by one person is a proprietorship, unless proven otherwise.

Family Limited Partnerships

Like the proprietorship, general partners have the right to manage partnership affairs and are personally liable for the debts and liabilities of the partnership. The general partnership is even more of a liability trap than the proprietorship, however, because general partners can incur liability because of themselves, their employees, and also their fellow partners.

■ Limited Partnerships

Unlike a general partnership, a limited partnership must be formally established; the law will not assume people operate a limited partnership. State laws control procedures to establish a limited partnership, generally requiring a certificate to be filed with the secretary of state and a registration fee.

A limited partnership has at least one *general partner* and at least one *limited partner*. The general partner(s) of the limited partnership have the same rights and liabilities of a partner in a general partnership—they have the right to manage the partnership business and unlimited liability for partnership debts. The limited partners, on the other hand, have a very limited right to partake in partnership business, but their liability is also limited to their investment in the partnership. They cannot be personally liable for partnership debts. Nonetheless, as owners of the partnership, partnership income is passed through to them. The following diagram visually describes a limited partnership:

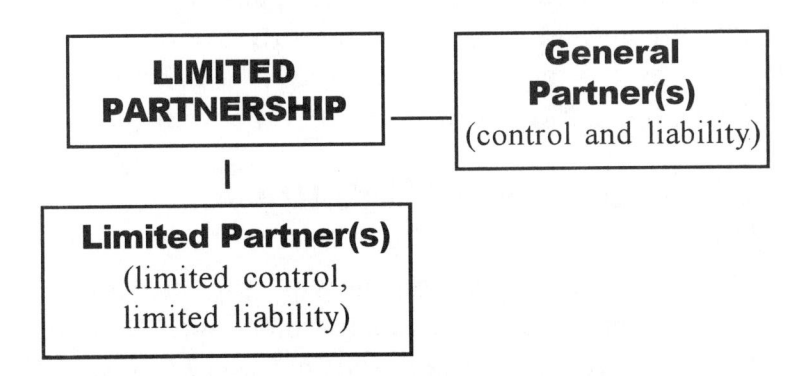

```
┌──────────────┐      ┌──────────────┐
│   LIMITED    │──────│   General    │
│ PARTNERSHIP  │      │  Partner(s)  │
│              │      │(control and  │
└──────┬───────┘      │  liability)  │
       │              └──────────────┘
┌──────┴───────┐
│Limited Partner(s)│
│(limited control, │
│ limited liability)│
└──────────────┘
```

■ Family Limited Partnerships (FLPs)

The family limited partnership (FLP) is a limited partnership, where family members, other trusted relatives, or friends are all the general and limited partners. Usually, the husband and wife are each general partners and their children the limited partners. This allows the parents to control FLP assets while gaining asset protection and tax benefits by sharing ownership with the children.

NOTE: *This and later chapters discuss FLPs using family members as limited partners, often with the husband-wife, 2-children model. However, a FLP does not require family members or a married couple. These are only examples of a* *common situation. If you are not married or have no children, there are ways to use FLPs with friends, your parents, other relatives, trusted professionals, or even other legal entities. An asset protection specialist can structure a FLP to your personal situation.*

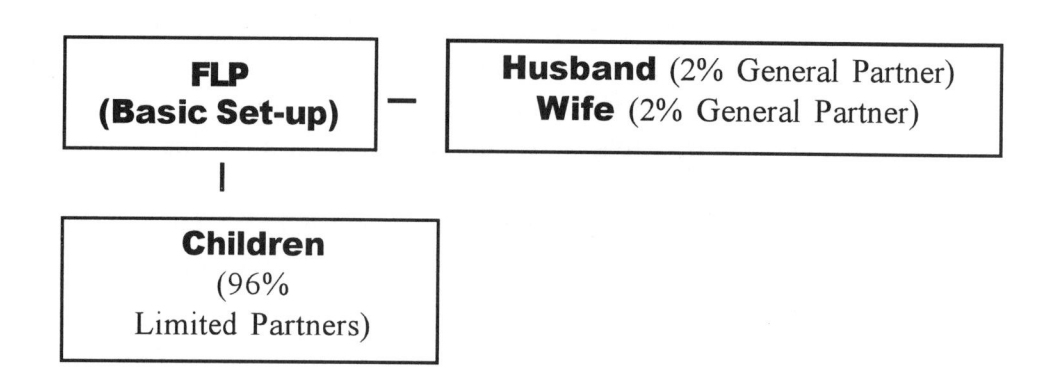

```
┌─────────────────┐     ┌──────────────────────────────────┐
│      FLP        │─────│ Husband (2% General Partner)     │
│ (Basic Set-up)  │     │ Wife (2% General Partner)        │
└─────────────────┘     └──────────────────────────────────┘
         │
┌─────────────────┐
│    Children     │
│     (96%        │
│ Limited Partners)│
└─────────────────┘
```

3 REASONS NOT TO OPERATE AS A GENERAL PARTNERSHIP

Although the headline makes this clear, we repeat: *Never* operate any business or practice as a general partnership! A general partnership is a creditor or plaintiff's dream and a partner's liability nightmare. It should not be part of anyone's asset protection plan. Why is a general partnership so dangerous? Consider **three hidden dangers of a general partnership:**

1. Partners Have Unlimited Liability for Partnership Debts

This tragic fact goes unrealized by many business people, professionals, and other entrepreneurs when involved in general partnerships. *They, in effect, personally guarantee every partnership debt and personally assume the risk for malpractice, accidents, and other liability sources of the entire partnership.* They fail to consider that their liability as a partner is *joint and several* with other partners. As explained earlier, a plaintiff who successfully sues the partnership can collect the full judgment from any one partner. An example:

Family Limited Partnerships

Case Study: *Jane and Ted's Real Estate Venture*

Jane and Ted were friends outside of their medical practices. They decided to go into a real estate venture together to refurbish old three-family homes and sell them as condominiums. Events went well for a while, but their real estate market went sour and they defaulted on a $650,000 loan to the bank. Jane was much wealthier than Ted, so the bank pursued Jane for the full amount, ignoring Ted.

2. Partners Have Unlimited Liability for Their Partners Acts

With a partner in a general partnership, you assume all the risk that the partner will cause a lawsuit. When the lawsuit arises from one partner's act or omission in the ordinary course of business, every other partner is personally liable. The dreaded joint and several liability then applies! If one of your partners gets into trouble, you can be personally liable for the entire amount—even if you were neither involved in the alleged incident, nor aware of it.

Think of the many ways a partner could get you into trouble: He commits malpractice, gets into a car accident while on partnership business, defrauds someone through the business, sexually harasses an employee, wrongfully fires an employee, etc. Multiply this risk times the number of partners in your partnership. You have a lawsuit liability nightmare! A real-world example:

Case Study: *Michael Gets Burned By His Partner*

Michael was the founding partner in a successful three partner medical clinic operating near Portland, Oregon. One of his partner's patients who was injured during treatment sued the partnership. The lawsuit alleged serious physical injuries, emotional distress, loss of work, and even punitive damages.

Settlement negotiations were unsuccessful and the trial jury awarded an extremely large verdict against the partnership, exceeding its liability policy limit. Since Michael was the wealthiest of the partners, the plaintiff's lawyer pursued him first, forcing Michael to pay the entire $250,000 amount (above the insurance policy limit) from his personal savings. Although Michael had absolutely no contact with the patient, nor participated in his treatment, he now understands the risks of a general partnership.

3. You May be an "Unaware" General Partner

A general partnership does not require a formal written agreement, as does a limited partnership. You can verbally agree to start a venture with another and create a general partnership, with all of its liability problems. Think about this whenever you start a new business venture with some one.

Even if you make no agreement to partner with another person, the law may impose general partnership liability on you if the general public reasonably perceive you as partners. You may already be part of a liability-ridden general partnership and not even know it.

> **Case Study:** *Roger Inadvertently Has Partners*
>
> Roger was one of four physicians who used a common office arrangement. They each had their own patients, which they did not share. They did, however, share a common waiting area, support staff, and accounting. Each physician had his own practice methods, set his own hours, and was not otherwise accountable to the others.
>
> When one of the physicians severely injured a patient as a result of an allergic reaction to a anesthetic gas, Roger and the two others had a rude awakening. Although only the treating doctor was negligent, all four were defendants in the lawsuit. The court found that the patient could reasonably conclude the four physicians were partners together because of their office set-up and common support staff. Therefore, the court allowed the plaintiff to proceed with the suit against all four physicians—as a general partnership, with each jointly and severally liable for the plaintiff's injuries.

HOW TO PROTECT YOURSELF IN A GENERAL PARTNERSHIP

We repeat our warning: *Do not run any business as a general partnership!* It is too risky. Rather, convert the business into a limited partnership, a C or S corporation, or a limited liability company. Despite our warnings, many professionals and businesspersons will continue their general partnerships or set-up new ones, because they do not want to change. One suggestion of how to set-up a general partnership for maximum asset protection purposes is then essential.

If you do use a general partnership, each partner should set up a corporation and the corporations should become the partners in the general partnership. This advice is followed by many medical professionals and attorneys using professional corporations (PCs). Each doctor or lawyer sets up a PC and the PC is the official partner in the partnership, not the professional personally. Structuring the partnership this way, the underlying corporate owner's personal assets remain protected from claims against the partnership. However, as with any corporation, the corporate formalities must be followed for asset protection.

HOW YOU FORM AN FLP

Forming your FLP involves two stages—legal formation and funding. We discuss each separately.

1. Legal Formation

An FLP, like any limited partnership, must be formed according to the laws of the state in which it is organized. Fortunately, most states have adopted the *Uniform Limited Partnership Act (ULPA)*, so the basic procedure is the same in most states. Essentially, you first draft a limited partnership agreement which contains the following:

- Name, address, purpose and duration of the FLP
- Capital contribution of each partner
- Percentage distribution of profits and losses among partners
- General partner compensation, if any
- Provisions for death, retirement, incapacity, bankruptcy of any partner
- Provisions for the assignment of any partnership interest, voluntary or involuntary
- Provisions for the termination and liquidation of the partnership

Once the partnership agreement has been prepared and signed, a certificate of limited partnership is filed with the appropriate state office.

2. Funding Your FLP

Funding your FLP means allocating the proper amount of FLP ownership to other family members and deciding what types of assets to transfer into the FLP.

a. Making the Transfers

In the typical situation, the husband and wife will transfer jointly owned assets into the FLP in exchange for partnership interests. The initial transfer might also include gifts to children of a partnership interests. Over time, the husband and wife may transfer greater interests to the children.

Case Study: *Woody and Marge*

Woody and Marge are married with three children Larry, Moe and Curly. Woody and Marge own a vacation property with $200,000 equity, cars with $25,000 equity, and stocks and bonds worth $275,000. They set up a FLP and transfer their assets into it—the FLP then is worth $500,000. When setting up their FLP, Woody and Marge each become 10% general partners (to fully control all assets), and are each 34% limited partners. The two still own 88% of the assets, but control them fully. The remaining 12% of the FLP ownership interests have been gifted by Woody and Marge to their children—4% of the FLP (equal to $20,000) to each child.

Woody and Marge have taken advantage of tax laws which allows up to $10,000 (or $20,000 for a couple) to be gifted annually without any gift tax due. In the first year, Woody and Marge have begun to transfer ownership while retaining control of their assets. Their children now own 12% of the FLP, yet Woody and Marge still have 100% control. They can continue to transfer 12% to their children each year.

b. Which assets should be transferred to the FLP

In the example of Woody and Marge, there was no mention of the family home. This was intentional. There are serious drawbacks to owning your primary residence through an FLP. First, the transfer may trigger a property tax reassessment of the home. Second, the transfer may activate a due-on-sale clause of your mortgage. Finally, such a transfer may cause you to lose the tax benefits when owning the home personally—the tax-free two year rollover and the $125,000 one-time exemption for owners over the age of 55. These drawbacks may be avoided when a FLP is used with a foreign asset protection trust. The safest bet is to have the FLP own assets other than the family home, unless asset protection is much more important than tax savings.

Another important tactic is to segregate *safe* assets from *dangerous* assets. One FLP should not own assets which may create liability along with assets which will not create liability.

Family Limited Partnerships

Other than concerns for the family home and tactics for segregating safe and dangerous assets, generally all assets can be transferred into your FLP. Stocks, bonds, antiques, jewelry, art, cars, boats, vacation property, rental property, interests in closely-held or family businesses, copyrights, bank accounts, CDs, or most other assets can be owned by your FLP. It is important that these transfers are made legitimately, changing registration and title documents, and using bills of sale.

c. Gift Tax Consequences

As in the case study of Woody and Marge, keep gift tax consequences in mind when you transfer FLP ownership interests. Working with an asset protection specialist will insure that you maximize your $10,000 annual tax free gifts, without using your lifetime gift tax exemption.

HOW FLPs POWERFULLY PROTECT ASSETS

FLPs are outstanding asset protectors because the law gives a very specific and limited remedy to creditors coming after assets in an FLP. When a personal creditor pursues you, and your assets are owned by your FLP, the creditor cannot seize the assets in the FLP. Under the ULPA provisions, *a creditor of a partner cannot reach into the limited partnership and take specific partnership assets.*

If the creditor cannot seize FLP assets, what can the creditor get? . . . a charging order. This is the exclusive remedy of a creditor attacking a partner in a limited partnership. Of course, assets owned in your name are vulnerable. But when assets are owned by the FLP, the best the creditor can do is to obtain a charging order; a very weak remedy indeed.

■ The Weaknesses of the Charging Order

The charging order is a court order which instructs the FLP to pay any income or distributions that would normally flow to you to your creditor, until the creditor's judgment is paid in full. Importantly, the charging order does not:

(1) give the creditor FLP voting rights; nor
(2) force the FLP general partner to pay out any distributions to partners.

Thus, the charging order means that if distributions are paid by your FLP, they should be paid to your creditor, not to you.

While this may seem like a powerful remedy, consider its limitations:

1. Only Available After a Successful Lawsuit

First, the charging order is only available after the creditor has successfully sued you, and won a judgment. Only then can your creditor ask the court for the charging order. While the lawsuit is proceeding, or while it is just a threat, FLP assets are completely untouchable.

2. Does Not Give Voting Rights — So You Stay in Complete Control

Despite the charging order, you remain the general partner of your FLP. You make all decisions about FLP assets; whether or not to sell, to pay income out, to shift ownership interests, etc. Your judgment creditor cannot vote you out because they cannot vote. Thus, as long as the creditor has a judgment against you, you make all decisions concerning the FLP, including the decision to refuse to pay distributions to partners. Perhaps you want to compensate yourself and your spouse as general partners by paying yourself a salary for running the limited partnership—this is 100% permissible. And, your creditor will still not get one red cent!

The charging order does not stop you from exerting complete control of the FLP assets—you manage them as if no charging order existed. It also does

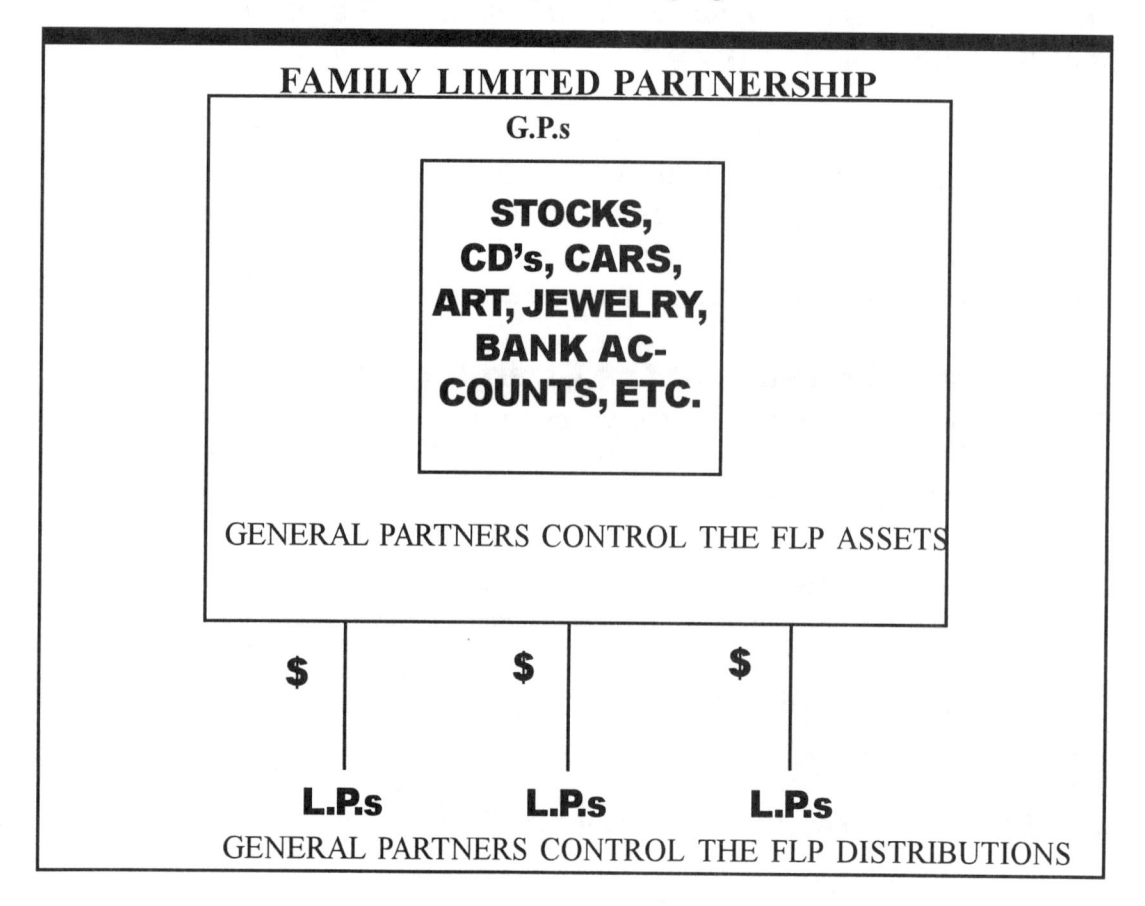

FAMILY LIMITED PARTNERSHIP

G.P.s

STOCKS, CD's, CARS, ART, JEWELRY, BANK ACCOUNTS, ETC.

GENERAL PARTNERS CONTROL THE FLP ASSETS

$ — L.P.s $ — L.P.s $ — L.P.s

GENERAL PARTNERS CONTROL THE FLP DISTRIBUTIONS

Family Limited Partnerships

not prevent you from paying yourself a salary and refusing to pay out distributions from FLP income. In fact, if your FLP simply owns cars, vacation homes, antiques, or other non income-producing assets, your FLP may not even have any income to distribute.

3. The Creditor Pays the Tax Bill

The real "kicker" is how the charging order backfires on creditors for income tax purposes. Because an FLP is taxed passed-through, the FLP does not pay tax; rather, the income tax is passed-through to the partners. Each partner is responsible for their percentage share of the FLP income, whether or not the income is actually paid out. Because a creditor who gets a charging order against you "steps into your shoes" for income tax purposes with respect to the FLP, your creditor will get your tax bill, and owe income taxes on FLP income, whether or not they received the income.

And, who decides whether or not to distribute the FLP income? . . . You and your spouse do, as the FLP general partners. The creditor thus gets the K-1 form and has to pay the tax on your share of the FLP's income even if you, as general partner, never decided to distribute the income to FLP partners. *Your creditor will pay income tax on earnings he never received. No wonder the IRS never pursues charging orders—they know it is a losing proposition!! Your creditor should realize the same.*

If a creditor thinks he will get more money out of a cheap settlement than from elusive FLP distributions, he will settle.

NOTE: *Remember, we are talking about creditors pursuing liabilities outside the FLP (or "inside protection")—putting personal assets like cars, vacation or rental real estate, stocks, bonds, etc., into the FLP to protect it from personal creditors. Creditors of the FLP, arising from debts of the FLP, can always seize FLP assets. For example, if a tenant of property owned by the FLP sued the FLP and won a judgment, she could pursue assets owned by that FLP. Hence, always segregate safe and dangerous assets.*

NOTE 2: *California limited partnerships face a possibility that a creditor can get more than a charging order, in very particular circumstances. See an asset protection specialist, if you live in California, to ensure that your FLP is drafted in a way that the charging order is the only remedy of a creditor.*

Case Study:
Woody and Marge are protected by their FLP

Return to the example of spouses Woody and Marge. Assume that Woody is a dermatologist with his own private practice. After two years of employment, Woody's assistant, Maribel, sues Woody for sexual harassment, and wins an award of $750,000. Woody's medical malpractice insurance, of course, does not cover this type lawsuit. Once Maribel discovers, through debtor's examination, that Woody and Marge's assets are owned through their FLP, what can she do?

She cannot seize the vacation home, stocks, and cars owned by the FLP. The ULPA provisions prohibit that. She also has no fraudulent transfer claim to try to undo the FLP. It was set up far in advance of her claim. She can get a charging order on Woody's 39% share of the FLP, but Woody and Marge still control the FLP. Maribel would probably end-up with no distributed profits, only a tax bill on dividends paid out by the stocks, which Woody and Marge never distributed. The charging order will not sound too inviting to Maribel, will it?

Maribel could look only to Woody's assets not owned by the FLP. As Woody had an incomplete asset protection plan, he did have assets exposed—copyrights and business interests in a film company worth about $75,000. Woody settled the judgment for just that—$75,000 cash. Woody and Marge's FLP helped them avoid financial disaster and settle the claim for pennies on the dollar. And, they never lost control of their assets.

You may wonder why we have such a protective laws for limited partnerships. The charging order law, which can be traced back to the *English Partnership Act of 1890*, is aimed at achieving a particular public policy objective—that business activities of a partnership should not be disrupted because of non-partnership related debts of one or more of the partners. The justification: since non-debtor partners and the partnership were not at fault, why should the entire partnership suffer? American law adopted this policy over the past 100 years, culminating in the charging order law of the ULPA.

Family Limited Partnerships

This background helps to explain why stating a business purpose for the FLP is important. It also helps to show that asset protection for FLPs is neither a loophole nor a passing fluke in the law. Rather, it is a specific policy intended by our partnership laws, with deep roots in our legal tradition.

4 TACTICS TO MAXIMIZE FLP PROTECTION

You understand the basic strategy for using FLPs—put your assets into the FLP so they will be protected from your non-FLP personal creditors. This is basic inside protection. Assets inside the FLP are protected against outside threats. There are more advanced tactics you can use with FLPs. This section describes these tactics, and you will see them come together again in the next section.

1. Have the Less Vulnerable Spouse Own Most of the FLP

If the FLP is formed by a two-spouse family, and one spouse is more vulnerable to lawsuits, have the less vulnerable spouse own more of the FLP. This is often the case for medical professionals. One spouse has the threats of medical malpractice lawsuits and other lawsuits arising from the practice, while the other faces relatively few lawsuit threats. For our discussion, assume that the husband is the high liability threat and the wife is low liability. Of course, while the roles could be reversed; the principle remains the same.

The husband would own only 1% of the FLP, all as general partner. The wife would initially own 99% of the FLP; 1% as general partner and 98% as limited partner. (Later, one can transfer ownership interests to children, other relatives, or loved ones.) If the wife's partnership interests were considered her separate property (not community property in those states with such laws), a judgment creditor of the husband could only receive a charging order against the 1% interest held by the husband. *With only 1% of the FLP subject to a charging order, the husband is in a great position to negotiate small settlements with even the most determined creditors.*

This tactic is especially important when income from the FLP is needed to support the family. For example, the FLP could own your savings, in the form of stocks and bonds. If you and your spouse needed its income to survive, you will not have the luxury to withhold FLP distributions, if a creditor obtains a charging order against your FLP interest. With only 1% of the FLP allocated to you, you ensure that 99% percent of FLP income will pass to your spouse, completely free of your creditor's claim.

There is one significant drawback to this tactic. It assumes that the less-vulnerable spouse is completely immune from lawsuits. We know this is not possible. However, the more equal the liability between spouses—through a business, real estate ownership, contractual obligations—the less attractive this tactic becomes. Further, this tactic has problems if there were a divorce; as one spouse would own much more of the FLP than the other. Nevertheless, if divorce is not foreseen on the horizon and if one spouse is relatively free from the lawsuit risks, this tactic can further protect family assets from lawsuits.

2. Use Multiple FLPs

This tactic, combined with tactic #3, is crucial for using FLPs effectively, as it was when using corporations. In fact, this same tactic should be employed to any legal entity—corporation, FLP, limited liability company, domestic trust, or even foreign trust. The reasons:

1. If any asset within a single FLP causes a lawsuit, all assets owned by that FLP are vulnerable. Multiple FLPs and segregating dangerous from safe assets, reduce this risk. Diversify your lawsuit risk for superior financial security.

2. Spreading your assets among a number of different legal entities (like FLPs), makes it more difficult for any creditor to come after your entire wealth. Practically, they must conduct more investigation, file more motions with the court, and perhaps even travel to different states. The more entities used, the more difficult it will be for your creditors to attack your wealth. The result: Creditors negotiate more favorable settlements.

3. Segregate Safe and Dangerous Assets in Different FLPs

In combination with tactic #2, the theory behind segregating dangerous and safe assets is to reduce the risk that lawsuits caused by one asset will threaten others. Safe assets are those which will not likely lead to lawsuits. Dangerous assets are more likely to bring lawsuits.

a. Safe Assets
Cash, stocks, bonds, mutual funds, CDs, life insurance policies, checking or savings accounts, antiques, artwork, jewelry, licenses, copyrights, trademarks, patents, among others.

Family Limited Partnerships

b. Dangerous Assets
Real estate—especially rental real estate, cars, RVs, trucks, boats, airplanes, interests in closely-held businesses, and others.

4. Use a Corporation or Limited Liability Company as General Partner

A general partner has unlimited personal exposure for debts and liabilities created by the FLP. This can be a significant drawback when the FLP is owning dangerous assets. Since you and your spouse will typically be general partners to control FLP assets, you will be personally responsible for any liabilities created by these dangerous assets. To protect you from this personal liability, use a corporation or LLCs for your FLP—especially when it will own dangerous liability-producing assets. You and your spouse can be the sole shareholders of the corporation or sole members of the LLC.

You and your spouse will own and control the corporation/LLC, which in turn runs the FLP as its general partner. You and your spouse do not face personal liability from dangerous FLP assets, yet retain complete control of them. Only the corporation or LLC has unlimited liability. Of course, the only thing it owns are the FLP general partner interests.

PUTTING IT TOGETHER: FLP CASE STUDY

Examine one case utilizing all the FLP tactics. Harry Gump, a 53-year-old anestheologist, and his wife Wilma, a day school teacher, have two teen-aged children and have the following assets:

	Asset	**Equity**
	Home	$150,000
Safe	Cash	$50,000
Assets	Mutual Funds	$550,000
	Antiques	$20,000
	Total Safe Equity	$770,000
	Rental Condo #1	$75,000
Dangerous	Rental Condo #2	$55,000
Assets	Interest in Medical Partnership	$380,000
	Cars	$20,000
	Powerboat	$30,000
	Total Dangerous Equity	$560,000
	TOTAL EQUITY	**$1,330,000**

The Doctor's Wealth Protection Guide

To provide the Gump's with maximum financial security using FLPs, we use between two and four FLPs. Let us examine each.

FLP #1: "Gump Safe Asset FLP"
Owns: Cash, mutual funds, and antiques. Total value = $620,000
Interests: Dr. Gump 1% owner as general partner
Mrs. Gump 1% owner as general partner, 98% as limited partner (before gifting interests to children, if desired)

Strategy: Because these assets are all safe, and not likely to cause liability, they can all be owned by one FLP. The family home is not included because of the adverse tax consequences noted earlier (Also, assume the Gumps live in Florida where homestead protects their home equity anyway). By isolating safe assets from dangerous assets, we ensure their security. Dr. Gump has only a 1% interest because he is far more likely to be sued, and because Dr. and Mrs. Gump are most comfortable with this ownership arrangement.

Result: All $620,000 is now safe from creditors or lawsuits. And, only 1% of the FLP income, if any, can be attached by a creditor who bothers to get a charging order. This will effectively encourage inexpensive settlements. Also, there is no gift tax due when the Gumps transfer assets to each other (husband and wife) or to the FLP.

FLP #2: "Gump Dangerous Asset FLP A"
Owns: Condo #1 and Condo #2. Total value = $130,000
Interests: Dr. Gump 1% owner as general partner (through an LLC)
Mrs. Gump 1% owner as general partner (through an LLC), 68% as limited partner
Each child 15% as limited partner

Strategy: These assets are dangerous because of the likelihood of lawsuits from tenants, guests, or neighbors. While one FLP owned both condominiums, a strong argument can be made to set up separate FLPs for each condo. Also, a corporation or LLC could well be used as the general partner, rather than Dr. and Mrs. Gump personally. The children each were gifted a 15% interest because the Gumps wanted to start reducing estate taxes, while giving up no control over their assets (See 2 sections ahead).

Result: Any lawsuit arising from the condos is isolated to the condos. All other wealth is shielded. Also, tens of thousands in estate taxes will be saved.

FLP #3: "Gump Dangerous Asset FLP B"

Owns: Cars and the powerboat. Total value = $50,000
Interests: Corporation or LLC as 5% general partner.
Corporation/LLC owned 50% each by Dr. and Mrs. Gump.
Mrs. Gump 95% owner as limited partner

Strategy: These assets are extremely dangerous, especially because the children drive both cars and the boat regularly. With a corporation or LLC as general partner, we protect the Gump's personal wealth from liability caused by the cars or boat. Yet, Dr. and Mrs. Gump still completely control the boat and cars through the FLP and LLC/corporation.

Result: All other wealth is shielded from lawsuits arising from car and powerboat ownership. Also, Dr. and Mrs. Gump achieve personal protection through the LLC/corporation.

Dr. Gump's medical partnership was not included in any FLP because the medical partnership agreement required that he own his shares personally. If Dr. Gump could have transferred his interests in the medical partnership to an FLP, we would set-up a fourth FLP to own the practice.

Without the FLPs, the Gump's family had over $1.1 million exposed to lawsuits (All of their net worth minus the homestead protection of their home equity)! Now, Dr. Gump, an obvious lawsuit target, has less than $15,000 worth of FLP interests exposed! And, the creditor must get a charging order to claim even those interests' profits. While the medical shares and the home need different protection devices, the Gumps are already on their way to total financial security using FLPs. And, they have relinquished no control while saving estate taxes!

HOW TO PROTECT YOUR BUSINESS OR PRACTICE USING FLPs

Protecting business/practice assets using FLPs relies on the same tactics as protecting personal assets. The business or professional person transfers business/practice assets of the proprietorship (e.g. owned in the businessperson's name) into FLPs. As described above, it is usually prudent to create several FLPs to own different parts of the business—to separate risks and to encourage small settlements. Usually, the best strategy is to separate the business into at least two FLPs—one to operate the business and one to own key assets. For example, a hotel operator might use one FLP to run the hotel and another to own

The Doctor's Wealth Protection Guide

the land and building. The asset-owning FLP would lease the land and building to the hotel-operating FLP. The building and land then would remain safe from any creditor of the operating hotel.

The above strategy works also for corporations and limited liability companies. To protect business and professional practices.

FLPs CAN SAVE YOU ESTATE TAXES

You see how FLPs can protect your savings and possessions from lawsuits and other creditors. This is a most important feature of the FLP. Equally important, however, is how the FLP can dramatically reduce or eliminate estate taxes, saving families tens or even hundreds of thousands of dollars. FLPs can make these valuable tax-savings available for you and your loved ones:

> *Remember—estate taxes are "death taxes"—whoever you leave your property to when you die will pay tax on everything you own when you die. After a tax-free amount, the estate tax rate quickly climbs from 37% to 55% and to 60% over $10 million. State inheritance taxes can add another 10 to 12 percent.*

■ Gift Partnership Interests to Save Estate Taxes and Keep Control

Because your estate only pays taxes on property owned at death, a common tax-saving strategy is to gift your property away during your life. The property goes to people you would leave it to when you die, anyway, and the government gets a smaller share. The main objection: you must give up control of your property while alive. If the FLP owns the asset(s), making yourself FLP general partner, and gifts FLP interests to intended beneficiaries, you get the best of both worlds. You still control the FLP assets while you are alive and bequeath your family and loved ones more wealth when you die, by paying the government less estate taxes.

Case Study: *Robert's Mutual Funds*

Robert Jones, a 63-year-old retired vascular surgeon, owned almost $1 million in mutual funds, and real estate assets. He set up an FLP to own the mutual funds, naming himself the sole general partner. He initially owned 95% of the partnership interests, gifting 1% each to his five grandchildren. Since this 1% was worth approximately $10,000, the gifts to each grandchild was tax-free.

Robert can continue to gift each grandchild $10,000 in FLP interests each year, completely tax-free. If Robert lives to age 75, he will give $600,000 fund FLP interests to his grandchildren ($120,000 each), tax-free. This $600,000 will no longer be in his estate, and not subject to estate tax. Because Robert's other assets put him in the 55% estate tax bracket, his tax savings using the FLP will be $330,000 (55% x $600,000). Because he is the FLP's sole general partner, Robert completely controls the mutual funds while alive and can distribute the income to himself or sell some of the funds for his expenses. Robert maintains control of his assets for his lifetime, pays less estate tax, and also provides more for his grandchildren.

■ Lower Estate and Gift Taxes Through FLPs

You may not want to gift your entire FLP partnership interests during your life. Instead, you will die owning FLP interests subject to the estate tax. But, what value will the IRS slap on the 37-55% tax on? It will not be: [your percentage ownership in the FLP] times [the fair market value of the FLP assets], as you might expect.

An important estate tax benefit of the FLP is that FLP interests enjoy discounted values by the IRS. The IRS realizes that a percentage ownership of an FLP which owns an asset is worth less than owning the asset outright. The IRS applies a *lack of marketability* discount, recognizing that your FLP interest is not really marketable—so its value should be reduced for tax purposes. There is very little market for FLP interests when the other partners are all family members. Who would want to own part of a mutual fund portfolio, when the other owners are five grandchildren?

Also, if you die owning less than 50% of the FLP, the IRS will apply the *minority ownership* discount to your FLP interest. There is very little market for interests in an FLP which others control.

The IRS may then value your FLP interest between 15% and 40% less than your percentage fair market value share. This translates into an estate tax savings of tens of thousands of dollars in larger estates.

Robert Jones' Mutual Funds Revisited

Assume that when Robert dies he still owns 40% of his mutual funds FLP interests—gifting 60% to his grandchildren during his lifetime. This 40%

partnership interest, as part of his estate, is subject to estate taxes. Assume also that the FLP mutual funds value is $2 million when Robert dies. His 40% interest in the FLP is then worth $800,000 (40% x $2 million).

For estate tax valuation, however, the IRS may agree that Robert's FLP interest is worth only around $500,000. The IRS will apply both the lack of marketability discount and the minority ownership discount. The lack of marketability discount exists because Robert's five grandchildren have part of the partnership so non-family members would not be interested in buying his interests. Also, under the FLP agreement, the FLP interests are not freely transferable. The minority ownership discount may be applied because Robert owns only 40% of the FLP when he dies.

These valuation discounts translate into an estate tax savings of about $150,000 ($200,000 x 50%). Because of the discounted valuation, discounts will not be used without an FLP.

Robert could have set-up a living trust owning his remaining FLP interests, rather than titled in his name. The FLP interests would then be with the *Robert Jones Revocable Living Trust* while he is alive. As Robert solely owns and controls his living trust, he completely controls the FLP partnership interests owned by his trust. When Robert dies, his partnership interests will pass outside probate, because they will be controlled by his living trust, not a will. Probate legal costs are around 5%, so a living trust saves Robert's survivors close to $40,000 ($800,000 x 5%).

Thus, gifting his mutual funds to his grandchildren through an FLP, taking advantage of IRS discounts on FLP interests, and owning his FLP interests through a living trust, saves Robert over $500,000 in estate taxes and probate fees! And, he lost absolutely no control over his funds while he was alive.

FLPs CAN ALSO REDUCE INCOME TAXES

An FLP also can save you tens of thousands of dollars, or more, in income taxes by spreading the income created by the FLP assets to the limited partners. Typically, FLP limited partners are children in lower tax brackets than the general partners, usually the parents. As this shows:

Case Study: Doug's FLP Reduces Family Income Taxes

Doug, a dermatologist, had taxable income of $100,000 from his investments, stocks worth about $500,000. In a 39% federal tax bracket his federal income tax on this income came to $39,000. To reduce his taxes, he set up an FLP.

The FLP was funded with the stocks. Doug and his wife were each 42% general partners, and his four children were gifted 4% limited partnership interests (16% total). Because each child's interest would be valued at less than $20,000 (4% x $500,000, less the minority valuation discount), no gift tax applied to the transfers to the children. But, because Doug and his wife were general partners, they controlled the stocks and mutual funds. Doug and his wife made these 16% transfers to their children annually for 5 years.

Under the FLP agreement, the children were taxed on their share of the FLP's income; which, after five years, become 80%. Thus, in year five, 80% of the FLP's taxable income would be taxed at the children's lower tax rate. So, when the FLP assets earned $100,000 in income, 80% of that income was taxed at the children's rate—15%. Thus, the federal tax bill with the FLP was: $7,800—39% on $20,000 (the parents' share); plus $12,000—15% on $80,000 (the children's share). Doug's family's tax savings?

Total tax with the FLP, Year 5:	$19,800
Total tax without the FLP, Year 5:	$39,000
Year 5 family income tax savings with the FLP:	**$19,200**

Plus, there were savings in years one through four! Also, under the FLP agreement, the general partners did not have to distribute any FLP income to the limited partners. This was totally within the discretion of Doug and his wife, as general partners. Thus, Doug and his wife could pay all FLP taxes with the income and re-invest the remaining proceeds.

COMPLY WITH REQUIREMENTS FOR YOUR FLP

To ensure the asset protection benefits and the tax advantages of an FLP, follow state regulations carefully.

- File the certificate of limited partnership with the proper state agency. File annual registration documents, pay all fees, and follow state law formalities or the law will treat the FLP as a general partnership—a liability trap.
- Treat the FLP as a separate entity with its own bank account. FLP expenses should be paid with FLP checks.
- Properly fund the FLP. All FLP assets should have their licenses, registrations, and titles changed to name the FLP as owner.
- LIMITED PARTNERS: Become involved with the management of the FLP or the law may treat you as a general partner. You would lose your limited liability and be personally liable for liabilities of the FLP. This is especially costly when the FLP holds dangerous assets.

SUMMARY

- There are two types of partnerships—*general* partnerships and *limited* partnerships. A family limited partnership is a limited partnership where all the partners are family members.
- General partnerships are liability traps—all partners have unlimited personal liability for the debts of the partnership, and for the acts of their partners.
- If a general partnership must be used, combine it with a number of corporations -- to serve as the partners.
- The FLP is a powerful asset protection device. It can protect both personal and business assets from creditors, while allowing you totally control your assets.
- The FLP is a powerful asset-protector because a creditor of an FLP partner cannot reach FLP assets.
- A creditor of a FLP partner can only obtain a *charging order* against the partner's FLP interest. If the FLP is set-up correctly, this charging order gives the creditor no control, no money, and a tax bill.
- Advanced FLP Protection includes: (1) having the less vulnerable spouse own most of the FLP, (2) using multiple FLPs, and (3) separating safe assets from dangerous assets.
- The FLP can also save you and your family estate taxes and income taxes while maintaining control of the assets.
- To take advantage of the asset protection and estate tax benefits of the FLP, follow all state law formalities.

CHAPTER 9:

LIMITED LIABILITY COMPANIES

The limited liability company (LLC) is a hybrid between the corporation and the limited partnership, and can combine the best qualities of both. Many corporate lawyers believe that the LLC will soon become the most popular legal entity for privately-held businesses.

Why is the LLC so desirable? Because it offers limited liability for its owners, which has long been associated with the corporation, while also offering single taxation, traditionally associated with the partnership. The LLC, a "hybrid" entity, offers the best of both worlds.

The LLC can also be an ideal asset protection tool, because the creditors of LLC members cannot reach LLC assets. This is very similar to the FLP. The LLC possesses many other benefits of the FLP, including significant estate tax benefits; and, can be used in many of the same ways.

The LLC is not perfect, however. Each state has its own LLC laws which must be followed. If the lawyer who drafts your LLC agreement is not careful, unintended tax or liability consequences may result. Also, since it is a new legal device, the LLC carries some uncertainty with it. For this reason, it may be wise to use a family limited partnership (FLP) when either device can accomplish the same strategy. Nevertheless, the LLC can be an extremely desirable legal entity for operating a business, establishing a personal company to fend off personal creditors, and for creating a tax-saving estate plan.

OVERVIEW OF THE LLC

The LLC is the first new legal entity to emerge since the 1950's, when the S corporation was born. The LLC initially appeared in Wyoming in 1977 to help mining developers attract foreign investors. Not until 1988, however, did the LLC became popular throughout the nation when the IRS allowed the LLC to be treated as a partnership for federal tax purposes. Like all partnerships, the LLC would have *single taxation*—LLC owners would be taxed, but not the LLC. This contrasts to the C corporation, which is subject to *double taxation*—the corporation pays tax on its income, and shareholders pay a tax on distributions.

The LLC could become the superior business organization in many situations because it could provide both the limited liability of the corporation and the favorable income taxation of the partnership. State legislatures soon passed laws authorizing this business form in their states. Nearly all 50 states have enacted LLC.

Because the LLC, like the corporation, exists by state law, there are variances in LLC rules. A lawyer familiar with your state LLC laws should draft your LLC agreement.

KEY LLC CHARACTERISTICS

Although the LLC is governed by state law, the following are common LLC attributes:

■ Formation

The LLC is formed by filing articles of organization with the state office in which corporations are formed. Usually, only one person must sign the articles and other LLC members need not be disclosed. All states require a business operating as an LLC to contain the words *limited liability company* or *LLC* and to maintain a registered agent in each state in which it is registered. Fees for forming an LLC—state filing fees and franchise tax pre-payment, range from $200 to close to $1,000 per year.

■ Ownership

Shareholders own a corporation, but the owners of the LLC are called *members*. A member may include a corporation, business trust, individual, U.S. citizen or non-U.S. resident, partnership (limited or general), or even another LLC. In most states, the LLC must include at least two members. A growing number of states allow one member LLCs.

Member voting may be *one member-one vote*, or proportional to the member's ownership in the LLC. Members can always dictate voting rules in their LLC agreement.

■ Duration
State rules differ on the length of time the LLC can exist. In many states, the LLC can exist for a predetermined maximum time period—30 or 50 years. Other states allow the LLC unlimited life, although this can negatively impact its tax status (see below). Several states, such as Virginia and Maryland, specifically prohibit unlimited life.

■ Powers
The LLC must have the powers necessary to conduct business. Some states restrict specific activities—farming, ranching, banking, and insurance. Professionals may generally use the LLC.

■ Management
The LLC may be managed either by its members, or by managers. If manager-controlled, there can be an individual manager or a group of managers. This flexible management structure—allowing centralized or spread-out management—is a great advantage of LLCs. If managers are selected to run the LLC, only they, and not members, can bind the company.

■ Transferability of a Member's Interest
A member may not transfer her interest without the consent of other members. In most states, consent must be unanimous; others allow majority approval.

■ Dissolution
The LLC dissolves upon the expiration of its stated life, upon vote of all members to dissolve, or upon the death, resignation, expulsion, bankruptcy, or dissolution of any member, unless the company is continued by the unanimous vote of the remaining members.

■ Taxed as a Partnership
The LLC is taxed as a partnership. Income and losses "pass-through" the LLC to the individual members. The LLC does not pay income tax. Its members do. Beware: If the LLC is not operated carefully, the IRS may disregard the LLC's partnership tax status and subject it to corporate *double taxation*. This does not occur for state taxation. Complying with IRS standards is crucial to avoiding an unintended federal tax.

■ Limited Liability of Managers and Members

Members, managers, agents, and employees of an LLC are not liable for the debts, contracts, or acts of the LLC, and have much of the same liability protection afforded the corporation to its officers, directors, and stockholders or limited partnerships and their limited partners—or *outside protection*. A manager's or member's personal wealth is isolated "outside" the range of general LLC debts and liabilities. They can only lose what they invest in the LLC. However, as with the corporation or FLP, this protection will not shield LLC members or managers from personal liability arising from torts committed personally or contracts signed personally.

■ LLC Assets are Protected from a Member's Creditors

This is *inside protection—if a member's creditor comes after the LLC property, the creditor cannot force a sale of the member's interest or any of the LLC assets. Nor, can the creditor vote on behalf of the debtor/member.* The member's creditor can only apply to the court for a *charging order*—an order which instructs the LLC to pay income or distributions that would normally flow from the debtor/member to the creditor—this is exactly the same as the "charging order" for FLPs. *The creditor can receive the financial rights of the debtor/member, but not the control rights.*

AN LLC CAN PROTECT PERSONAL ASSETS FROM PERSONAL CREDITORS

An LLC can provide inside protection for personal assets such as cars, home, vacation real estate, stocks, etc. so that your personal creditors cannot seize them. This includes the IRS or an ex-spouse. A creditor cannot get to the assets owned by the LLC because they are not your assets.

All the plaintiff can do, after he wins a judgment, is apply to the court for a charging order to instruct the LLC to pay income or distributions due from you to the creditor until the creditor's judgment is paid. The charging order does not (1) give the creditor LLC voting rights, or (2) force the LLC manager to pay distributions to members. It only means that if distributions are paid, they are paid to your creditor, not you.

The charging order is as futile a remedy when applied to LLCs as FLPs. As the manager of your LLC, you decide if, when, and to whom you will pay distributions. Your judgment creditor cannot vote you out because they cannot vote. As long as the creditor has a judgment against you, you can refuse to pay distributions to members. You can compensate other members by paying them a salary for services, and pay yourself a manager's salary. Your creditor cannot seize your salary through the charging order, but needs a wage attachment, which is restricted to a certain amount.

As with the limited partnership, the "poison pill" of the charging order against LLCs is that it backfires on creditors for income tax purposes. Because an LLC is taxed like a partnership—income tax passes through to members—a creditor with a charging order against your LLC interest also receives an income tax bill for your share of the profits. The creditor receives the K-1 and must pay the tax on your share of the LLC's income, even if you decide never to distribute income to LLC members. *Your creditor thus pays income taxes on earnings he never received—a losing proposition.*

The hollowness of the charging order means that your creditor will more likely agree to a small settlement. Why would they sue you just to get a remedy which gives them no money, no control and a large tax bill? It would not make sense. Talk to the plaintiff's and creditor's lawyers at the outset of any lawsuit or collection procedure. *You'll probably reach a favorable settlement at the outset —before the expense, time, and hassle of defending a claim begins.*

HOW THE LLC PROTECTS YOU FROM BUSINESS CREDITORS

As demonstrated in earlier chapters, running any business involves serious lawsuit risks. The business may fail to pay its debts, its employees may have car accidents, customers may be injured in the business, disgruntled ex-employees may sue for discrimination or sexual harassment. Protecting your personal wealth from these and other business risks is essential today. The LLC accomplishes this goal: Outside protection of the LLC is as strong as the corporation's—if the LLC formalities are followed, only LLC assets are exposed to LLC creditors and plaintiffs. The personal wealth of LLC members is untouchable. When considering a corporation, examine the LLC first. You will get the limited liability of the corporation, while paying less tax on business profits.

Case Study: Elizabeth's Restaurant Revisited

Remember Elizabeth from chapter 7? She declared bankruptcy after she was personally hit with a devastating judgment for her restaurant employee's car accident. Had Elizabeth set up her restaurant as an LLC, not a proprietorship, her personal wealth would have been protected. The worst thing that could have happened would be that the LLC would be forced to liquidate. Elizabeth's personal assets would have remained completely safe. Also, with the restaurant operated as an LLC, Elizabeth would have paid less tax than she did when she ran it as a proprietorship. This could not be said for a C corporation.

For more advanced business protection, we often employ LLCs with the same strategies discussed previously for corporations and limited partnerships. While these are developed further with examples in chapter 12, the two most important are: (1) Use multiple LLCs and (2) Isolate safe assets from dangerous assets in these multiple LLCs.

THE LLC IS ESPECIALLY USEFUL FOR PROTECTING REAL ESTATE

Using an LLC to own real estate is desirable for several reasons. First, real estate, especially rental real estate, is a dangerous asset. The LLC's ability to isolate an owner's personal wealth from liabilities arising from real estate is quite valuable. Combining this personal protection with a favorable tax treatment has the LLC emerge as the preferred way to hold real estate, especially rental real estate.

CASE STUDY: Sam's Condominiums

Sam, a surgeon, owns two mortgage-free luxury vacation condominiums in Newport (condo A and B) which he alternately rents out in the summers and year-round. Sam has owned other rental property and realizes it is only a matter of time until a tenant, guest, or neighbor sues. Sam's state recently passed LLC legislation and he asked us whether he should have an LLC own his two condominiums.

Sam was right when considering the LLC. It turns out he had two other prospective members in mind—his two children in their 20's to whom he intends to bequeath the condominiums. We advised Sam to set up two LLCs; one for each condominium.

While that required an additional $1,000 in registration fees, this extra expense is less than 1% of the value of either condominium. With two LLCs, Sam protected his other personal wealth from liabilities arising from either condominium and isolated each condominium from creditors of the other.

If a tenant from condo A sued, they would sue LLC A, and could reach only asset owned by LLC A. Condo B, and Sam's other personal wealth, would be untouchable. With Sam's LLCs set-up properly, there were no state or federal income taxes on the LLCs. He and his children were taxed personally.

THE LLC ALSO SAVES ESTATE TAXES AND PROBATE FEES

Estate taxes are "death" taxes on everything you own when you die. After a $650,000 non-taxed amount, these taxes quickly hit a maximum rate of 55%. To reduce estate taxes, attorneys are now using LLCs as they have traditionally used FLPs for years.

However, there is much less certainty in how the IRS looks at these strategies with LLCs, compared with FLPs. Most tax attorneys believe that LLCs will enjoy the same estate tax benefits as FLPs, but the IRS has not yet definitely ruled. Conversely, a FLP is more a "sure bet" because the IRS has ruled many times on FLP estate and gift tax planning. Therefore, if estate tax planning is your goal, use an FLP rather than LLC. The LLC can be as effective for asset protection, but for estate tax planning, the FLP is still more reliable. Nevertheless, the following are the key ways an LLC can save you estate taxes and probate fees:

■ LLC Assets Avoids Probate and can Continue to Operate

Assets owned by your LLC do not go through probate. Only your interest in the LLC will. However, if you structure your LLC so your intended beneficiaries eventually own most of the LLC when you die, these beneficiaries will control the LLC and its assets when you die. Your beneficiaries can effectively control the LLC assets or business, while the probate process for distributing your remaining membership interests continues. As probate can last several years, this continued control can be crucial for an operating business or real estate investment.

Remember, consider a living trust to avoid the costs, delay, and publicity of probate. Your trust can own the LLC membership interests while you are alive and pass it to your beneficiaries when you die, completely avoiding probate (see below). This automatically saves your family probate fees on your LLC interest—usually 4-5% of its value.

■ Gifting LLC Membership Interests Lets You Maintain Control While Saving Estate Taxes

The last chapter explained how FLPs allow you to save your loved ones estate taxes when you die while still allowing you control over partnership assets while alive. The FLP accomplishes this by making you the controlling general partner of the FLP, while gifting passive limited partnership interests to your intended beneficiaries during your life.

You achieve this goal with an LLC. Transfer asset(s) to an LLC, make yourself the LLC manager, and gradually gift LLC interests to your intended beneficiaries. As the LLC manager, you control the LLC assets, yet gradually move LLC interests out of your estate, using tax-free gifts of $10,000 per donee per year. The LLC interests also have discounted values because of lack of marketability and lack of control. This means you can gift more than a mathematical $10,000 value of LLC interest per year to each recipient.

Like the FLP, the LLC allows you to control the LLC assets while alive, and give your family and loved ones more wealth when you die, by paying less estate taxes.

Case Study: *Robert's Mutual Funds Revisited*

Recall Robert Jones, the 63-year-old retired vascular surgeon with almost $1 million in mutual funds and real estate. Assume that instead of creating an FLP, he sets-up an LLC to own the mutual funds. He makes himself the sole manager. He initially owns 92.5% of the membership interests, gifting 1.5% each to his five grandchildren. While this 1.5% was, on "paper," worth approximately $15,000, his interests were discounted close to 30% because of the two IRS discounts—lack of marketability and the lack of control attributable to the minority interests. This brings the value of his transferred interests within $10,000 tax-free gift limit.

Robert can continue to gift each grandchild $15,000 worth of LLC interests each year, completely tax-free, as long as these discounts are applied. If Robert lives to 73, he can gift a total of $750,000 worth of mutual fund LLC interests to his grandchildren ($150,000 each), tax-free. This $750,000 is no longer in his estate, nor subject to estate tax. Because Robert's other assets put him in the 55% estate tax bracket, the tax savings from the LLC will be $412,500 (55% x $750,000). And, as the LLC's sole manager, Robert completely controls the mutual funds while alive, and he can distribute income to himself or sell funds for his expenses, pay less estate tax, and provide more for each grandchild.

■ Estate Taxes Are Reduced When Assets Are Beqeathed Through LLCs

You will probably not be able to, nor want to, gift your entire LLC membership interests. Any LLC interests owned at death are subject to the estate tax. However, the IRS applies the same discounts when valuing property for estate tax purposes that it does for gift tax purposes with discounts for lack of marketability and lack of control. Through these discounts, the IRS may assign a value to your LLC interest, 15% to 40% below its *economic value*. This can save thousands of dollars in estate taxes.

Robert Jones' Mutual Funds Revisited

Assume that when Robert dies he still owns 40% of his LLC membership interests, having gifted 60% to his grandchildren. These membership interests, as part of his estate, are subject to estate taxes. Assume that the LLC mutual funds are worth $2 million when Robert dies. His 40% interests in the LLC is then mathematically worth $800,000 (40% x $2 million).

For estate tax valuation, however, the IRS may agree that Robert's remaining LLC interests are worth about $500,000. The IRS will apply the lack of marketability discount because (1) Robert's 5 grandchildren have stakes in the funds so non-family members would not buy his interests and (2) because LLC interests are not freely transferable. The minority ownership discount applies because Robert owned only 40% when he died. A valuation discount in this situation might be around $300,000 which translates into a tax savings of $50,000 ($300,000 x a 50% estate tax). These discounts would not exist if he owned the mutual funds outright.

Robert's living trust could own his remaining LLC interests. While alive, Robert solely owns and controls his living trust, and completely controls the LLC membership interests owned by his trust. When Robert dies, these membership interests pass outside probate, because they are controlled by his living trust, not a will. With probate costs around 5%, a living trust saves Robert's heirs nearly $40,000 ($800,000 x 5%).

Gifting his mutual funds to his grandchildren through an LLC, taking advantage of IRS discounts on LLC interests, and owning his LLC interests through a living trust, saves Robert nearly $200,000 in estate taxes and probate fees, and he never loses control of his funds.

WHEN THE LLC IS YOUR BEST BUSINESS FORM

As mentioned earlier, the LLC is superior to other legal entities in many ways. This section outlines the LLC's advantages over the C corporation, the S corporation, the limited partnership, and the general partnership.

■ Advantages of the LLC over the C corporation

1. No double-taxation for federal or state income tax;

2. No double-taxation on liquidation;

3. Ability to allocate income and losses; and

4. Other tax advantages associated with contributing appreciated property to the LLC, which do not occur with C corporations.

■ Advantages of the LLC over the S corporation

1. LLCs can have more than 74 members, S corporations are restricted to 74 stockholders;

2. LLCs can make special allocations of income and losses, while S

corporations must make allocations pro rata based on percentage ownership;

3. Other tax advantages associated with LLCs when a member dies and the LLC continues to operate.

■ Advantages of the LLC over the Limited Partnership

1. A limited partnership must include at least one general partner who is personally liable for partnership debts and liabilities. The LLC need not have any member or manager personally liable for LLC debts and liabilities. (Remember, the personal liability of a general partner can be shielded by a corporation or an LLC).

2. Although limited partners enjoy single-tax treatment and limited liability, in most states, limited partners lose their limited liability by participating in the management of the partnership. Members of the LLC, on the other hand, are permitted to be active in the LLC's business, while retaining limited liability.

■ Advantages of the LLC over the General Partnership

A general partnership offers no limited liability whatsoever. Each partner is jointly and severally liable for partnership liabilities. LLC members completely avoid this trap; they are neither jointly and severally liable for the LLC debts nor debts of other members (except for professional LLCs, in some states).

REQUIREMENTS FOR FAVORABLE INCOME TAX TREATMENT

As long as an LLC is established according to the laws of its state, the state taxation authority will always tax an LLC's income favorably; as a partnership. This was not the case for federal income tax until the IRS promulgated the "Check the box" regulations in 1997. These rules allow the individuals or professionals creating the LLC to choose its treatment for federal tax purposes. Simply, you need only to "check the box" for tax treatment as a partnership and that is how you will be taxed. The IRS may, of course, audit the returns and structure of the LLC to see if it may lose the single-tax status, but this choosing of treatment gives practitioners much more security in how the entity will be taxed than they had previously.

If you try to get too cute with your LLC, incorporating three or four corporate factors, the IRS may decide that your LLC is more like a corporation than a partnership. If so, your LLC would have to pay tax on its income and so would the LLC members on any income distributed to them. For this reason, if you are setting up an LLC in a flexible state, it is crucial that you have a corporate attorney who is familiar with LLCs and with your intended use of your LLC to prepare LLC documents.

DISADVANTAGES OF THE LLC

The limited liability company, although quite desirable in many circumstances, is not perfect. Definite disadvantages may exclude it from being considered in certain situations. Rather than compare these disadvantages to any particular alternative, simply understand its main drawbacks.

■ Not Available to the Sole Proprietor

Many states require at least two members to form an LLC. Even in those states that allow one-member LLCs, the IRS taxes a single-member LLC as a corporation. Its income tax advantage, therefore, is lost for any sole owner.

Overcoming the disfavored tax treatment of single-member LLCs by using a corporation as your second member will not work. The IRS taxes such a structure as a corporation, even when states allow it.

■ Not Always Available for the Professional Practice

Many states prohibit LLCs for physicians, attorneys, and other professional practices. California, for example, prohibits LLCs for any professional licensed by the state. Before using an LLC for a professional practice, check with an attorney familiar with your state's LLC laws.

■ Formation Involves Expenses

Forming an LLC requires a state filing fee and, in many states, a deposit on income tax for the upcoming year—usually between $200 and $1,000, which compares to a corporation.

■ Risk of Planning Error

An error in LLC planning can destroy the LLC tax advantage. This risk is not prevalent for corporations and partnerships.

■ Uncertain Estate Tax Benefits

While the LLC may be as effective as an FLP for saving estate taxes, many estate planning strategies used for FLPs remain untested with LLCs.

■ Dissolution Dilemma

When unanimous vote of all members is required to continue the company after the death, bankruptcy, retirement, etc., of a member, one member can become a hold out, and make unreasonable demands on the other members to assure continuation of the company. Fortunately, the IRS recognizes the use of majority vote in these situations to continue the company. LLC articles of organization/operating agreement should require only a majority vote to continue the company.

OFFSHORE AND DOMESTIC LLCs: Why "For Value" Is Important

Thus far, the discussion has been about domestic LLCs -- those set up in one of the 50 states. However, LLC legislation is increasingly being adopted in the offshore jurisdictions you will learn about in chapter 11 -- Nevis, in fact, is the leading offshore jurisdiction in terms of LLC legislation.

While we will leave most of our discussion of offshore LLCs to chapter 11, it is enough to say here that they are extremely useful tools as part of offshore planning as well. Especially important is the fact that when one sets up an LLC, one takes back LLC interests.

Thus, this transfer is "for value" and not a gift -- as it is when one transfers assets to a trust. Because it is "for value", the transfer has a much less chance of being characterized as fraudulent under the fraudulent transfer laws discussed in chapter four. This is an important benefit for LLCs and FLPs, when compared to trusts for asset protection purposes.

CONCLUSION: THE LLC IS AN EXTREMELY USEFUL TOOL

The LLC can play a very useful role for asset protection. It is often the best way to operate a privately-held business, simply because it provides asset protection benefits for its members while allowing pass-through income tax status. If you own a private business, consider the LLC.

The LLC also can be an effective personal wealth protector, functioning like a limited partnership, to shield personal assets from personal creditors. Combine this use with its likely estate tax advantages, and the LLC becomes a desired tool to own personal and family assets.

SUMMARY

- The LLC, a relatively new legal entity, can operate businesses and own assets. It combines the limited liability of a corporation with the favorable income tax treatment of a limited partnership.
- The LLC's other important attributes are its flexible management arrangement and restricted transferability of ownership.
- The LLC powerfully protects personal assets from personal creditors. As with an FLP, a creditor of an LLC member cannot seize LLC assets. He can only get a hollow *charging order* against the LLC interest.
- The LLC powerfully protects your personal wealth from the creditors of your business—as powerfully as a corporation will
- The LLC is not perfect. It also has advantages and disadvantages versus the other type legal entities.
- The IRS will not grant an LLC favorable income tax treatment, if the LLC has too many corporate characteristics.
- IRS "check the box" regulations allow you to choose how the LLC will be treated for federal income tax purposes.
- Overall, the LLC is an excellent asset protection tool—one that plays a role in most asset protection plans.

CHAPTER 10:

USING TRUSTS TO PROTECT YOUR WEALTH

For years, America's richest families have used trusts to protect their wealth and to save taxes. The general public is, only now, utilizing trusts. In fact, trusts are probably the most misunderstood of all legal devices. Many people simply do not understand how trusts work, and wrongly believe that they are only for the super-rich.

This chapter explains what a trust is, and the role it can play in your asset protection plan. A number of different trusts used in asset protection planning are covered, each with its own place and use in specific situations. One trust not covered in this chapter is the "foreign asset protection trust," also called the "offshore trust." This tool is sufficiently important enough to deserve its own chapter with other offshore strategies and entities.

WHAT IS A TRUST?

A trust is a legal entity, often misunderstood by the general public. The following definitions and diagram should help you understand a trust and how it functions.

A. Definitions

1. TRUST: The trust is essentially a legal arrangement where one person holds property for the benefit of another. The person who holds the property is the *trustee*. He holds the property for the *beneficiary(ies)*.

A trust is created by a trust document which specifies that the trustee holds property owned by the trust for the benefit of the beneficiary of the trust. The trust document also establishes the terms of how the trust should be administered, and how the trust assets should be distributed during the lifetime of the trust as well as after the trust is terminated.

2. GRANTOR: The Grantor is the person who sets-up the trust. Usually, the person who transfers property into the trust. Also called, *Trustor* or *Settlor*.

3. TRUSTEE: The trustee(s) are the legal owners of the trust property. The trustee(s) are responsible for administering and carrying out the terms of the trust. They owe a fiduciary duty to the beneficiaries—an utmost duty of care that they will follow the terms of the trust document and manage the trust property properly. A trustee may be a person, such as a family member or trusted friend. The trustee can also be an institution such as a professional trust company or trust department of a bank. More than one trustee are called *co-trustees*.

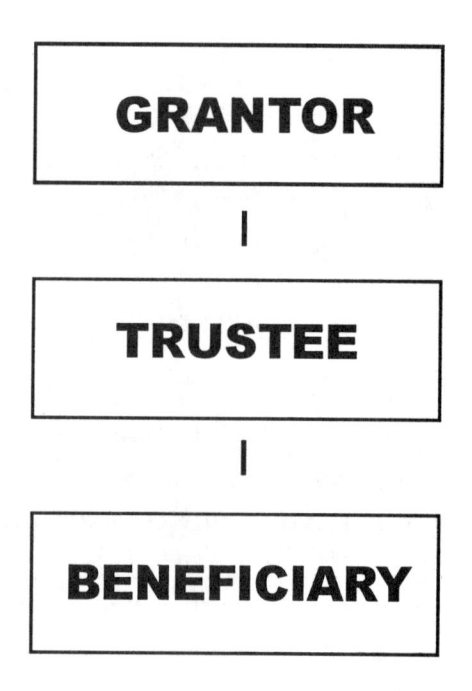

```
┌─────────────┐
│  GRANTOR    │
└─────────────┘
      │
┌─────────────┐
│  TRUSTEE    │
└─────────────┘
      │
┌─────────────┐
│ BENEFICIARY │
└─────────────┘
```

The trustee as the legal owner of any assets owned by the trust, and has "legal title" to the assets owned by the trust. For example, assume that Dad wants to set-up a trust for his children, Son and Daughter. Dad wants his brother, Uncle, to serve as trustee. If Dad transfers his house into the trust, the title to that house will be with "Uncle, as trustee of the Dad trust."

Using Trusts To Protect Your Wealth

4. BENEFICIARY: The beneficiary (or beneficiaries) is the person for whom the trust was set-up. While the trustee has legal title to assets owned by the trust, the beneficiary has *equitable title* or the rights to the trust property. The beneficiary can sue the trustee if the trustee mismanages the trust property or disobeys specific instructions in the trust.

The beneficiary may be the same person as the grantor, and can possibly be the same person as the trustee. For asset protection purposes, *the trustee, beneficiary, and grantor, cannot all be the same person.*

5. FUNDING: Funding the trust means transferring assets to the trust. *A trust that is "unfunded" has no property transferred to it. It is completely ineffective.* You must title assets to the trust if you want trust protection as with any other legal entity/asset protection tool discussed previously.

To title real estate to the trust execute and record a deed to the property. Bank and brokerage accounts can be transferred by simply changing the name on the accounts. Registered stocks and bonds are changed by notifying the transfer agent or issuing company and requesting that the certificates be reissued to the trust. Other assets, such as household items, furniture, jewelry, artwork, etc., are transferred by a simple legal document called an *assignment* or *Bill of Sale*. Your asset protection specialist can transfer assets simply and quickly.

> Remember: legal entities used in asset protection planning often separate *ownership* from *control*. The trust also separates ownership and control. **The trustee controls trust assets, but beneficial ownership is with the beneficiaries.** The grantor, on the other hand, has relinquished control and ownership.

B. TRUST CLASSIFICATIONS
Trusts follow these classifications:

A. Revocable: A revocable trust is one that you, the grantor, can revoke and undo at any time.

B. Irrevocable: An irrevocable trust is one that you cannot revoke or undo once established.

C. Inter vivos: An inter vivos trust takes effect during your lifetime.

D. Testamentary: A testamentary trust takes effect at your death. Testamentary trusts are usually created in wills, living trusts, or other documents taking effect at death. All testamentary trusts are irrevocable: you cannot come back to life to undo the trust.

LIVING TRUSTS: ILLUSIVE ASSET PROTECTION

Living trusts are excellent devices for avoiding probate. They also effectively sidestep the hidden dangers of joint tenancy. However, *living trusts provide absolutely no asset protection!* Many people think that because a living trust is a trust it somehow protects their assets from creditors, lawsuits and other threats. Nothing is further from the truth!

■ Revocable Trusts do not Protect Assets

Living trusts provide absolutely no asset protection because they are revocable. As a revocable trust, the grantor of the living trust can undo the trust at any time during her lifetime. This is a great benefit of the living trust for probate avoidance and estate planning purposes. You, the grantor, can change the trust whenever you wish to change who receives your savings when you die. This greatly comforts those setting up living trusts—to know that they can change their living trust at any time, just as they could a will. However, while revocability is good for estate planning goals, it renders a trust useless for asset protection. Remember this simple rule: *revocable trusts are vulnerable trusts!*

■ Creditors can "Step Into Your Shoes" and Revoke the Trust

Revocable trusts are useless for asset protection, because revocable trusts allow the grantor to undo the trust. If the grantor's creditors want to seize assets owned by a revocable trust, they simply need to petition the court to "step into the shoes" of the grantor. If you have a living trust or any other revocable trust to shield assets from creditors, your creditors can easily ask the court to step into your shoes and revoke the trust themselves. Its assets will no longer be owned by the trust, but by you personally. The creditors then have all the rights and privileges to seize these assets, now owned by you.

■ Other Benefits of Living Trusts

Despite its weakness for asset protection planning, the living trust is still commonly used in asset protection plans. It is the ideal way to own FLP interests, LLC membership interests, or other interests in entities that will provide protection.

Corporations, trusts, FLPs, LLCs, and other legal entities can protect assets owned by them —such as real estate, stocks, cars, bank accounts, etc. You and your family members will own the legal entities. However, you should not own these entities in your own names, but in the name of your revocable living trusts.

With these legal entities owned by your living trusts, rather than in your own name, you later save estate taxes and expensive probate fees. You get the best of both worlds: protecting your assets while alive and saving your family estate taxes and probate fees when you die. For more about living trusts, including how to use it to save estate taxes, see the Appendices.

IRREVOCABLE TRUSTS: THE ASSET PROTECTION TRUST

While revocable trusts offer no asset protection, irrevocable trusts are important for asset protection. Once you establish an irrevocable trust, you forever abandon the ability to undo the trust and reclaim property transferred to the trust. With an irrevocable trust, you lose both control of the trust assets and ownership.

■ Why Irrevocable Trusts Protect Your Assets

Irrevocable trusts protect assets for the same reason that revocable trusts do not. Revocable living trusts do not provide asset protection because creditors can step into your shoes with such a trust. Assets owned by a revocable living trust are vulnerable to lawsuits and creditors.

An irrevocable trust brings opposite results. Because an established irrevocable trust cannot be altered or undone, your creditors cannot step into your shoes and undo the trust, any more than you can. Assets in an irrevocable trust are immune from creditor attack, lawsuits, and other threats. An irrevocable trust carries a heavy price—you must give up control and ownership of the asset to gain protection.

When does such a heavy price make sense? When you (1) would inevitably gift the assets to the beneficiaries, and (2) do not foresee needing the assets for your own financial security. When both factors are satisfied, your "price" is not particularly heavy. You do not personally need the assets and the trust will accomplish what you would do yourself—distribute the assets to your beneficiaries (usually children) at some future time.

■ 3 Pitfalls to Avoid With Irrevocable Trusts

Keep three cautions in mind:

1. You cannot reserve any power to revoke, rescind, or amend the trust or retain any rights, either directly or indirectly, to reclaim property transferred to the trust. Simply, there can be no strings attached.

2. You cannot assert authority on how trust property will be managed or invested.

3. You, as the trust's grantor, cannot be its trustee. Nor can you appoint a trustee not considered arm's length: your spouse, close relative or even a close personal friend. Courts closely examine the relationship between the grantor and the trustee to determine whether the trustee is only the grantor's "alter ego." If there is such a relationship, courts will ignore the trust and allow creditors to reach the trust assets.

TIP: *A corporate trustee, such as a bank or a trust company, are much less likely to be judged as an alter ego, thereby giving your trust an added layer of security.*

TWO CLAUSES YOUR IRREVOCABLE TRUST SHOULD HAVE

Two clauses are extremely important for an irrevocable trust intended for rock-solid protection. These clauses are important not necessarily to protect you, the trust creator, but for shielding your beneficiaries from their creditors.

1. Spendthrift Clause

The spendthrift clause allows the trustee to withhold income and principal which would ordinarily be paid to the beneficiary, if the trustee feels the money could or would be wasted, or seized by the beneficiary's creditors. This clause accomplishes two goals. First, it prevents a wasteful beneficiary from spending trust funds or wasting trust assets. This is especially important to many grantors who set up trusts with their children as beneficiaries. If you worry that money in trust for your children would be wasted if not controlled, then use a spendthrift clause. The trustee can then stop payments if your child spends too quickly or unwisely.

Secondly, the spendthrift clause protects trust assets from creditors of the beneficiaries. Beneficiaries may now be young, but as adults, they will face the same risks we all face: lawsuits, debt problems, divorce, a failing business, etc.

Using Trusts To Protect Your Wealth

The spendthrift clause protects trust assets from your children's creditors, by allowing the authority to withhold payments to a beneficiary with a creditor. If the beneficiary and trustee are arm's length, the creditor has no power to force the trustee to pay the beneficiary. The creditor only has a right to payments actually paid by the trustee. He cannot force the trustee to make disbursements.

2. Anti-Alienation Clause

The anti-alienation clause also protects trust assets from the beneficiary's creditors. Specifically, the anti-alienation clause prohibits the trustee from transferring trust assets to anyone other than the beneficiary. This, of course, includes creditors of the trust beneficiary(ies). Thus, while the spendthrift clause allows the trustee to withhold payments if a creditor lurks, the anti-alienation clause goes one step further—it prohibits the trustee from paying trust income or principal to anyone but the named beneficiaries.

Case Study: *Jerry and His Kids*

Jerry, an orthopedist, had a sizable investment portfolio, including $200,000 in mutual funds which he planned on leaving to his two children, Steve and Stephanie. Jerry knew that he and his wife could live quite comfortably without these mutual funds, and he wanted to save estate taxes and provide security to his children. Jerry, however, was concerned that his kids would unwisely spend the funds.

We established an irrevocable trust for Jerry and named his local bank trust department as trustee. Jerry told the trust officer about his concerns for the funds, and Jerry's wishes were incorporated into the trust document.

Although Steve and Stephanie were only 12 at the time, Jerry and his wife funded the trust with $20,000 worth of mutual fund interests each year—so the gifts to the trust were completely tax free. The trust was made irrevocable, so that if Jerry or his wife were sued, their creditors could not seize these funds. The trust also had anti-alienation and spendthrift clauses, so that the funds would be protected from his children's poor spending habits as well as from their creditors.

139

Jerry realized that the trust would eventually be substantial in value. He also recognized the possibility that his children will someday have creditor or divorce problems. With this irrevocable trust, Jerry protected these funds from his creditors, gifted them tax-free to the trust, provided for his children's future (which he intended to do through his will or living trust), and did so in a way that fully protects the funds from his children's creditors.

5 TIPS FOR AN IRONCLAD IRREVOCABLE TRUST

You can greatly increase the asset protection for your irrevocable trust with five tactics:

1. FUND THE TRUST EARLY: As with any asset protection strategy, avoid fraudulent transfers. Set-up the trust and fund it before a lawsuit arises. You greatly ensure that your trust cannot be undone by a creditor crying "fraudulent transfer."

2. USE AN INDEPENDENT TRUSTEE: Do not be the trustee of your own trust. The best trustees are completely independent: a bank or professional, such as an attorney or accountant. Less desirable are close family friends.

3. STATE A NON-PROTECTION PURPOSE FOR THE TRUST: It is usually desirable to state a non-protection reason in the trust document. Courts are less likely to set aside a legal entity, such as a trust, established for estate planning purposes or to provide support for a family member. Often, we write this non-protection purpose in the trust Preamble.

4. THE BENEFICIARY SHOULD NOT BE THE GRANTOR: If the beneficiary is the grantor, courts will likely disregard the trust and allow the grantor's creditors to seize the trust assets.

5. KEEP ACCURATE RECORDS: Operate the trust in a businesslike way. Keep accurate records of all transfers to the trust, as well as disbursements of income and principal to beneficiaries. This is another benefit of a corporate trustee. They keep accurate records.

4 USEFUL IRREVOCABLE TRUSTS

Four irrevocable trusts are particularly useful in asset protection planning.

1. THE IRREVOCABLE LIFE INSURANCE TRUST

Life insurance is more than insurance—it is an important asset. In fact, your life insurance policy may have a substantial cash value. Even "noncash" life insurance policy is an important asset because you rely on it to provide income and support to your family when you die. Further, life insurance is highly recommended as a tool to pay estate taxes due when you die—because funds are available immediately to your survivors, without the delays or expenses involved with liquidating tangible assets. We always recommend that clients protect their life insurance with an irrevocable life insurance trust. Without such a trust, an important bedrock of your family's financial security is vulnerable to creditor and lawsuit attack.

■ Features of the Irrevocable Life Insurance Trust

An *irrevocable life insurance trust (ILIT)* is an irrevocable trust which contains only a life insurance policy. Like other irrevocable trusts, the ILIT requires a written document, trustee, beneficiary, and terms for the trust distribution. A properly drafted ILIT also has a preamble stating that the purpose of the trust is tax savings involving a particular life insurance policy.

In essence, the ILIT owns a policy which insures your life. The policy itself will name the trust as beneficiary so when you die, the insurance company pays the proceeds to the ILIT trustee. Then the ILIT trustee will follow your trust instructions on what to do with the proceeds, including paying the ILIT beneficiaries you name in the trust.

The ILIT can either be funded or unfunded. With an unfunded ILIT, the life insurance policy is either fully paid when transferred to the trust, or provisions are made in the trust document for the future funding of premiums (such as you agree to make payment to the trust, so it can pay the premiums). In a funded trust, the grantor transfers to the trust, in addition to the policy itself, adequate income-producing assets to pay off future premiums—usually bonds, annuities, or income-producing stocks.

Whether the trust is unfunded or funded, future payments on the policy must be made from the trust funds. You, as the grantor of the trust, cannot directly pay for the insurance premiums. The trustee must pay premiums from the trust account, otherwise, you lose creditor protection.

■ An ILIT Protects You

Because the ILIT is irrevocable, it protects the life insurance cash value and proceeds on distribution from your creditors. As life insurance policy is an important asset for the future financial security of your spouse, children, and other beneficiaries, this trust is a crucial asset protection tool. Because you no longer have any ownership or control over the insurance policy, and cannot change policy beneficiaries or change terms of the policy. Your creditors cannot "step into your shoes" and seize any policy proceeds or cash value.

■ An ILIT Can Save Estate Taxes

As important as the asset protection benefits of an ILIT are the estate taxes it can save. *An ILIT can save you hundreds of thousands of dollars in estate taxes!*

An ILIT saves you estate taxes because the trust, rather than you personally, own the life insurance policy. Thus, the policy proceeds will not be part of your *net estate* when you die and will not be subject to the estate tax.

Assume that you are single when you die and your estate is then worth $1 million, $400,000 of which is life insurance. Let us also assume that you have the full $650,000 exemption available . Your estate will have to pay taxes on the remaining $350,000—an estate tax bill of about $150,000! An ILIT eliminates that $400,000 life insurance value from your estate, thereby saving over $150,000 in estate taxes!

■ An ILIT Gives You More Control

The ILIT gives you much more control over what happens to the policy proceeds than you can get from a bare insurance policy. With an insurance policy alone, your only decision is whom to name as beneficiaries. The insurance company simply pays these people when you die. An ILIT, on the other hand, allows you to control not only who gets the proceeds, but, even more importantly, what exactly happens to the funds when you die.

The ILIT trust document can provide that the trustee will pay your estate taxes and other costs (taxes due on IRAs or other retirement plans probate costs, legal fees, other debts, etc.) before paying trust beneficiaries. The trustee can pay the beneficiaries directly or pay them over a period of months or years. You can incorporate spendthrift provisions and anti-alienation provisions to protect against your beneficiary's (children) financial problems or their spouse's financial woes. An ILIT gives you all of the protective benefits of a trust arrangement.

Using Trusts To Protect Your Wealth

NOTE: *Another benefit of the ILIT is that it prevents court interference if a beneficiary becomes incompetent. Many insurance companies will not pay life insurance proceeds to incapacitated persons. Instead, they will ask the court what to do. An ILIT avoids this complication—the insurance company pays the ILIT trustee, who does exactly as you instructed in the trust.*

■ Requirements for your ILIT

Your ILIT, for maximum protection, must follow guidelines:

1. **MAKE THE PROPER TRANSFERS:** You must fully fund the ILIT with the insurance policy in order to gain its protective value. Contact your insurance carrier and change the ownership of the policy to the trust. Make the trust the beneficiary of the policy. Remember, the trust is the beneficiary of the insurance policy. The trust beneficiaries (spouse, child, etc.) will eventually receive the proceeds as you instructed in the trust document.

2. **THE TRUST MUST PAY THE PREMIUMS:** One indication of ownership is who pays the policy premiums. If you continue to pay the policy premiums while the trust is the owner of the policy, the courts may disregard the ownership of the policy and consider you the owner. This allows your creditors to "step into your shoes" and take the policy proceeds away from your family members. The policy would also be in your estate for estate tax purposes. The trust must pay premiums out of trust funds.

3. **YOU CANNOT BE TRUSTEE:** You must *not* be the ILIT trustee yourself. You may name your spouse, adult child, or another trusted individual as trustee. Corporate trustees are often preferred because of their familiarity with ILITs, and their reliability in following trust instructions and paying premiums promptly.

2. THE IRREVOCABLE CHILDREN'S TRUST

If you have children to whom you want to gift assets, an irrevocable children's trust (ICT) can offer both tax savings and asset protection. Property transferred to such a trust, (1) can no longer be reached by your creditors, (2) is no longer a part of your estate for estate tax purposes, and (3) at least some income from the trust assets can be taxed at the children's lower income tax rates. These three reasons make children's trusts increasingly popular.

The ICT is also called a *Section 2503(c) Minor's Trust* (because the Internal Revenue Code Section 2503(c) controls the taxation and asset protection benefits of this trust). The ICT must include a trust document, and a trustee who has legal title to the trust assets. As long as the trust is in force while the child beneficiary is under 21, neither your creditors, nor the child's creditors can seize the trust assets.

However, when the child reaches legal age, 21, the child has the absolute right to demand the trust assets. As an irrevocable trust, you, the grantor, have no rights to hold back trust assets and prevent the child from obtaining what is now owned by the trust. It is possible to extend the trust until a later age, but only if the child (now 21) consents in writing.

However, if the child (now adult) demands his share of trust assets, the trustee must deliver them. For this reason, carefully consider your child's demeanor and expected attitude towards trust property when they reach the age of 21. You no more want to lose trust assets to an irresponsible 21 years old than you do to creditors.

3. THE IRREVOCABLE CHARITABLE REMAINDER TRUST

This sounds like an extreme measure to protect assets by gifting them to a charity. But, under our tax code, you can often give away much of your property to charity and still enjoy it during your lifetime. Many people find this is an effective way to gift assets they would ordinarily give to charity anyway, while still enjoying asset protection benefits and tax advantages while alive. With a *charitable remainder trust (CRT)*, you can gift property to a charity and protect it from creditors while retaining an income stream for your life and still have the value of the property go to your heirs.

A CRT is an irrevocable trust. You, as grantor, select a tax exempt charitable organization as the beneficiary of the trust principal. By creating this trust, the tax law considers you as making a charitable donation. You can claim a tax deduction for the fair market value of the assets contributed to the trust. Although you have gifted the asset's "principal," the law still allows you to take a fixed amount of annual income from the trust as the income beneficiary. In this way, you get a tax deduction now while enjoying the income from your assets until you die. To understand how a CRT works, consider this example:

Using a CRT to Gift your stock portfolio

Assume that you have $200,000 in stocks purchased 15 years ago for only $60,000. If you sold that stocks to invest in treasury bonds for a stable conservative retirement income, you would pay about $28,000 in capital gains tax on the profit. Upon your death, assuming the stocks were still worth

$200,000, your estate would pay another $88,000 in estate taxes, if you were in the highest estate tax bracket. Deducting these two taxes, your heirs receive only $72,000 from the original $200,000 value.

Now, instead of selling your stocks, you transfer it to a CRT. You can require that you receive the same income you would receive from treasury bonds for the rest of your life. How? By making yourself the CRT's income beneficiary. This is perfectly permissible. Now, you can deduct the $200,000 donation as a charitable contribution, and with the money saved using the deduction, you buy life insurance which would give your heirs more than $72,000 they would have received had you not used a CRT. You get a large tax deduction this year, the same fixed retirement income as with treasury bonds. And, you help charity.

WARNING: *This is a simplification of a CRT. There are often many other tax considerations with a CRT including estate income tax and capital gains tax issues. Further, this example only makes sense for someone with appreciated assets, who requires a fixed income, and where the CRT's fixed income adequately covers one's retirement years, even when considering inflation. Nonetheless, for many people who would give to charity upon their death, a CRT can be an effective tax-saver and asset-protector.*

4. THE IRREVOCABLE MEDICAID TRUST

A medicaid trust is an irrevocable trust to protect an individual from the cost of catastrophic illness. Basically, the medicaid trust ensures that the principal amount in the trust cannot be counted by the government to disqualify you from Medicaid assistance. Set-up properly, you can enjoy some ownership benefits of what is in the trust, while still qualifying for Medicaid nursing home benefits.

ALASKA AND DELAWARE TRUSTS

There is a great deal of interest in Alaska and Delaware. Both states recently enacted legislation allowing the formation of special trusts in their jurisdiction which give certain estate tax benefits and asset protection. While the estate tax possibilities may be worth exploring, here we will discuss the asset protection attributes of these trusts.

The Alaska and Delaware trusts are touted as good alternatives to the FAPT. Arguably, Americans would be more comfortable with a U.S.-based trust than a foreign trust. That is their selling point.

Both the Alaska and Delaware trusts offer good protection from future creditors. However, these trusts do not seem to offer much more protection than could be obtained from a well-drafted irrevocable trust in any other state.

The main flaw with these trusts is that they can not adequately protect you from the claims of present creditors and certainly not as effectively as an offshore trust can. While foreign trusts do not recognized U.S. judgements or court orders, Alaska and Delaware must, as a constitutional matter, recognize and enforce judgements from another state. For this reason alone, we do not usually use Alaska or Delaware trusts for our clients.

TRUSTS FOR BUSINESS OWNERS

Many trusts as effectively protect business assets as they do personal assets. For more discussion on trusts beneficial for business protection, see Chapter 12 *Advanced Protection for Business Owners*.

CONCLUSION: TRUSTS MAY BE AN IMPORTANT PART OF YOUR ASSET PROTECTION PLAN

Your asset protection plan will likely involve at least one trust. Most people have at minimum, an ILIT and Living Trusts for both spouses. If you have life insurance, do not forego the asset protection benefits and tax savings of the ILIT. Also, a Living Trust is a necessity for everyone—to avoid the costly, time-consuming mistake of a will.

If you have children, or other beneficiaries who may have creditor or spending problems, then irrevocable trusts are often ideal for passing wealth while frustrating creditors. Recall Jerry and his children—Jerry saved taxes, while providing for his children, and protecting mutual funds from his creditors, his children's creditors, and his children's spending habits—all with an irrevocable trust.

The next chapter covers one specific trust which is a top asset-protector—the foreign asset protection trust.

SUMMARY

- A trust is a legal entity where one person (the trustee) holds property for the benefit of another (the beneficiary).
- To be effective for tax or asset protection purposes, the trust must be funded (i.e. have assets transferred into it).
- Living Trusts are excellent for avoiding probate, the pitfalls of joint tenancy, and estate taxes. However, they provide no asset protection benefits.
- To protect assets from creditors and other threats, the trust must be irrevocable. Since you cannot undo the irrevocable trust, neither can your creditors.
- The Spendthrift clause and the Anti-Alienation clause protects trust assets from your beneficiaries' creditors and your own.
- For a rock-solid irrevocable trust—fund it early, use an independent trustee, state a non-protection reason for the trust, separate grantor from the beneficiary, and keep accurate records.
- The *Irrevocable Life Insurance Trust (ILIT)* is essential for everyone with life insurance. It protects the insurance from all threats, saves estate taxes, and gives you more control than a bare policy does.
- Remember: the ILIT premiums must be paid by the trustee with trust funds, the policy must be owned by the trust, and you cannot be the ILIT trustee.
- The *Irrevocable Children's Trust (ICT)* and the Irrevocable *Charitable Remainder Trust (CRT)* are two important trusts for saving taxes and protecting wealth.
- A total asset protection plan may utilize a number of trusts, depending on the assets owned and your estate plan.

CHAPTER 11:

FOREIGN ASSET PROTECTION PLANNING AND OTHER OFFSHORE STRATEGIES

*With the offshore entities, you have the most powerful asset protection tools available. In this chapter, we explain the basics of the **Foreign Asset Protection Trust (FAPT)** and how you can use one effectively to protect your family wealth. You will learn what a FAPT is, the mechanics of how it protects your assets, why a FAPT can provide you with investment benefits, and which countries are the best places to set up your FAPT.*

*This chapter also highlights several other offshore strategies and structures that can protect assets. The most significant -- the **offshore limited liability company (LLC)**, which can allow the client greater control than the FAPT and also provides a stronger defense to any fraudulent transfer claim which may arise.*

*Finally, we have left the discussion of one of the most powerful offshore entities, the **closely held insurance company (CIC)**, also called the **"captive" insurance company,** out of this chapter. Because its tax benefits are even more valuable than its asset protection qualities, we have placed most of our CIC discussion in the financial "Special Bonus" section found in chapter 18. Make sure you read the CIC discussion in that chapter as well.*

THE OFFSHORE REVOLUTION

Using foreign jurisdictions to protect wealth has been a popular strategy for estate and family-wealth planning since the early Roman days, when emperors attempted to preserve their riches for their descendants. It was also used by the Crusaders, who left their homes and savings behind for foreign ventures. Nevertheless, offshore planning has never been as popular as it is today -- due primarily to the use of the foreign trust.

Today there are over $2 trillion in foreign trusts! Most are established in *offshore havens* or *offshore financial centers*. (A list of such havens is located later in the chapter). Because they have favorable tax, banking, privacy, estate planning, and asset protection laws, these offshore havens are extremely desirable countries in which to set-up a trust. In fact, wealthy individuals and families from around the world have established trusts in these countries for decades. Only in the last ten years have middle-income professionals, entrepreneurs, and other savvy business people started taking advantage of this opportunity.

You may be one of the many under the misconception that a foreign trust is in some way illegal—that they are only used by drug-dealers to launder money or avoid taxes. Certainly, some offshore trusts and bank accounts are used for illegal purposes. Of the $5 trillion in all offshore entities including trusts, LLCs, bank accounts, CICs, and other offshore investment structures, about 10%, or $500 billion, are illicit money-laundered funds. While there is illegal money in offshore havens, *roughly 90% of the funds in offshore entities —close to $4.5 trillion—is legal and legitimate.*

Further, *a FAPT does not avoid U.S. taxes*. A FAPT has no tax consequences at all—it neither helps nor hurts you. The FAPT only protects your wealth from future threats, and to provide you an offshore investment structure.

WHY A FAPT WORKS

The FAPT protects assets so well because of the concept of *jurisdiction*. American courts only have jurisdiction over persons or property located within the U.S. They cannot control people or property in other countries. Some foreign countries do recognize judgments by U.S. courts and enforce them as they do judgments in their own country. Your FAPT would be in one of the many offshore havens which refuse to recognize foreign judgments, including U.S. judgments. *To fight your FAPT in these havens, your creditor must sue the trust in the haven courts.*

Foreign Asset Protection Planning and Other Offshore Entities

The trustee is the legal title owner of trust assets. If the trustee of your FAPT is not located in the U.S.— such as a foreign trust company with no U.S. ties—a U.S. court cannot order the trustee to turn over assets to your American creditors.

Even if a U.S. court has no jurisdiction over a foreign trustee, if trust assets are located in the U.S., an American court could control them. The court could order real estate deeds changed, or order the seizure of local bank accounts or stocks of U.S. corporations, etc. That's why, when a serious threat arises, you must have a significant portion of your vulnerable wealth offshore. *This way, no American court has jurisdiction over either the trustee or the trust assets and is powerless over your FAPT.*

Because an American court is powerless to recover assets from your FAPT, creditors seeking assets from the FAPT must file suit in the foreign haven. This can be extremely time-consuming and expensive. Further, these countries have laws which are extremely protective of debtors, making it virtually impossible for a foreign creditor to win a judgment against your trust.

A creditor trying to reach your FAPT assets will almost certainly agree to a quick and relatively inexpensive settlement. *Many plaintiff attorneys, in fact, settle as soon as they learn that you have a FAPT.* Most attorneys do not know how to sue the trust, and those that do, understand that it is seldom worth the effort. *Thus, using a FAPT is the best way to encourage settlements and even discourage lawsuits before they occur.* Few contingency lawyers will take a case if they are to be paid only if assets are recovered from a FAPT. It's a losing proposition.

NOTE: Because FAPTs lower lawsuit exposure, *many physicians with astronomical malpractice premiums have lowered their coverage, due to their FAPT. With a lower policy limit and less wealth exposed, these doctors greatly diminish their attractiveness to potential plaintiffs.* Yet, because their wealth is protected through their FAPT and other entities, they enjoy much more security than if they maintained high-cost insurance but, did not otherwise protect their assets.

THE FAPT STRUCTURE

■ Typical Trust Elements

The FAPT, *"Offshore Trust" " Foreign Situs Trust"* or, *"Asset Protection Trust"*, has the same trust elements described in the previous chapter.

1. Grantor: You, or you and your spouse.

2. Trustee: Usually, there are initially two co-trustees—you and a foreign trust company. For asset protection purposes, the foreign trustee must have no ties to the U.S. so U.S. courts have no power or control over the trustee. The foreign trustee will be a professional trust company, which charges annual fees based on the amount in the trust.

Foreign trust companies are large, trustworthy firms with excellent track records and are typically bonded. Funds in the trust are normally as secure as in a U.S. bank (considering our Savings and Loan debacle, we say your savings are safer offshore).

You, your asset protection attorney, and your trustee will together set-up your trust. You must be comfortable that your trustee is reputable and understands your wishes and desires. A strong working relationship between the three of you will ensure your FAPT will shield you against any and all threats.

3. Beneficiary: Although this is not advisable for asset protection purposes, certain havens allow you to be the sole beneficiary. Other havens allow you to own a *reversionary interest*, which gives you access to trust assets after a certain term, usually ten years. Until your spouse and children (or anyone else you name) would be the current beneficiaries. You can still obtain trust funds through loans and gifts.

4. Trust Agreement: Sets out the trustee's duties and includes many important provisions described later in the chapter.

■ Unique FAPT Elements

1. Foreign Trust Situs: *Situs* means *place* or *location* for your trust to be registered—a foreign country whose laws will govern the trust. This will be one of the offshore havens, such as Nevis, Bahamas, the Cook Islands, or another haven listed later in the chapter. Essentially, you use the haven's trust laws, although you may never transfer your assets to that haven. For this reason, *(a) the FAPT should* *explicitly state that it is governed by the foreign situs' law, (b) the trustee should be located in the same country.*

2. The Protector: The Protector is an independent person or entity chosen by you (the grantor) who acts like a watchdog over the foreign trustee. Obviously, you must trust anyone you appoint as Protector. The Protector typically has the power to remove the trustee and the Protector's consent is required for major acts by the trustee, such as adding a beneficiary, selling key assets, making purchases or disbursements, etc. The Protector's powers can be as broad or limited as you decide.

The Protector provides protection against mismanagement by the foreign trustee; especially important when you are removed as a co-trustee—which happens when a lawsuit or other threat emerges. U.S. Protectors must also then resign (as will be explained later).

6 PROVISIONS TO IMPROVE YOUR FAPT

The following provisions ensure that your trust gives you maximum protection.

1. Discretionary Clause: This states that the trustees are not required to make regular distributions of income and principal. Instead, the trustee has sole discretion of disbursements. If you could demand distributions, so could your creditors. Rather, the trustee must be able to say "I don't have to pay anyone anything unless I decide to."

Of course, your trustee normally will pay you whatever you want, if a creditor is not lurking. As one trustee we worked with admits, "We have total discretion of what and when to disburse. However, we seriously consider the grantor's wishes." You usually phone the trustee and disbursements are wired to you.

2. Irrevocability Clause: The FAPT is usually set up for a number of years, typically ten or twenty years. Until then, the trust cannot be revoked. The trust assets then go to the trust beneficiaries, typically you, your spouse and/or your children. Even with a trust, there are ways to return money to you—usually through loans from the trust to you (see later in the chapter).

After the trust period expires, the trust dissolves. However, the clause should permit the trustee to extend the term of the trust if you experience a lawsuit, divorce, or other creditor pressure towards the end of your trust term. Also, the trust should allow the trustee to change beneficiaries or to add beneficiaries with the consent of the Protector. If you get divorced, remarried, or have additional children, you can alter the FAPT to adjust to new family circumstances.

3. Anti-Duress Clause: If a U.S. court orders you to repatriate trust assets, this clause prohibits the trustee from obeying your directions. In fact, any order made to the trustee, while under duress from a creditor, must be ignored under this provision. This makes U.S. courts ineffective. Even if the court threatens to hold you in contempt for not repatriating the assets to the U.S., you have a perfectly valid defense—it is impossible to direct the trustee because the trustee will not listen to you under the anti-duress clause. This defense is called *impossibility of performance.*

4. Flight Clause: This clause allows the trustee to transfer the trust to a different country if (1) a creditor's challenge to the trust appears likely to succeed, (2) the local government is unstable, or (3) a new tax law makes the trust a poor investment.

In this way, you can tell a creditor: *"First you must come to the Cook Islands and hire a lawyer there to fight my trust—because (a) U.S. courts have no power over my Cook Island trust and (b) my trustee will not listen to me because I am under duress.*

Then, while you are paying a local lawyer to fight my trust at trial, if the trustee sees that you may be successful, he will transfer the trust to another haven and appoint a new trustee. If you do these things, the new trustee will move the trust elsewhere, and so on and so on . . ."

You can see how effectively the FAPT encourages quick pennies on the dollar settlements. Even the most determined creditor would rather settle than try to hopscotch around the world spending countless time, energy, and money along the way.

5. Clause Giving the Foreign Trustee Power to Remove U.S. Co-Trustee

Because local U.S. co-trustees (like you) can be forced by an American court to turn over trust assets, the trust must permit the foreign trustee to remove American co-trustees when there are lawsuits, creditor threats, divorce threats, etc.

6. Clause Defining "Excluded Persons"

This clause states that the following people are excluded from becoming beneficiaries, trustees, or protectors under the trust: creditors of the settlor (your creditors) or anyone else appointed by a court. This ensures the trust cannot benefit anyone other than your beneficiaries.

WHY TRUST ASSETS ARE UNTOUCHABLE

Here we more fully explain how FAPTs protect assets so effectively.

1) U.S. Courts Cannot Control the Trust

As you learned, an American court needs jurisdiction to control something—whether a person, property, or legal entity. We structure your FAPT so that a U.S. court has no jurisdiction over the FAPT or its assets. We (1) use a foreign co-trustee with no U.S. contacts and, (2) transfer trust assets offshore when trouble arises. Because the trustee and the trust assets are beyond the reach of an American court, your creditor must sue the trust in its foreign haven.

2) U.S. Courts Cannot Threaten Contempt of Court

A common question is, *"Can an American court order me to return FAPT assets to the U.S., and if I don't, can the court throw me in jail for contempt?"*

Contempt of court is a remedy courts use to force people to comply with court orders. If you do not follow a court order when you have the legal ability to do so, a judge can fine and jail you until you comply. The person punished for contempt has *the keys to the jail in his pocket -- meaning the person has the power to satisfy the court's order and get out of jail.* Often times, people are punished for contempt when they refuse to testify without a legal privilege. If they chose to testify, they would be released.

With a properly-drafted FAPT, you are not vulnerable to contempt of court because the FAPT document will not give you the legal ability to force the trustee to transfer assets back to the U.S. First, the trust is irrevocable and you cannot remove the trustee or revoke the trust. Also, the trust directs the trustee to ignore your pleas anytime there is creditor duress or a court order. Thus, the trustee must obey the trust and ignore your pleas. For these reasons, you can not bring back the trust assets and can not be in contempt of court for failing to do so.

There is one exception in the law of contempt which applies to impossibility of performance. You cannot claim impossibility of performance when ignoring a court order, and thereby avoid contempt, if you created that impossibility. For this rule to apply, there must be a close connection between the creation of the impossibility and the order. If a significant time passes between the creation of the trust and the court order, a judge will less likely find that you created the impossibility with the intention of ignoring the court order.

For this reason, your FAPT should be established before any creditor threat arises. A judge can not hold you in contempt when you set-up your FAPT years before a lawsuit. If your FAPT is set-up and partially funded well in advance of any lawsuit, it will be impervious to attack and you will be immune to contempt. Remember: The earlier your FAPT is established, the better!

3) Offshore Havens are on Your Side

A number of foreign countries compete for offshore financial business. A large part of this business is attracting asset protection trusts. Why not? . . . It is a $2 trillion business.

To attract asset protection business, these offshore havens compete against each other with laws that make it extremely difficult to find out about and successfully sue a trust in their country. The most important protective laws follow—there are many more. While most offshore havens have much of this legislation, each country's laws are different:

- **Strict Privacy Laws:** These laws prevent banks and trust companies from disclosing the beneficiaries of trusts or owners of bank accounts.
- **No Contingency Fee Attorneys/Local Attorneys Only:** This means that any creditor attacking transfers to your FAPT must hire another lawyer in that country.
- **Bond Required:** Certain havens require a bond to be posted when filing a lawsuit because, in these countries, the loser pays the winner's legal fees. This is the "British Rule." The bond is often required to cover tens of thousands of dollars for legal fees, making the prospect of suing even more expensive.
- **Tough Burden of Proof:** In many countries, a plaintiff must prove you fraudulently transferred assets beyond a reasonable doubt; an extremely difficult standard. In our legal system, this standard is only for criminal cases. In your FAPT haven, however, any civil suit to get at your trust assets may have to satisfy this difficult burden of proof.
- **Favorable Statute of Limitations Period:** As mentioned in previous chapters, the *statute of limitations* is the time period within which a lawsuit must be brought. When the time expires, the lawsuit will not be allowed. In certain asset protection offshore havens, lawsuits against the trust must be commenced in the haven's courts within two years from when the legal right to sue arose.

Case Study: *Lon's FAPT Protected by the SOL*

Lon is a plastic surgeon who set-up a private practice in May 1993, and signed an agreement to purchase certain medical equipment in August 1993. While the equipment was extremely expensive, Lon thought it would save him money and eventually bring him more business. Lon signed personally on the note which accompanied the purchase agreement.

Unfortunately Lon became quite ill over the next 18 months and could only practice medicine about 25% of the time in 1994 and 1995. With sagging revenues, personal expenses, and his own medical costs, Lon then fell far behind in his payments to the medical equipment distributors beginning in December 1993. In November 1994, the distributors sued him—for the entire $650,000 balance.

Lon set-up his FAPT and funded it in March 1993—before he had set-up his private practice. The FAPT came well before he signed the contract for the medical equipment (August 1993) and well before on payments (December 1993). Thus, there was no fraudulent transfer and no way a court could find he created the impossibility of not being able to bring the trust funds back when the distributors finally sued.

Assume the distributors sued Lon in the U.S. and, after discovering he had a FAPT, wanted to sue the FAPT in the offshore haven. Assume these distributors are the most determined of creditors. The lawsuit, filed in November 1994, would probably reach the American courtroom by the end of 1996. If the case and debtors' exam went quickly, and the distributor moved fast, they could probably bring suit in the offshore haven in early 1997.

At this point, even if they did sue the trust in the foreign haven, they would be barred because the two year statute of limitations would have expired. If they sued on the contract, their right under contract to sue commenced when Lon was first delinquent (in December 1993), more than two years passed so they cannot sue. If they sued for fraudulent transfer—that Lon's liquidating his stocks and sending the cash to the FAPT was fraudulent—it will depend on when Lon made such a transfer. Assuming he did so more than two years ago (early 1995), he would be completely protected. If so, the statute of limitations would bar this lawsuit as well.

WHY USING OFFSHORE TRUSTEES IS LOW RISK

You now understand why the FAPT protects your wealth so well and why a FAPT almost always leads to settlements with creditors. Nevertheless, you may still have an insecurity, as many people initially do, that the foreign trustee cannot be trusted. You too may be nervous about giving another party in a foreign land control of your assets. This is understandable.

You will eventually realize, as you set-up a FAPT, that your savings will be just as secure in a FAPT as in your local bank. While nothing substitutes for meeting and building a relationship with your foreign trustee, the following checks and balances are put on any foreign trustee:

- **Screening:** Select trustees who have a good reputation in the financial community. Or, use a large trust company with at least 50 partners, or companies which have been established for 50 years or more. Many of the world's largest and oldest trust companies (without U.S. ties) have offices in the leading offshore havens—the Cook Islands, Nevis, the Bahamas, the Cayman Islands, the Isle of Man, and many others.
- **Bonding Requirement:** Use trust companies that are fully bonded so your funds are insured against any mismanagement or embezzlement by the company.
- **Use Co-trustees:** Multiple trustees are often advisable with each consenting to any major disbursement or transaction. Before any threat arises, you may be one of the co-trustees, so much of this issue is moot. However, even when you are removed as co-trustee, you may employ two trust companies to jointly manage the trust—providing a double-layer of protection against mismanagement.
- **Use Trust Protectors:** The Protector watchdogs the trustee, in that the Protector's consent is also required for major transactions. The Protector should be another foreign company, that need not be removed when trouble arises.
- **A Secure System:** With these checks and balances from you, the chance that your trustee will steal is extremely low. Even if such an incident did occur, the trust company and the entire offshore country itself would likely pay the loss to the beneficiary immediately. Neither a trust company nor offshore haven can afford a bad reputation with offshore investors.

2 FAPT STRATEGIES

The basic setup of the FAPT itself (trustee, Protector, etc.) is the same no matter which strategy you use, but there are two ways a FAPT asset protection plan can be established. The first involves simply establishing a FAPT and funding it with liquid assets, such as stocks, bonds, mutual funds, etc. This is a *True FAPT* strategy. It is easiest to set-up and gives the strongest protection from the outset. The second strategy, called the *Flexible FAPT,* uses a FAPT in conjunction with an FLP. Before any threat arises the FLP owns the assets and the FAPT owns most of the FLP. Once a threat appears, the FLP is liquidated and most of the equity is transferred offshore to the FAPT. Examine each strategy in more detail.

1) The True FAPT

The following diagram illustrates what the True FAPT arrangement looks like. The FAPT is set up and funded before any threat arises. Decisions for you and your attorney include the following:

- How much of your savings do you want to transfer to the FAPT before any threat appears? The benefit of transferring more is that you ensure that these amounts are immune to a fraudulent conveyance claim and to the claim you created the impossibility of not bringing them back. Also, funds offshore gives you access to the lucrative foreign investments not available in the U.S. The downside: You may not feel as comfortable transferring that much of your wealth out of the country. If comfort is of paramount concern, remember: You can still be a co-trustee of the FAPT until a threat arises.
- When do you want the foreign co-trustee to remove you as co-trustee and when do you want to transfer the remaining funds offshore (i.e. activate phase 2)? This occurs when a lawsuit, divorce, or other threat appears on the horizon.

Tip: *Keep in contact with your asset protection lawyer. If anything occurs which you think may lead to a lawsuit, or anticipate trouble on the horizon, tell your lawyer. You can both then evaluate whether or not (or how much) to transfer offshore.*

Phase 1: No threat

Liquid assets are sent offshore to the FAPT (foreign co-trustee manages with you as co-trustee and Protector).

- invest in foreign stocks/bonds/funds
- use large, stable investment firm

1) Loan money back to you as you direct (explained later)
2) Distribute principal/income to beneficiaries as you direct

Phase 2: Threat Emerges
More liquid assets sent offshore to the FAPT (foreign co-trustee manages with Foreign Protector and U.S. Protector, with veto powers only)
- invest in foreign stocks/bonds/funds
- use large, stable investment firm

1) Loan money back to you as you direct (explained later)
2) Distribute principal/income to beneficiaries as you direct

2) The Flexible FAPT
With the Flexible FAPT, you set up a FLP to own wealth that will eventually end up offshore in the FAPT (as in the diagram earlier). Before any threat arises, you alone (or, you and your spouse) are general partners of the FLP, while the FAPT owns the limited partner interests. Recall that you can have total control of FLP assets with only a small percentage ownership, as long as you are general partners. Therefore, the FLP is typically structured so that you and your spouse each own 1% of the FLP as general partners, while the FAPT owns 98% of the FLP as a limited partner (see diagram).

You then keep all your wealth within the U.S. until a threat arises when the limited partner (the FAPT foreign trustee) liquidates the FLP. It is crucial that the FLP agreement specifically grants the general partner the ability to dissolve the FLP and turn FLP assets into liquid assets, such as cash. Once liquidated, 98% of the equity in FLP assets will be transferred to the FAPT offshore. As with the "True" FAPT arrangement, when the threat arises, the foreign co-trustee must remove you and any other U.S. co-trustees or Protectors.

Phase 1: No threat
FLP owns the assets to be protected in the structure
General Partners: You and Spouse each with 1%
Limited Partner: FAPT foreign trustee in the name of the FAPT 98%

Phase 2: Threat Emerges
FLP liquidated by foreign trustee and you as co-trustee removed funds sent offshore to the FAPT (foreign co-trustee manages with Foreign Protector, U.S. Protector with veto powers only)

- invest in foreign stocks/bonds/funds
- use large, stable investment firm

1) Loan money back to you as you direct (explained later)
2) Distribute principal/income to beneficiaries as you direct

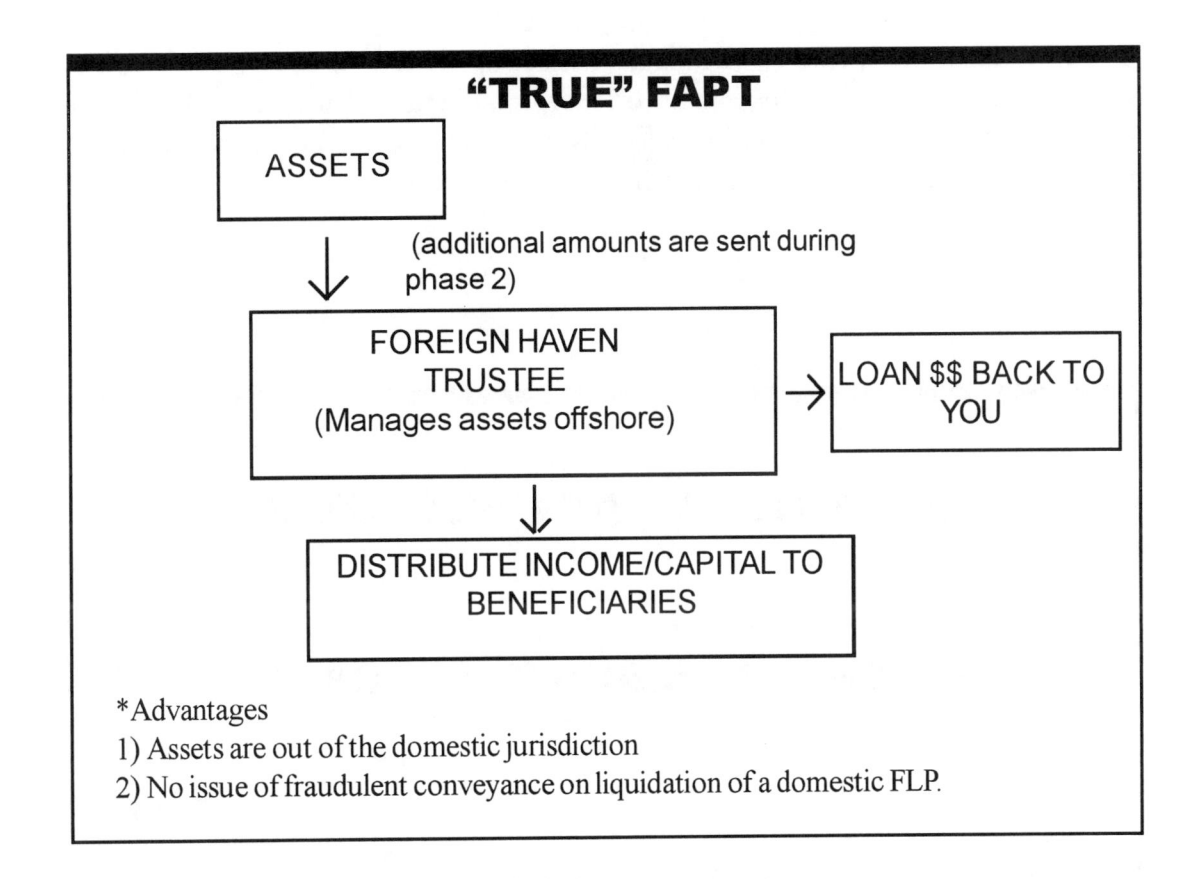

"TRUE" FAPT

ASSETS
↓ (additional amounts are sent during phase 2)

FOREIGN HAVEN TRUSTEE
(Manages assets offshore) → LOAN $$ BACK TO YOU

↓

DISTRIBUTE INCOME/CAPITAL TO BENEFICIARIES

*Advantages
1) Assets are out of the domestic jurisdiction
2) No issue of fraudulent conveyance on liquidation of a domestic FLP.

One of the main drawbacks of the flexible arrangement is the possibility that the liquidation of the FLP will prompt a fraudulent transfer claim. Recall that earlier you learned that it is fraudulent to transfer assets when you know about *probable* creditors, but it is permissible if they are simply *possible* creditors. For this reason, the FLP liquidation must be completed sufficiently before there is any probable creditor.

There can be negative tax consequences that result from the liquidation of the FLP, such as losing FLP valuation discounts and taxable gains on any appreciated property owned by the FLP. Your asset protection lawyer should understand these consequences and recommend how to minimize them.

3) Which FAPT Arrangement Is Best?

The key to this answer is your comfort level. The true FAPT structure is more sound for asset protection purposes, especially if the FAPT is fully funded before a creditor threat arises. The true FAPT is not as likely to be found fraudulent as the FLP liquidation in the flexible FAPT arrangement. Nonetheless, many clients are more comfortable with their assets in the U.S.

The answer to the question "which FAPT set-up, if any, is for you?" involves considering your comfort level with offshore planning and investing. If you are committed to securing your and your family's financial security, you must consider the FAPT as security you cannot get from any other structure.

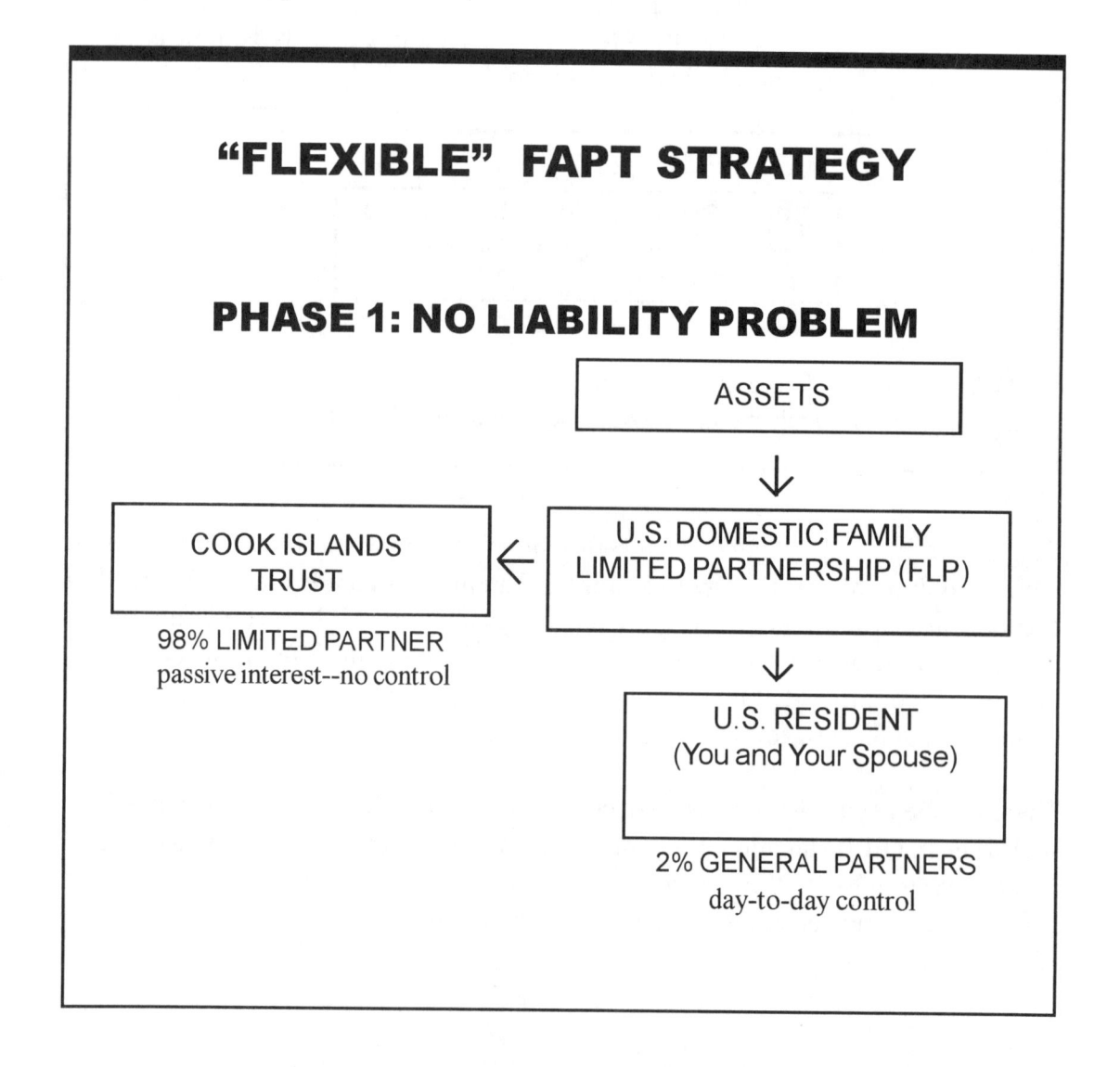

"FLEXIBLE" FAPT STRATEGY

PHASE 1: NO LIABILITY PROBLEM

ASSETS
↓
U.S. DOMESTIC FAMILY LIMITED PARTNERSHIP (FLP) → COOK ISLANDS TRUST

98% LIMITED PARTNER
passive interest--no control

↓
U.S. RESIDENT
(You and Your Spouse)

2% GENERAL PARTNERS
day-to-day control

Foreign Asset Protection Planning and Other Offshore Entities

---

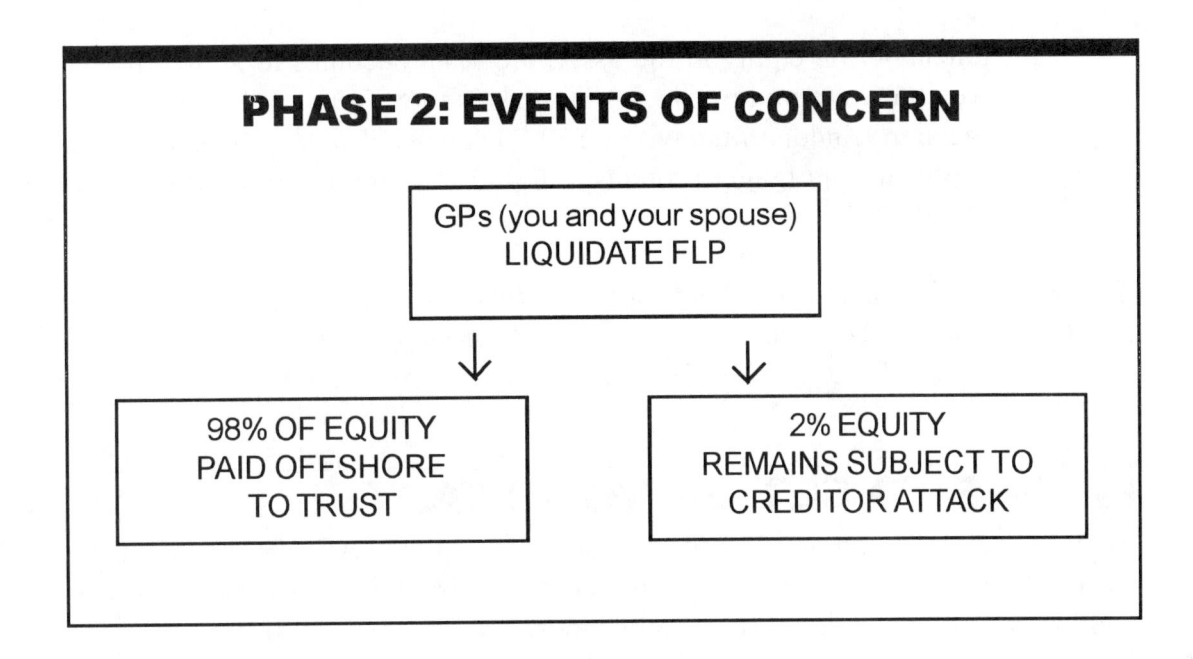

```
┌─────────────────────────────────────────────────────────┐
│            PHASE 2: EVENTS OF CONCERN                   │
│                                                         │
│              ┌─────────────────────────┐                │
│              │  GPs (you and your spouse) │             │
│              │      LIQUIDATE FLP       │               │
│              └─────────────────────────┘                │
│                   ↓               ↓                     │
│      ┌──────────────────┐  ┌──────────────────┐         │
│      │  98% OF EQUITY   │  │   2% EQUITY      │         │
│      │  PAID OFFSHORE   │  │ REMAINS SUBJECT TO│        │
│      │    TO TRUST      │  │  CREDITOR ATTACK │         │
│      └──────────────────┘  └──────────────────┘         │
└─────────────────────────────────────────────────────────┘
```

HOW YOU GET YOUR MONEY OUT OF YOUR FAPT

A common question is: "Can I get any money out of the trust when the trust is irrevocable?" The answer is "Yes." During phase 1 of the FAPT set-up, you will either a) not have sent much offshore (Flexible) or b) Be co-trustee (both). As co-trustee, you can tell the foreign trustee how much and when to send funds to you in the U.S. Modern technology makes these transfers quick. Because there is no creditor problem, the duress clause does not apply and the trustee will most likely follow your wishes.

Even during phase 2 you can get money back from the FAPT without interference from your American creditor. One way is to have the FAPT trustee pay distributions to your spouse, children, or other persons you normally support. Because the money is not sent to you, your creditors can not seize it. Yet, you still benefit from these transfers because the FAPT is paying people you would ordinarily support. Or, you can ask your trustee to loan you money from the FAPT. The transfer should have all the formalities of a loan—a formal note signed by you to dispute any claim that the loan is a gift.

TIP #1: *Use the trust to secure assets you own in your name in the U.S., such as your home, car, artwork, etc. This accomplishes two objectives:*
   1. The opportunity to file a security agreement or mortgage for the loan thereby making the loan rock-solid.
   2. It protects the secured asset as the *friendly* loan from the FAPT.

Encumbering equity in the asset, the asset becomes less attractive to creditors. Example: The FAPT may loan $50,000 secured by your vacation condominium with a $60,000 equity. The loan, like any other legitimate mortgage, protects $50,000 in condominium equity from creditors.

TIP #2: *If the loan is a balloon-payment loan, you owe no payments to the FAPT until, maybe, 20 years down the road—long after this creditor has gone away and probably long after the FAPT itself has been dissolved.*

WHERE TO SET UP YOUR FAPT

Another common question is, "Where should I set-up my FAPT?" Although there are a number of important considerations, and a long list of possible offshore havens, U.S. asset protection specialists usually choose one of a few countries.

a. Considerations in Choosing a Country

Factors you and your attorney will consider in choosing a FAPT haven:

- Favorable, definite, and protective trust laws
- Political, economic, and social stability
- Reputation in the offshore investing community
- Taxation, if any, on trusts set-up by non-residents
- Language barriers
- Modern telecommunications, banking, legal, and accounting services.
- Geographic accessibility, time zone, etc.

b. Possible Offshore Havens

The following are possible offshore havens—including those used primarily for tax planning, privacy concerns, and asset protection planning:

Antigua, Aruba, Bahamas, Barbados, Belize, Bermuda, British Virgin Islands, Cayman Islands, Cook Islands, Costa Rica, Cyprus, Gibraltar, Grenada, Guernsey and Jersey, Isle of Man, Labuan, Liechtenstein, Luxembourg, Madeira, Malta, Mauritius, Monaco, Montserrat, Nauru, Niue, Netherlands Antilles, Nevis, Panama, Seychelles, Switzerland, Turks and Caicos, and Vanuatu.

c. Most Popular FAPT Locations

Although many of the countries listed above could be used for an offshore trust, U.S. asset protection specialists consistently use certain havens for asset protections trusts. Because these countries have the highest rating considering these factors—

their protective laws regarding trusts are most important. If taxation or privacy are more your concern, you may use a different country.

You will probably establish your FAPT in a haven where your asset protection lawyer already has contacts and is most familiar with the trust process. West coast asset protection attorneys are most familiar with the Cook Islands. East coast attorneys usually use one of the Caribbean nations.

1. The Cook Islands

The Cook Islands, located in the South Pacific, is the pre-eminent haven for asset protection. The country's 1989 and 1991 trust law amendments, in fact, coined the term "asset protection trust" first.

The Cook Islands satisfy the previously listed factors with flying colors. Their laws are detailed, unambiguous, and extremely protective. Further, they have been in existence for over 5 years and asset protection lawyers throughout the U.S. have established FAPTs.

2. Nevis

Nevis, an island nation in the Caribbean, recently enacted powerful asset protection legislation: The *Nevis International Exempt Trust Ordinance of 1994*. The Nevisian laws incorporate many of the best asset protection provisions of the Cook Islands laws. Examples of these provisions include a 2-year statute of limitations for fraudulent transfers and an explicit rule not recognizing foreign law with regards to local Nevisian trusts.

Many East coast asset protection lawyers use Nevis as the haven to set-up FAPTs. They consider their protection as strong as the Cooks, and find that Nevis is much more accessible from the East Coast (3 hour plane flight); often important to the client who wants to visit the trust site or meet trustees before transferring large sums of money.

3. Bahamas, Caymans, and other Caribbean Nations

Many Caribbean nations are offshore financial havens because they do not subject local trusts and business corporations to taxes. For asset protection, though, the Bahamas and the Cayman Islands are usually considered excellent. *The Bahamas* guarantees immunity from all foreign judgments to individuals who set up Bahamian trusts. Also, the Bahamian statute of limitations for fraudulent transfer claims is two years—an extremely short period, attractive for asset protection purposes. Further, the Bahamas has other pro-asset protection laws and is extremely accessible from the U.S.

The *Cayman Islands* may be the best-known foreign offshore havens because of books and movies like *The Firm* by John Grisham. This is *not* surprising because over $460 billion is deposited in the Caymans—more than in New York City! Unfortunately, many references to the Caymans make it appear that most of this money is there illegally—when this isn't true.

The top attorneys and accountants establishing CICs for asset protection and significant tax planning use the *British Virgin Islands*. Thus, the jurisdiction used often depends on the type of entity and benefits sought.

4. Isle of Man and Channel Islands

The Channel Islands are island nations located near Britain and are part of the British Commonwealth. The Isle of Man, Guernsey, and Jersey are principal offshore financial centers. While Jersey's laws for trusts are quite protective for asset protection, all are relatively strong. Further, there are long-standing, world-class trust companies and financial institutions there. Although less accessible than the Caribbean havens, U.S. asset protection lawyers often use trustees in these havens to administer trusts in Caribbean nations.

FOREIGN INVESTING OPPORTUNITIES WITH YOUR FAPT

Today, our world is a global village. No longer are American stocks, bonds, and mutual funds the only safe, lucrative investments. In fact, the opposite may be true. Economists and financial analysts agree that most of the economic growth in the next 50 years will occur in Asia, Eastern Europe and other developing nations, like India and Vietnam. Why restrict your investment portfolio to American investments when you can diversify your risk and enjoy better returns by also investing in foreign markets? Do what sophisticated advisors, pension managers, corporate financiers, and savvy investors have been doing for many years—take advantage of the global marketplace!

How much do you now have invested in foreign markets? Leading advisors recommend 15% to 50% of your total investments should be invested in foreign markets. Your FAPT can be the perfect vehicle to begin this expansion.

The Securities and Exchange Commission makes it almost impossible for foreign countries to sell their stock in the U.S., so you will typically need an offshore entity to purchase foreign stock for you. The FAPT is so valuable for foreign-market investing because it allows you to access lucrative investments you would

Foreign Asset Protection Planning and Other Offshore Entities

not be able to take advantage of here. With the increased returns from foreign-market investing, you can possibly pay for your FAPT within a few years. Consider these investments for your FAPT:

- **Offshore Bank Accounts:** Banks in the Caymans, Hong Kong, or Switzerland often pay much higher interest than American banks with no more risk. And, the currency of your investment may also appreciate against the U.S. dollar.

- **Foreign Mutual Funds:** To diversify against recessions in the U.S. and to invest in a particular country (China), area of the world (Asia) or industry (telecommunications). Beware of hidden tax traps if the fund is not a PFIC-QEF fund. We have seen many people get into trouble with the IRS by unknowingly investing in mutual funds which were not qualified for tax-favored treatment by the IRS. Speak with one of the authors if you want more information on this subject.

- **Offshore Annuities:** Lets you achieve diversification and (possibly) tax-deferral. Most popular are Swiss annuities. They are offered by some of the world's most respected Swiss firms, many of which we have close working relationships with.

TAXES AND YOUR FAPT

Contrary to common myth, you will not save taxes with a FAPT! A FAPT is tax-neutral—income taxes, gift taxes, estate taxes, and excise taxes are unaffected, unless an American citizen illegally fails to report foreign income to the IRS.

Strict privacy laws in the offshore havens prevent local banks or trust companies from reporting income to the IRS. However, U.S. law puts the burden on the American citizen to report income from all sources, regardless of where it is earned. Americans with foreign bank accounts or FAPTs must report the income to the IRS. Understand your responsibility.

WHAT YOUR FAPT TRUST COMPANY WILL REQUIRE

Trust companies in the most protective offshore havens will not help you establish a FAPT if transfers to the FAPT are blatantly fraudulent. Trust companies and havens do not want a reputation as an oasis for deadbeats and money-launderers, which might jeopardize the protectiveness of its laws. The concern, of course, is that other countries' legal systems then might not honor its rules due to the violation of basic international treaties. Legitimate foreign trust companies will make certain that any trust it establishes has no appearance of impropriety, and may make you:

1. Complete and sign an affidavit of solvency; extremely effective in fighting later claims of fraudulent transfers.
2. Prepare and sign a statement of net worth, often authenticated by a C.P.A.
3. Provide your latest IRS Return.

THE #1 REASON TO OWN A FAPT

The FAPT is one of the top asset protection tools. It is virtually impenetrable. Only the most diligent, determined, and unreasonable creditor would even attempt to seize FAPT assets.

The most important benefit of the FAPT is that you will discourage lawsuits and force creditors into early and favorable settlements. Once creditors and their lawyers realize that your wealth is owned by a FAPT, they know they will never get it. It just does not make sense for them to spend time or money. It's not worth the fight. The alternative? . . . give up the lawsuit or accept a "pennies on the dollar" settlement. Whether you discourage a lawsuit or negotiating one quick cheap settlement, your FAPT will have paid for itself many times over.

THE NEVIS LLC

In recent years, Nevis, a small Caribbean Island, has gained a reputation for financial privacy and asset protection. A new weapon has been added to Nevis' wealth preservation arsenal: The *Nevis Limited Liability Company*. This can be an important alternative to the FAPT.

While most states and many foreign jurisdictions recognize limited liability companies, the Nevis LLC is particularly popular because of its many unique features.

- **Flexible Management Structure**

The Nevis LLC can be either member-directed or managed by an outside foreign director. For asset protection purposes, the LLC should be controlled by an outside director, particularly if a debtor member owns a significant interest and can be compelled to change management to one who would obey a U.S. court order.

Foreign Asset Protection Planning and Other Offshore Entities

- **Charging Order Protections**

If you have a judgement creditor, the creditor can only obtain a charging order against your LLC interest. This entitles the creditor only to your share of any distributions from the LLC. The LLC interest cannot be seized nor can the creditor vote your interest or exercise other member rights, such as the inspection of books and records. (See chapters 8 or 9 for more on "charging order" protection).

Interestingly, Nevis law imposes U.S. income tax liability for the debtor-member's share of the apportioned profits, notwithstanding whether the creditor received a distribution. These same protective features are found with U.S. limited partnerships and LLC's, but usually not with offshore entities designed to shelter wealth.

Properly structured, a Nevis LLC can delegate virtually all powers to the managing director, who like a Trustee of an offshore trust, can ignore U.S. court orders to repatriate assets. If the LLC has two or more members, an operating agreement provision requiring a unanimous member vote to change the managing director will stifle a court order compelling one debtor member to replace the director. Conceptually, the Nevis LLC then assumes the same protective characteristics of the offshore trust, except that the debtor member may retain an interest in the LLC and, derivatively, its assets.

- **Avoid Fraudulent Transfer Claims**

Unlike the situation with an offshore trust, where you have to "gift" assets to the trust, using a Nevis LLC, you can make a *qui pro quo* transfer of assets for LLC interests. Thus, if you are in litigation or have an existing creditor, under Nevis LLC ordinances, you can place assets into the LLC and avoid a claim of fraudulent conveyance -- as long as your membership interest is proportionate to the contributed capital. Under Nevis law, even a promise of a future contribution by other LLC members can be used to achieve proportionality, thus giving you total flexibility when making transfers to the Nevis LLC.

In this respect, the Nevis LLC can be more protective than both a foreign trust or limited partnership and can be legally used regardless of your financial situation.

In addition to strong asset protection capabilities, the Nevis LLC boasts several other significant features:

- The Nevis LLC has minimal reporting requirements, and it is not subject to the foreign trusts' new reporting requirements.

- The LLC is typically less expensive to establish and maintain than a FAPT.

- If the LLC conducts business in the U.S. and has U.S. source income, it can be structured for profits to flow to the owners or managers as specified in the operating agreement.

- Officers and directors are immune from company liability, and creditors can not pierce the corporate veil.

- There are no requirements to keep minute books, hold annual director or member meetings, or observe other customary corporate formalities.

- As with its domestic FLP and LLC counterparts, the Nevis LLC can similarly save estate taxes through discounted valuations. You may also easily gift interests in the LLC and maintain all income rights and management control of the company.

- The Nevis LLC may be owned by an offshore trust in lieu of an IBC and can also be used in combination with domestic entities, such as FLP's and domestic irrevocable trusts.

- The Nevis LLC may be set-up quickly and is usually less costly to form and maintain than an offshore asset protection trust.

- Nevis is an outstanding privacy haven and is politically and economically stable.

While many asset protection attorneys now use the Nevis LLC in place of an offshore trust, there are still instances where the trust may be preferable, particularly when estate planning is an objective. Nonetheless, it is an alternative structure for offshore asset protection planning that should always be considered.

THE CLOSELY-HELD INSURANCE COMPANY (CIC)

The CIC (also called "captive" by lay people) is the most powerful offshore planning vehicle when it comes to legitimate U.S. tax planning -- combined with significant asset protection features as well. In fact, the CIC is the only commonly-used offshore planning entity designed to legitimately save U.S. citizens income and capital gains taxes. While many marketers -- and even shady professional advisors -- may entice clients to go offshore because of the tax savings, that savings usually boils down to not disclosing some part of the offshore planning. Often, this is tantamount to tax fraud.

Because of its tax planning benefits, we have chosen to include our discussion of the CIC in chapter 18 -- under tax planning. We strongly urge you to read that section now. The CIC is a tool not to be ignored by physicians -- it is simply that valuable!

SUMMARY

- An offshore revolution is underway. Over $5 trillion is invested in offshore financial centers. Most entities are 100% legitimate.
- The FAPT works because American courts do not have jurisdiction (power) over trusts in which the assets and the trustee are out of the U.S.
- The best offshore havens make it virtually impossible for a creditor to undo your trust.
- Foreign trustees are extremely secure. They are screened, bonded, and reports of embezzlement are nonexistent.
- You have many offshore havens to choose from: The Cook Islands, Nevis, the British Virgin Islands, and others.
- A FAPT is tax-neutral. You still pay income tax to the U.S. on income earned abroad.
- The Nevis LLC may replace the FAPT in many circumstances -- because it allows greater flexibility than the FAPT.
- The Nevis LLC allows avoidance of fraudulent transfer claims because you exchange assets for LLC interests.
- The CIC is a powerful asset protection and tax planning vehicle.
- The CIC is the only offshore vehicle designed to legitimately save U.S. taxes.
- See chapter 18 for more on CICs.

CHAPTER 12:

ADVANCED PROTECTION FOR PROFESSIONALS AND BUSINESS OWNERS

This chapter marks the third major segment of this book. The first segment explained the threats to your financial security. The second segment explained the various tools asset protection lawyers use to protect clients from the lawsuit threat, or "building blocks" of a fortress surrounding your savings and property.

In this third segment, we explain strategies for protecting assets in certain situations. This chapter focuses on safeguarding a privately-held business or professional practice. Future chapters deal with shielding wealth from particular creditors, the IRS, divorce, or bankruptcy. While the specific focus of each chapter differs, essentially they each are examples of applying the strategies and tools explained in the second segment.

This chapter has two objectives: (1) protect your personal finances from your business or practice debts and (2) shield your business or practice from its creditors. The first challenge is covered briefly—because the personal protection from business/practice debts was covered more thoroughly in earlier chapters. Making the business or practice a rock-solid fortress is the focus of this chapter.

TWO BUSINESS ENTITIES TO AVOID

This section answers the question; *"How do I protect my personal savings from my business debts and liabilities?"* We address this issue because business owners risk being sued personally because of their businesses. *Private business owners are among the most vulnerable lawsuit targets and face the "triple threat" of liability—*

1. **liabilities from their place of business** (slip and fall lawsuits, etc.),
2. **liabilities from their business operations** (discrimination claims, bad debts, defective products, etc.) and
3. **liability for employees' acts** (car accidents, etc.).

We do not focus on this issue in this chapter because we already dealt with it in earlier chapters—specifically, those covering corporations, limited partnerships, and limited liability companies (LLCs) and trusts. Nonetheless, the issue of protecting personal wealth from business claims is important enough to warrant this section. In fact, of the 20 million businesses operating in the United States, over 5 million do so as proprietorships or general partnerships—dangerous personal liability traps for the business owners.

■ Why a Proprietorship Should be Avoided

Chapter 7 discussed a *proprietorship* — a business arrangement where you operate a business without establishing a legal entity. Essentially, the pitfalls of the proprietorship are that you automatically guarantee every contract, deal, act by employee, or other action on the part of your business. The business and you are legally the same. *You gamble your family's personal financial well-being on the success of the business.*

The harsh reality is that 90% of our nation's businesses fail within the first five years. So, this is an unwise gamble. Why allow a business failure to bring personal financial ruin? It does not have to be that way if you use protective legal entities.

■ Why a General Partnership is Always the Most Damaging Business/Practice Entity

Operate your business as a proprietorship and you gamble your family's savings on the success of your business. *Operate as a general partnership and you gamble on the success of your partners' businesses.* Remember, a general partnership is created whenever you begin a venture with another person without creating a particular legal entity, like a corporation or LLC. You can have a general partnership and not know it, depending on the reasonable perception of the general public.

With a general partnership to run a business or professional practice, you (1) effectively guarantee the debts your partners incur and (2) assume liability for their acts and omissions, as well as your own. Further, because of joint and several liability, you can be held liable for the full damages for acts in which you were not even involved. For these reasons, a general partnership is the most dangerous form of business organization.

Avoid a proprietorship and general partnerships. With a limited partnership, LLC, or corporation, you can have all the upside potential of your business with less downside risk.

■ Caution For Entrepreneurs

Most business owners are optimists who look at their business as a grand opportunity. However, most entrepreneurs see through rose-tinted glasses—they see only the upside potential, confident that their venture will beat the odds and avoid failure. When considering how to structure their business, entrepreneurs usually ignore asset protection entirely. If they have any defensive strategy, it is to maximize write-offs if the venture incurs losses. In most cases, they ignore the many possible ways to structure a business defensively, so as to maximize the protection of their investment. Given the short odds of success, such narrow-mindedness usually becomes quite costly in the end.

Yes, your business may become the next Microsoft or McDonald's. Nevertheless, an "optimism only" attitude is extremely dangerous. Why? Because without considering the downside of your business venture, you ignore the simple and effective steps you can take to minimize your personal exposure. Don't ignore defensive planning. Instead, follow this advice, which we give all business owners:

"Aim for the best, plan for the worst"

FLPs, LLCs, AND CORPORATIONS SAVE TAXES WHILE CONTROLLING YOUR BUSINESS

Previous chapters explained how you can use FLPs, LLCs, and corporations to save on estate taxes, income taxes, and even probate fees. The basic strategy—transfer assets now in your name to the legal entity and then gift interests in the entity to family members or other beneficiaries.

This general structure saves you estate taxes and probate fees when you die because these assets are no longer owned by you and much of the legal entity interests will have been transferred to your beneficiaries before your death. The strategy saves you income taxes because much of the partnership/LLC/corporation income is shifted to beneficiaries (usually children) with a lower tax bracket. Finally, you fully control the business for as long as you want to by making yourself the FLP's general partner, the LLC's manager, or the corporation's director and only voting-stock shareholder.

While we previously discussed this strategy with respect to individual assets or groups of assets, it works perfectly when applied to your privately-owned or family-owned business.

Again, the procedure has four steps: (1) Establish an FLP, LLC, or corporation, (2) Transfer all assets and debts from the business to the new legal entity, (3) Become the controlling partner, manager, or voting shareholder of the entity, (4) Gift passive interests to children and other beneficiaries over your lifetime.

Another important benefit to structuring your business in this manner is that it makes it much easier to pass business interests to the next generation when you die.

TWO ADVANCED STRATEGIES TO CONSIDER

This and the following sections explain strategies for protecting the business/practice from risks involved in its daily operation. These risks include lawsuit claims and the possibility that your business will have cash flow shortages, be unable to pay debts to banks or suppliers, or go bankrupt.

The question, then, is *how to structure your business, so it has the highest chance of survival and prosperity. In other words, to make your business/practice as much an ironclad fortress as your personal financial structure.*

NOTE: *We usually use the word "business." But remember, these concepts apply to your professional practice just as well.*

■ Use Multiple Legal Entities

Don't put all your eggs in one basket: You have probably heard this advice since you were a child. But, did you know this advice would be so valuable for running a business? The same principle applies. *Do not let one lawsuit, bad loan, or under-performing business unit destroy your entire business/practice.* Using multiple corporations, LLCs, or limited partnerships, you isolate the threats and keep them from jeopardizing the healthy parts of your business.

You already know why a corporation, LLC, or limited partnership is essential. However, in today's lawsuit-crazy, ultra-competitive world, operating with one layer of protection is not adequate. Company graveyards are full of businesses which operated under one legal entity. For your business to be a true ironclad fortress, operate it using multiple legal forms. You then double, or even triple, the chances that your business will survive any threat that comes its way. The next section shows concrete examples of how you can use this strategy in any type company.

Always remember to enjoy valuable business protection from a corporation, LLC, or a limited partnership, you must follow their legal formalities and treat each legal entity as separate under the law. It means getting tax identification numbers for each entity, paying taxes separately, use distinct checking accounts, never commingle funds, using separate stationary and business cards, etc. Only if you operate each entity separately will the courts treat them separately and uphold the protection each is designed to provide.

■ Separate Safe Assets From Dangerous Assets

This strategy goes hand-in-hand with *Using Multiple Entities*. In fact, one reason to use multiple corporations, LLCs, or limited partnerships, is to effectively insulate valuable safe assets from the riskiness of the dangerous assets. This is especially important when your business has both significant safe and dangerous assets. If your business owns both types of assets, you need multiple legal entities.

SAFE ASSETS: Inventory, accounts receivable, non-dangerous machines (computers and other office equipment), cash and other liquid investments, copyrights, trademarks, patents, licenses, etc.

DANGEROUS ASSETS: Real estate, heavy machinery, cars, trucks, equipment able to injure workers or patients, and other liability-prone assets.

Why risk losing your valuable safe assets to creditors and lawsuits arising from your dangerous assets? That is the gamble you take when you own all your business assets through one legal entity. Instead, *limit your downside— isolate liability-prone assets in one entity, leaving your safe assets protected in another.* This is smart defensive positioning—essential in today's brutal business environment!

Case Study:
Elizabeth's Restaurant Revisited

Remember Elizabeth, the restaurateur, in chapter 7? Her successful restaurant was forced to close because of a lawsuit. Had she incorporated the business, or used an LLC, she would have protected her personal wealth from the lawsuit. Even better, however, would have been using two corporations or LLCs; one to own dangerous restaurant assets, like the delivery car, and one to operate the restaurant.

If Elizabeth had multiple entities and segregated her safe assets, she would have protected her personal wealth from the lawsuit, and continued operating restaurant. All she could lose would be assets owned by her "dangerous assets" corporation or LLC—like the delivery car and perhaps other dangerous equipment. The rest of the restaurant could operate; unaffected by the lawsuit.

STRUCTURE YOUR TYPE OF BUSINESS FOR MAXIMUM PROTECTION

No matter what type of business you own, you can transform it into a creditor-proof, lawsuit-proof financial fortress. The challenge is to determine how to implement the two strategies to your particular business. You then have the *asset protection battle plan* for your business. The specific blueprint depends on the structure and nature of your business.

1. One Company With Multiple Business Units: Use A Distinct Legal Entity For Each Business Unit

- A company which operates a restaurant and a catering service
- A medical partnership which renders surgical services to a hospital and operates a separate walk-in surgical center
- A lumber company which manufactures lumber products, sells its products at retail outlets, and performs construction consulting work

What do these companies have in common? They all have multiple business units which perform distinctly from each other. It would be a terrible mistake to operate these different business units under one legal entity. Instead, each should operate under its own corporation, LLC, etc. This way, a lawsuit or creditor of one unit is isolated from the assets of the remaining units. Consider this:

Case Study:
Westside Surgical Group: Before and After

The Westside Surgical Group rendered surgical services to a hospital and also operated a separate walk-in surgical center in a bordering neighborhood. Before consulting us on how best to structure their operations, the 6-surgeon group operated both the in-hospital services and the walk-in clinic under their general partnership. In so doing, these well-intentioned physicians walked a liability tightrope. Any slip and fall accident at their walk-in clinic or severe collision by their clinic x-ray delivery car could threaten their thriving 10-employee $4 million-per-year surgical practice. Similarly, an outrageous malpractice award or employment-related lawsuit in their medical practice could jeopardize their growing walk-in clinic. It was only a matter of time until one business threatened the other.

Fortunately, the doctors implemented asset protection planning before serious damage occurred. After learning about their business organization and company goals, we developed their "financial fortress blueprint," which had two phases. In phase 1, the doctors would reduce their personal liability arising from their surgical practice. While they could not use an LLC or limited partnership under their state law, professional corporations were used with each surgeon, establishing his own professional corporation, and then becoming the partner in the general partnership. That way, the personal liability of any one physician was then limited to his own errors, not to the acts or omissions of the other partners. Also, the doctors had all of the control and tax characteristics, as before.

In phase 2, we separated the surgical practice from the walk-in clinic. A S corporation was formed to operate the clinic, with each of the doctors a 1/6th shareholder in the new *Westside Surgical Clinic, Inc.* Each doctor's personal wealth was then protected from the liabilities of the clinic. Further, by incorporating the clinic, the surgeons effectively separated their business risks. Their clinic can no longer threaten their medical practice, and vice versa. And, because it is an S corporation, the doctors continue to enjoy pass-through tax status.

The doctors had not originally structured their businesses this way because: (1) they had not been advised to do so; and, (2) they incorrectly assumed structure would be extremely expensive to set-up. In the end, the additional costs for the new fortress-like arrangement are less than $5,000 annually—less than .01% of their annual revenues. This is very cheap insurance!

2. For one Business Unit with Multiple Locations or Outlets: Use a Distinct Legal Entity for Each Location or Outlet

- A dry-cleaning business with 16 locations throughout the state
- A chiropractic practice with four clinics around the city
- A taxicab company with 100 cabs

What do these companies have in common? They each operate one type business in multiple outlets. That's right—even the taxicab company has multiple locations because the business is conducted in different taxicabs. Do not put all your eggs in one basket. Create a separate protective basket for each business location. If one location fails, it is isolated to the one location . . . and the rest of your business continues unscathed.

Case Study: *Metropolis Chiropractic Offices*

Metropolis Chiropractic Offices is partially owned by Jack, the chiropractor who set-up his first office over 15 years ago in a wealthy suburb. It was initially established as a professional corporation and continued to operate it as such. Throughout the first 10 years, Jack's practice grew, as did his good reputation and the opportunity to expand his practice to additional locations.

Over the next five years, Jack established three new offices, two in neighboring suburbs, and another in the city's downtown business district. They operated under the original professional corporation. While the two suburban offices were relatively small, the downtown location was even larger than Jack's original office. Jack hoped the downtown office would be his real money-maker, but he was wrong. Within three years, the two new suburban locations were operating profitably, as was Jack's original location. However, the downtown location turned out to be a nightmare.

The downtown location could not attract patients. Perhaps it was because a renewal program for office's neighborhood never took hold; or, because most people left downtown after work, and obtained care where they lived. Regardless of the reason, the downtown location operated deeply in the red, losing so much money that it threatened to financially cripple the entire corporation. Jack channelled cash from the other three offices to pay creditors of the downtown location. The cash crunch soon got so bad that Jack considered bankruptcy for the entire corporation.

Jack's problems could have been avoided had he established each chiropractic office under a separate corporation. While this may not have saved his downtown office from financial woes, it certainly would have isolated it. Its failure would be a bankruptcy of only that office, not Jack's entire operation. If the office had operated under its own legal entity, it is likely Jack could have negotiated favorable settlements with its chief creditors—the bank (on an operating cash loan), the landlord (on the lease), and medical suppliers (on equipment). By operating as one corporation, Jack precluded this possibility. After all, why should creditors settle when they can claim the assets of all four offices?

Learn from Jack's mistake and use multiple legal entities for multiple locations or outlets.

3. One Business Unit with a Single Location or Outlet: Use At Least Two Legal Entities; One for Dangerous Assets and One for the Safe Assets

- A men's clothing store
- A orthopedist's sole office
- A consulting company

Each operation has one outlet and one line of business. But, like the businesses in the previous examples, these ventures can also benefit from multiple entities. These businesses can effectively segregate safe assets from dangerous assets by using multiple entities.

Case Study: *Dave's Orthopedist Office*

Dave is an orthopedist who operates one successful medical office. Concerned after a friend suffered a devastating lawsuit judgment for a personal injury claim, he asked us how he could best protect his practice. We learned that in addition to owning expensive equipment in his office, Dave also owned the building housing the office—both owned personally.

First, we advised Dave to set-up a professional corporation in which to operate the business. This may help protect personal assets from future non-malpractice claims. Second, Dave formed a family limited partnership (FLP) to own the building. The FLP, owned by Dave, his wife, and his children, leased the office to the professional corporation (see next section). Should any patient sue, Dave's building would not be vulnerable.

Third, Dave set-up an LLC to own the medical equipment to be leased to his professional corporation. This protected the equipment. Dave effectively isolated his asset (the building) from his practice; and, safeguarded other valuable assets (his medical equipment).

Even within a multiple-entity structure, each business unit or location should be as lawsuit-proof and creditor-proof as possible. This is the best structure: a multiple entity business, where each unit segregates dangerous from safe assets.

ASSETS YOUR BUSINESS SHOULD NEVER OWN

Your operating business or practice must never own valuable assets. Usually, this is real estate, whether in the form of outright ownership or a valuable below-market lease. For many businesses, location is everything. In others, their most valuable assets may be copyrights, patents, or even high-tech equipment. Whatever the valuable asset, do not let the operating company own it!

Why don't you want your operating company owning this valuable asset? Because if the operating entity owns the asset, the creditors of the operating business can claim it. Your strategy: make your operating business as poor as possible. Then, creditors and lawsuit plaintiffs have little to gain by attacking the business. Establish other legal entities to own valuable assets and then lease or license these assets to the operating business entity. The following tactics illustrate this strategy:

- If your business owns real estate: Have a separate entity to own the real estate and lease it back to the operating company asset. Make the tenancy month-to-month, so it has the least valuable assets as an operating company. Remember: less value for the operating company means less attractiveness for creditors. Also, document the sale and lease-back, and follow legal formalities (i.e., the business must pay rent to the other entity).

- If your business has a valuable lease: Have a separate entity own the lease and have your operating company sublet it on a month-to-month basis. This is especially crucial if your business depends on its location. Again, all formalities between the entities must be followed.

    If your business hits hard times, you can always close-up shop and your creditors cannot claim the lease. They can only claim the operating entity's sublet, until the end of the month. Next month, you can set-up the same business using a different legal entity in the exact same location! Your lease-controlling entity sublets the same location to your new business. You have effectively secured your valuable location, while protecting it from creditor and lawsuit threats.

- If your business owns other extremely valuable assets such as copyrights, trademarks, patents, high-tech equipment, etc., have another entity own these asset(s) and then license or lease them to the operating business. By now, you understand the tactic, but always follow legal formalities in the transactions. If not, you could lose your protection.

USING MORTGAGES AND SECURED LOANS TO BEAT CREDITORS

Most people think of mortgages as a burdensome obligation. They believe, "the only good mortgage is one that is paid." But, to turn your business into a creditor-proof fortress, you must see the silver lining in every mortgage—that it shields the secured assets from other creditors. After all, what creditor would want an asset already mortgaged for its full value to another creditor? The trick, of course, is to find a *friendly creditor* who can shield your business assets through his mortgage but who is unlikely to foreclose on the mortgage.

Where can you find such a friendly creditor? Look around. Do you have a relative who loaned you money to begin the business? Our client Robert did, when he started his desktop publishing firm five years ago, with a loan from his uncle. Now, Robert's business is quite successful. So, why not draw up a legitimate mortgage on his valuable computer equipment in favor of his generous uncle? His uncle does not even care if he is paid back now, but the mortgage stands as a barrier against other creditors.

Other possible friendly creditors include the following:

- **You** — loans to the business from your personal funds should be secured with a mortgage on key assets. Consult your asset protection attorney, as these transactions must be by the book to be upheld.

- **A Friendly Supplier** — perhaps you have a friendly supplier? The supplier would much rather have you fall behind in payments on accounts payable during tough times then to lose you completely as a customer. Why not give this supplier a mortgage on your business assets? You know he won't come after your business and the mortgage will keep other wolves at bay during your business' tough times. Perhaps you can agree to protect his assets in the same way he is securing yours. This arrangement shields you both.

- **A Friendly Lender** — using the same theory as with the supplier, a friendly banker or other lender may be helpful. If you know your lender would be less likely to put pressure on you than other creditors, why not give the lender a security in your business assets? Often, a matter of months is all it takes to turn a failing business around. If you have a line of credit with the lender already and you think he will be more lenient than other creditors, give him the mortgages. The time and flexibility you gain may save your business during tough times.

FIVE WAYS TO GET QUICK CASH FOR YOUR BUSINESS

Almost every business goes through a periodic cash-crunch. Revenues are less than expected, loan payments and utility bills continue, employees need to get paid, withholding taxes are due . . . the list goes on. One software company, in fact, suffered a cash-drought so severe that utilities were discontinued. Fortunately, they raised enough to pay the utilities and have some working capital. Now, the software company is a $10 million a year business. But, it might have all been lost in those critical months back in 1990.

Surviving a cash crunch can be the difference between long-term survival and a bankruptcy/liquidation. During such a cash-crunch, the goal is to turn unessential business assets into cash as quickly as possible.

1. Collect Accounts Receivable

Many business have overdue accounts—buried cash! Aggressively pursue delinquent customers. If your business needs cash ASAP, then offer the customers a heavy discount on their accounts for cash today—say 50% off. This may motivate even the slowest-paying customer. If you have a personal relationship with the customer, make the phone call yourself. Do not delegate it to an underling who does not understand the importance of finding the funds.

2. Sell Accounts Receivable

Factoring companies make their business out of buying and collecting other businesses' receivables. Put them to work for you when you have a cash-crunch. Often, they are more effective for collecting cash than you would be. After all, it is their business specialty. Another benefit of an outside factor is that it lets you focus on the real problems facing your business (ineffective marketing efforts, poor cost controls, etc.).

Factoring companies typically buy receivables owed by business customers with acceptable credit and they charge approximately a 10% fee on the accounts. Nevertheless, if your accounts qualify for factoring, it is a key way to beat a cash-crunch.

3. Sell Idle Equipment

Many cash-shy businesses have idle equipment or machinery lying around. Often the business acquired equipment in anticipation of a new project which did not materialize. So why keep the equipment if you now need cash?

4. Rent Unused Space

Do you have empty offices or space in your business? If so, rent or sublet these areas to other businesses, and pocket more cash.

5. Negotiate With Key Suppliers

A friendly supplier can often help you protect your business assets from other less-understanding creditors. Similarly, a friendly supplier, especially one that relies heavily on your business, may forego payments on his accounts, temporarily, while your business fights to survive. If this supplier is reasonable, he will see that harassing you about your debts will only push the business closer to insolvency—where nobody wins. Convince him to take less now if it will help you stay in business.

THE PITFALLS OF BANKRUPTCY

Most business owners see bankruptcy as the end of a long road of frustration and disappointment—their last option, when all other attempts at salvaging the business have failed. Do not take this limited view of bankruptcy.

Instead, see bankruptcy as a powerful bargaining chip—one that can force even the most disagreeable creditors to develop plans and favorable settlements. We have seen the threat of bankruptcy lead to negotiated deals with creditors that have saved many businesses.

Nonetheless, bankruptcy can be the best option for a troubled business. Perhaps cash flow problems are too severe, business products are no longer in demand, or a new competitor obsoletes the market. Whatever the reason, the business can not sustain itself. Bankruptcy should then be considered. There are 1.5 million bankruptcies each year. Many are small businesses.

We cover the specifics of bankruptcy in a later chapter—both personal bankruptcy under Chapter 7 and business reorganizations under Chapter 11 and 13. The key point is that most business owners do not correctly plan before filing bankruptcy. Pre-bankruptcy planning is essential for successful reorganization or liquidation. Proper planning saves you much of your investment and the business itself may emerge stronger. Without proper planning, you stand to lose much of your business and personal finances. BEWARE: NEVER FILE FOR BANKRUPTCY WITHOUT FIRST CONSULTING AN ASSET PROTECTION SPECIALIST.

THE TWO GREATEST THREATS TO YOUR FAMILY BUSINESS ... AND HOW TO PROTECT AGAINST THEM

FAMILY BUSINESS OWNERS: The greatest threats to the continuity of your family-owned business may not be competition, creditors, or even lawsuits. They are (1) divorce and (2) an inadequate succession plan.

■ A Disruptive Divorce

If you get divorced, you could lose up to one half of your business to an ex-spouse. Alternatively, if you gift or sell a large percentage of the business to an adult child who gets divorced, a large portion of the business will also be lost. Why? Because your ex-daughter-in-law or son-in-law will likely end-up with half of your child's share—which could be a controlling interest. With the divorce rate over 50%, expect this kind of fight in your family business.

The *Wall Street Journal* (June 19, 1996) detailed the need to protect the family-owned business from the ex-spouses of family members. They reported many stories of family businesses attacked in the divorces of elder and younger family members alike. In the typical situation, the family patriarch gifted substantial family business stock to a child who works in the business.

When there is a divorce, a nasty fight ensues for as much of the child's share as possible—using the share to demand high dividend payments or threaten liquidation! One fight in California tied-up a family-owned real estate business in litigation for over a year, seriously disrupting business operations.

Avoid this! An antenuptial agreement can prevent such a disaster from befalling your family-owned business. Your family has worked too hard to build the business. Do not let poor asset protection planning be the reason it falters. Your business fortress planning *must* include divorce protection for yourself and other family members.

■ An Inadequate Succession Plan

A succession plan provides for the succession of the business after you retire. It is as essential as the estate plan, which provides for the distribution of your assets when you die.

Lack of a succession plan has destroyed many family-owned businesses after the businesses' founders retire. Nearly two-thirds of family-owned businesses never reach the second generation, in part because of bad feelings, infighting, and uncertainty that result when there is no structured plan of who should take over what parts of the business, when, and how.

Nothing substitutes for the advice of a lawyer who is knowledgeable about business law and estate planning. The following are essential preventative tips:

1. All family members should consider the eventual change of control. Do not wait until the last minute! Start 10-20 years in advance for a smooth transition.

2. Take care of yourself. Separate your own financial security from the business'. Otherwise, your future will be tied to it.

3. Be truthful with your children. If you have already decided whom you want to run the business when you are gone, tell everyone now. Otherwise, false hopes will linger.

4. Create a graceful exit. For children not chosen to lead the company, leave a graceful exit, perhaps a cash-out. This reduces resentment.

CONSULT A PROFESSIONAL

Protecting business assets and creating a healthy business is a complicated specialty. Your business structure must be tailor-made to your business operations, future strategy, and personal management. Obviously, expert advice is invaluable.

SUMMARY

- Never run a business or practice as a proprietorship. It risks all your personal wealth.
- Running a business or practice as a general partnership is even worse—you gamble your personal finances on your acts and those of your partners. If you use a general partnership, make corporations the partners.
- A corporation, LLC, or a limited partnership is usually the preferred way to structure a business—you have less risk and exposure. You can also save taxes, probate fees, and keep 100% control.
- "Aim for the best, plan for the worst." Structure your business defensively, as a creditor-proof lawsuit-proof fortress.
- No matter what type business you own, or its operational structure, for ultimate protection: (1) use multiple legal entities and (2) segregate safe assets from dangerous assets.
- Your operating business should never own valuable assets, like real estate, copyrights, hi-tech equipment, etc.
- Mortgages from friendly lenders or suppliers can protect you from hostile creditors and lawsuits.
- Bankruptcy is an effective bargaining chip. However, if it is a real option, do pre-bankruptcy planning with an asset protection specialist.
- If your business is family-owned, protect it from its two greatest threats: (1) divorce of a family member and (2) a flawed sucession plan.

CHAPTER 13:

LEGALLY SHIELD YOUR ASSETS FROM THE I.R.S.

This chapter explains strategies and tactics effective against the most powerful creditor in the world—the Internal Revenue Service. While the IRS is extremely powerful, as you will learn, it is not limitless. There are many ways to legally prevent the IRS from seizing your assets if you owe back taxes. In fact, you can settle with the IRS and pay them less than you owe.

Ten million Americans personally owe the IRS back taxes, and many more owe payroll taxes from their defunct businesses. Each of these people should read this chapter. Why? Because most people make costly mistakes when dealing with the IRS. They either lie, illegally hide assets, or are so intimidated by the IRS that they give away too much. Either way, they end-up in a much worse position than if they had consulted an asset protection lawyer.

Treat the IRS like any other creditor. Position yourself defensively and protect your assets first. As always, proper timing in protecting assets against the IRS is crucial. After you are fully protected, you can approach the IRS to make good on your debt...possibly paying pennies on the dollar to settle.

THE IRS WILL EVENTUALLY FIND YOU

Whether you owe the IRS back taxes or previously failed to file returns, hiding from the IRS is not a wise solution. We have seen many taxpayers "go underground" for years, but eventually the IRS tracks them down. A vast IRS computer network, tied to state and federal computers, is almost foolproof. Voluntarily come forward to pay your bill, before the stress of looking over your shoulder becomes too much.

While the IRS will eventually find you, it is possible to sidestep the taxman temporarily. The IRS computer is network slow, but methodical, like a tortoise. Without any action on your part, it may take years for the IRS to locate you. If you move around more quickly, like a rabbit, you may be able to forestall the IRS for many years. You are not preventing your day of reckoning, however, only delaying it. This delay has a cost. Interest and penalties accrue each day. Also, you will receive far less cooperation from IRS officers if they believe you intentionally avoided them.

3 POWERFUL IRS WEAPONS

The IRS is the most powerful creditor in the world. While it is a slow-moving beast, once the IRS catches-up to you, it wields awesome power to take your assets. Its principal weapons in this regard are the tax lien, the levy, and seizure. While you may remember these tools from earlier, they are much more effective in the hands of an IRS officer.

■ Tax Lien

The tax lien is usually the first serious collection remedy. You will receive a notice that a tax lien is coming, 10 days before the lien is to be filed. The lien is like an all-encompassing mortgage. It encumbers all your assets! This makes it virtually impossible to sell, refinance, or get credit to purchase any major assets, including a home or automobiles. In essence, a tax lien destroys your credit. This can be financially crippling. And, the lien stays in effect as long as the IRS can enforce the tax liability against you, which is currently 10 years.

▪ Levy

The IRS can attach money owed to you by third parties, through its power of levy. Before levying, the IRS must give you a 30-day written notice of its intent to levy. Once notice is given, the IRS simply contacts the third-party. In this manner, the IRS can take your:

- Checking or savings accounts
- Stocks, bonds,
- Cash value life insurance
- Keoghs and IRAs
- Inheritances
- Interests in partnerships
- Accounts receivable

▪ Seizure

If your tax bill remains unpaid, the IRS will eventually seize and sell your assets at a private or public sale, unless you discharge the taxes in bankruptcy or make some type settlement agreement. Before any seizure, however, the IRS must give you a 30-day written notice, as with the intent to levy. The process of the tax sale is similar to the previously described procedure for ordinary creditor foreclosure sales.

YOUR MOST INSECURE ASSETS

The IRS officer handling your case has wide discretion on which assets to seize first. The officer will consider the ease with which the service can seize the asset and convert it to cash to pay the tax bill. He will also consider the importance of the asset to the taxpayer. For this reason, a taxpayer's home is usually the last asset seized by the IRS. Considering these factors, the foregoing assets are most vulnerable to IRS liens, levies, and seizures:

- ▪ Savings and checking accounts
- ▪ Cars, boats, airplanes, RVs with significant equity
- ▪ Accounts receivable
- ▪ Stocks, bonds and other debts due to you

A taxpayer's wages, IRAs/Keoghs, or family home is not exempt from the IRS. Nonetheless, the service usually takes these assets only when other measures fail to resolve your tax problem.

2 WAYS TO PROTECT YOUR BANK ACCOUNT FROM IRS LEVY

Your bank account is probably most vulnerable to IRS levy because it gives them quick cash and they already know about your accounts, in most cases. Nevertheless, you can protect it.

- Use a corporation, LLC, or FLP to own the bank account then "borrow" from the legal entity to pay your personal expenses. As always, the loan should be documented so the court does not treat the entity as your "alter ego" and allow the IRS to go after the account, despite the "corporate," "LLC" or "FLP" name.

- Use your personal name but open account(s) in small banks—those the IRS will not easily target as they "canvass" your region for accounts owned by delinquent taxpayers. Large and slow-moving, the IRS does not have the time to check every bank looking for accounts to seize. Instead, they usually check the 10 or 20 largest banks in the area.

You will need to move the bank account periodically because eventually, the IRS will catch up with any one account. There is nothing illegal about this. You can legally move your money wherever you want, as many times as you want, as long as the funds are owned by you. Just remember: if you complete a financial disclosure form, you must truthfully disclose where your accounts are at that moment. Of course, nothing prevents you from moving the funds later that day, before the IRS can pounce!

ASSETS THE IRS CANNOT TAKE

Contrary to popular belief, the IRS cannot take everything you own. However, the list of exempt assets is short and insignificant. The IRS cannot seize:

- Food, fuel, furniture and other personal effects up to $2,500
- Undelivered mail
- Tools and books required for your business—up to $1,100
- Income needed to provide court-ordered child support
- Unemployment, worker's compensation, public assistance and job training benefits
- Clothing and school books

- Pension payments of retired railroad personnel, military disability benefits, or benefits for those on the Armed Forces Honor Roll

How scant this list is? Most surprising to many people is that the family home is not on the list. As explained earlier, the homestead exemption as state law does not protect you against federal government creditors, like the IRS. Delinquent taxpayers lose their homes everyday to IRS seizure. Do not let your case go that far!

■ How to Remain in Your Home if it is Seized

If the IRS does take your house, it must give you 90 days between the date of seizure and the day of the public sale. During that time, you can remain in the home. Further, once the house is sold, you have six months to "redeem" your tax bill—pay it off entirely and get your house back. Otherwise, the new owner can begin eviction proceedings to get you out. By knowing and exercising your rights, you can possibly live in your house for over 200 days, rent and mortgage-free.

■ How to Reclaim Personal Property Seized by the IRS

If your personal property is seized by the IRS, all is not lost. You can reclaim the property, if:

1. You negotiate an acceptable installment agreement to pay the tax debt.

2. You recover the property, enabling you to pay the tax debt. This often occurs when business assets are seized—if you can show that the operating business will become current or pay its tax obligations faster if the equipment, etc. is returned.

3. You post a bond or give other collateral equal to the unpaid tax.

4. You file bankruptcy under chapters 7, 11, or 13. Once you file, the IRS can only proceed with collection with the permission of the bankruptcy court (See later section).

HOW TO KEEP THE IRS FROM TAKING YOUR BUSINESS

The IRS favors certain types of businesses—the minority-owned and operated, those with loans from the SBA and other federal agencies, and a high-profile business. These factors and others can convince IRS officers to be lenient on your business. We handled IRS officers in Ken's case (below) using that strategy.

Case Study:
IRS Officers Stalled From Taking Ken's Business Equipment

Ken, a medical supply manufacturer, fell on hard times. He lost a few accounts and was unable to sell an adjacent building in a depressed market. To keep the business operating, Ken used cash earmarked for withholding taxes to pay suppliers, utilities, and payroll. After three consecutive quarters of not paying withholding taxes, IRS officers moved. First, came the customary notices to pay-up or collection enforcement would ensue. Ken felt he had no options, thinking "I don't have the cash to pay, and I'm still operating at a loss." An IRS officer phoned Ken for a meeting threatening to seize Ken's equipment and inventory unless the tax was paid.

Ken gave us a power of attorney, so the IRS had to deal with us. They could no longer contact Ken directly. This left Ken less stressed which helped turn the business around. We argued that the IRS should not seize business assets, pointing to the difficulty of selling these assets: They would generate cash better through the business than at an auction; The business has an SBA loan; It assisted the Red Cross for years; Employed over 50 people in a small community; And, had a strong reputation. . . all to stop a quick seizure and sale which would surely do-in Ken's company.

Fortunately, these arguments helped us negotiate. Ken could pay the taxes over the next 12 months, or when the building was sold at a profit, which ever came first. This saved Ken's equipment from seizure, and saved Ken's business from a final blow.

AVOID THIS CRUCIAL MISTAKE WITH THE IRS

A taxpayer's most common mistake is to voluntarily extend the statute of limitations on collection action. IRS officers realize that taxpayers generally do not understand what such an extension means and casually have the taxpayer sign for an extension. More aggressive officers use the extension as a bargaining chip, promising leniency if the statute is extended. Do not be fooled. Never extend the statute of limitations on tax collection voluntarily!

What does such an extension do? The IRS has 10 years from the date of tax assessment to collect taxes (it used to be six years). After that 10-year period, the taxes are discharged, and the IRS must give up all efforts to collect the tax. For that reason, every year, the slow-moving IRS allows thousands of claims for overdue taxes to expire—they did not get around to enforcing tax collection before the statute ran out. However, if you extend the statute, the IRS can continue to collect until the extension runs out. Usually another five or 10 years.

The IRS pushes for extensions most aggressively when the 10-year period is about to expire. This, of course, is exactly why you should not sign such an extension. After all, if the IRS could not collect the taxes against you in the first nine years, what will make them more successful now? Do not let the IRS "back in the ballgame." Refuse any extension agreement.

PROBLEMS WITH JOINT OWNERSHIPS AND TRUSTS

Trusts or joint ownership pose special IRS problems.

■ Trusts

Transferring assets to a trust can be a successful tactic against the IRS. Generally, the IRS only seizes property held in the delinquent taxpayer's name, or jointly-held property, or property owned by the taxpayer's spouse, if they filed jointly. The IRS usually has no right to take property owned by a third-party, such as a trust. Nevertheless, the IRS will seize property held in trust if:

- ■ The transfer was fraudulent — Like other creditors, the IRS can argue that a transfer to the trust was fraudulent and have it undone

The Doctor's Wealth Protection Guide

by the court on that basis. As discussed, timing is critical to the success of a transfer. If the transfer was completed before any tax problem arose, the trust assets will be safe from IRS attack.

- The trust is revocable — The IRS can "step into your shoes" and revoke the trust to claim trust assets. Use *irrevocable* trusts to protect against the IRS, with no "ownership strings" attached.

■ Joint Ownership

Jointly-held property, like all co-ownerships, is a double-edged sword. It can be protective, but usually makes assets more vulnerable. Consider these general rules with joint ownership collectors, and remember joint property can include both real property (land and buildings) and personal property (cars, bank accounts, etc.):

- For joint filers — Joint ownership provides no protection. If you and your spouse file taxes jointly, you essentially each guarantee the tax bill of the other. This is why the IRS encourages joint filing by granting lower tax rates. They prefer both spouses "on the hook" for the entire bill. If you file jointly, the IRS can seize any property owned individually by either spouse and all jointly-owned property, including community property and tenancy by the entirety property.

- For separate filers — Protection is only for the non-liable owner's share. As previously explained, this type of asset protection leaves much to be desired. The creditor, here the IRS, can force the sale of the entire property and simply pay the non-debtor owner his share of the sale proceeds. This is undesirable protection, if any at all.

With tenancy by the entirety property, the IRS has much more power than an ordinary creditor coming after one co-owner. Chapter 6 outlined that as a state law protection, the tenancy by the entirety shield does not necessarily effect federal agencies like the IRS. Therefore, the IRS can claim tenancy by the entirety property just like joint tenancy property. The IRS can force a sale of the entire property to satisfy the debt of one co-owner.

THE 4 BEST ASSET PROTECTION STRATEGIES VS. THE IRS

If you owe significant back taxes, engage in asset protection before approaching the IRS. You want less wealth exposed when you negotiate a payment plan or settlement. Without asset protection planning, the IRS will levy your savings and seize your property. With an asset protection in place, you negotiate from a position of strength, with much less to lose through levy, seizure, and even garnishment.

Protecting assets against the IRS is much like protecting against any other creditor, except that state law protections do not work against the federal tax collectors. Trusts, federal exemptions, and even joint ownership can be effective against the taxman. The four most effective strategies for protecting your savings against the IRS are as follows:

1. An Offshore Trust

Whether it be a flexible set-up with a *family limited partnership (FLP)*, or a straight funding of a foreign trust, the use of a *Foreign Asset Protection Trust (FAPT)* is the most powerful tool against the IRS. The IRS, like other creditors, can only seize assets in your name. For assets owned by another legal entity, the IRS must, allege a fraudulent transfer and try to get the asset back from the legal entity.

Thus, to recover FAPT assets, the IRS must also fight the trust in the foreign haven, using foreign attorneys. Even more than the run-of-the-mill creditor, however, the IRS is usually too bureaucratic and slow-moving for such a fight. The IRS attempts to chase a foreign trust in criminal cases where (1) the trust held drug money and laundered funds, (2) millions of dollars in taxes were owed, and (3) they work in conjunction with the justice department.

If your case is simply a civil claim for back taxes, the FAPT will in most cases force the IRS officer to settle for the value of assets they can actually reach. The IRS will likely treat the trust assets as untouchable and look only at available assets and future earnings for determining a payment plan or settlement amount.

2. Domestic Legal Entities (FLP, LLC, Corporations)

Domestic legal entities used against the IRS are as effective as using them against other domestic creditors, like banks and lawsuit plaintiffs. The IRS simply cannot come after assets not owned by you, unless they can undo the transfer as fraudulent. Thus, as explained in earlier chapters, by transferring your assets into corporations, family limited partnerships, and limited liability companies, you can effectively keep those assets out of the grasp of the IRS, no matter how much you owe. Remember: the sooner you make such transfers, the better.

Also remember, the IRS has some remedy if the underlying interests in these entities are owned by you personally. Whatever percentage you own in a corporation, the IRS can take those shares. Similarly, to the extent that you have FLP interests or LLC membership interests, the IRS can get a charging order against such interests. However, as noted, the IRS knows how useless a charging order is and they rarely, if ever, come after FLP or LLC interests as a result.

Legal entities act as a powerful motivator for a favorable settlement or payment plan. IRS officers are not attorneys. They are overworked and underpaid. They have many cases on their desk that they just want to close. Your complex maze of irrevocable trusts, FAPTs, FLPs, LLCs and corporations, are not easily pierced. Assets clearly in your name and your earnings, are two sources of cash which they target.

3. Debt Shields

Debt shields are friendly mortgages, when protecting business assets. A debt shield is a mortgage or security interest on your assets, held by a friendly creditor. Friendly creditors can be friends, relatives, your business (if you have the tax problem), suppliers (if your business has the tax problem), or anyone who would agree to be a creditor of record on your property but who is unlikely to enforce the debt against your interests.

Debt shields deter the IRS from seizing assets because IRS officers only seize assets if there is equity to justify the expense. For example, if you own a sports car with $25,000 equity, the IRS would probably receive about $15,000 at a quick sale auction. Assume the costs of seizing the car and the sale are about $3,000. Without a debt shield, the IRS officer would seize your car, because the sale would give the IRS a recovery.

Assume instead that a friend has a mortgage on the car for $20,000. Using the $15,000 quick-sale value, it is not worth it for the IRS to lien and seize your car.

4. Convert Wealth from Non-Exempt Assets to IRS Exempt Assets

This is similar to the strategy we presented in Chapter 5, except the list of exempt assets is shorter because many state-only exemptions do not apply to IRS collection. For example, the IRS may come after IRAs, annuities, life insurance cash value, and even ERISA-qualified pensions.

HOW TO SETTLE IRS TAXES

If you owe the IRS more than you can feasibly pay, you can make a deal with them to pay less than you owe and discharge your tax debt in full. There are three different programs under which you may be relieved from part or all of your tax debt:

- **Abatement:** With an abatement, the IRS cancels all or part of interest accrued and/or penalties assessed on the tax you owe. Often, the interest and penalties will exceed the tax, so this cancellation can be extremely valuable for many taxpayers.

- **Hardship Status:** If you obtain hardships status, also called "temporarily uncollectible," the IRS ceases collection activity against you. Although your debt will not be officially erased, the IRS only starts collection activities again if your financial situation improves. For many elderly taxpayers who owe back taxes, this designation is as effective as a complete forgiveness of their debt.

- **Offer In Compromise:** With a successful offer in compromise (OIC), the IRS forgives your entire debt for a fraction of what you owe. In essence, you settle for pennies on the dollar. Most successful OICs are lump sum payments, although the IRS accepts short-term payment plans even on low settlement amounts.

Revamped in 1992, the OIC program now allows thousands of taxpayers to settle their past debts and rejoin the tax system. In 1994, for example, over 20,000 OICs were successful, settling for an average of 15% of the original tax! Using this system, the IRS collected over $150 million in revenue. Both taxpayers and the IRS agree that this program should be increased so more delinquent taxpayers can settle their past debts and move forward as tax-paying citizens.

WHY BANKRUPTCY MAY NOT CANCEL UNPAID TAXES

Many people incorrectly believe that bankruptcy will clear them of tax bills. Before filing for bankruptcy, understand the type of taxes you owe and the type of bankruptcy you are considering. The two most common taxes are either (1) personal income taxes or (2) withholding taxes assessed to you as the officer or director of a company. Withholding taxes are never dischargeable in any type of bankruptcy. They stay with you until paid, settled through an OIC, or until you are given hardship status.

- **Chapter 7** — This type bankruptcy is called *straight* because it is a straightforward discharge of most debts by a liquidation of nonexempt assets. Personal income taxes are dischargeable in bankruptcy filed under Chapter 7. However, only taxes assessed at least three years prior to the bankruptcy filing are discharged. Newer taxes and liens in effect before filing bankruptcy remain. Thus, the IRS could force the sale of liened assets even after you file Chapter 7. Finally, Chapter 7 will not help if you filed a false claim or understated income. If you later owe more because of an audit, this new amount will survive bankruptcy.

- **Chapters 11/13** — These bankruptcies are not liquidations like Chapter 7, but are re-organizations of the debtor's financial affairs. With these bankruptcies, you do not lose your assets, but have to pay your tax debt in full over time—usually 3-5 years. The IRS must follow the orders of the bankruptcy court regarding the payment schedule of overdue taxes.

CONCLUSION: AN ASSET PROTECTION LAWYER IS A KEY TAX ADVISOR

The best person to help you when the collection arm of the IRS is chasing you is an asset protection specialist— not an accountant or enrolled agent. They know nothing about how to legally protect assets from the revenue officer's tools. Not even a tax lawyer has this knowledge—his/her expertise is shielding your property when your tax bill is undisputed. Only the asset protection specialist can buy you the time you need to re-organize your finances, make you look "paper poor" to the IRS officer assigned and help you on your way to a favorable installment plan or settlement.

SUMMARY

- You cannot hide from the IRS forever. Eventually they find you.
- The three powerful IRS weapons: The *Lien, Levy,* and *Seizure.*
- Liquid assets are the most vulnerable—especially bank accounts which can be protected by using legal entities or smaller banks.
- Certain assets are exempt from the IRS and you do have rights to reclaim your home seized by the IRS.
- There are arguments which often persuade IRS officers to give troubled businesses time to pay their taxes.
- Never voluntarily extend the statute of limitations for tax collection.
- Joint ownership can deter the IRS; irrevocable trusts are much more effective.
- The best strategies against the IRS: Offshore trusts, other legal entities, debt shields, or convert wealth to exempt assets.
- You can pay less taxes than you actually owe through abatements, hardship status, and offers in compromise. You must, however, be guided by an expert in order to be successful.
- Bankruptcy may help you discharge old tax bills, depending on the type tax and the type bankruptcy.
- Call an asset protection specialist when under attack by the IRS to shield your savings and to put you in the best position to negotiate with IRS revenue officers.

CHAPTER 14:

SAFEGUARDING ASSETS AGAINST DIVORCE

The lawsuit threat comes in many forms, from traditional civil lawsuits, to IRS collections, to bankruptcy. Nonetheless, the most powerful threat to many American's financial security is the divorce. Over 50% of all marriages in this country end in divorce—and that percentage grows to almost 75% for second marriages. Divorce, an emotionally devastating experience, can be a financially devastating experience, as well.

Millions of Americans each year, in fact, are frustrated with the financial consequences of their marital dissolution. They may not receive what they believe they deserve or lose personal assets intended for children, or family assets intended to remain within the family, such as family businesses. Many of these scenarios could be avoided—with proper advance planning.

Asset protection in divorce is not about hiding assets from a soon-to-be ex-spouse. Nor is it about cheating or lying to keep your wealth. Rather, it concerns resolving issues of property ownership and distribution, before things go sour. By agreeing up-front what will be yours and what will be theirs, you save money, time, and emotional distress in the long-run. In fact, this type asset protection planning inevitably benefits all parties, except the divorce lawyers.

In this chapter, you will see how to create a rock-solid premarital agreement or post-marital agreement—one that will withstand attack, and be binding upon divorce; how to overcome objections to signing such an agreement; and, how to properly act in accordance with one. In addition, we explain savvy tactics for the soon-to-be divorced, such as how to prevent the soon-to-be ex-spouse from hiding assets and how to maintain good credit during a divorce. Finally, we touch on the risks of cohabitation and how to avoid them.

WHY DIVORCE CAN BE FINANCIALLY DEVASTATING

Most Americans do not have to read newspapers to see how devastating a divorce can be financially. While high-profile divorces involving tens of millions of dollars illustrate the point dramatically, most of us only need to look to family or friends to see how a divorce turns into a financial upheaval. The prevailing attitude towards divorce comes from a recent movie. In the film, Ivana Trump explains her theory of divorce to three ex-wives, played by Goldie Hawn, Diane Keaton, and Bette Midler. "Don't get even," she says, "get everything!"

Combine this fight-for-everything attitude with the terrible odds of getting a divorce (close to 50% for first marriages, 75% for second marriages) and you have a very serious threat to any married person's financial security. In fact, a divorce threatens not only former spouses, but also their families and possibly their business partners as well. To truly understand how a divorce affects the finances of the participants, you must first understand how property is divided when the marriage is dissolved.

■ Community Property States

Nine states have community property laws: Arizona, California, Idaho, Louisiana, Nevada, New Mexico, Texas, Washington, and Wisconsin. If your divorce occurs in one of these states and there is no valid pre- or post-marital agreement, the court will divide equally any property acquired during the marriage, other than inheritances or gifts to one spouse. Even the appreciation of one spouse's separate property can be divided, if the spouse spent efforts during the marriage on that property. Obviously, how the asset is titled is not the controlling factor. When the asset was acquired and how it was treated are much more important.

■ Equitable Distribution States

Non-community property states are called *equitable distribution* states because courts in these states have total discretion to divide the property *equitably* or fairly. The court will normally consider a number of factors in deciding what is "equitable," including the length of the marriage, the age and conducts of the parties, and the present earnings and future earning potential of each former spouse. The danger of equitable divorces is that courts often distribute both non-marital assets (those acquired before the marriage) as well as marital assets (those acquired during marriage), in order to create a "fair" arrangement. In this way, *courts often split-up property in ways that the ex-spouses never wanted or expected.*

■ Examples of "Disaster Divorces"

The following are examples to help you consider whether you and your family are adequately prepared to divorce:

1. A couple marries, each for the second time, and each with adult children from a previous family. Without any pre- or post-martial agreement, they title many of the wife's previously separate income-producing properties (such as her rental apartment units) into the name of the new husband to save income taxes this way. Within two years of the marriage, they divorce. The husband gets half the rental units (in addition to alimony and other property), even though both spouses understood that the wife intended them to go to her children. The court simply ignored their understanding, giving half the properties to each spouse.

2. A couples marries, each for the first time. Over the next 20 years, the husband acquires more ownership in his family's bakery business. His father, the founder, gradually transferred shares to him. At 42, he is the majority owner. Unfortunately, he and his wife then undergo a bitter divorce with the ex-wife granted half the husband's bakery business as community property. She then forces (1) high dividends and (2) a sale of the company to a competitor.

3. An internal medicine resident gets married. She and her husband discuss her medical education and agree that she should not have to later compensate him for his greater financial contribution in their early years. However, they file for divorce eight years later. The husband considers the wife's professional degree as marital property, so he claims a share in her earning potential. The court agrees, even though the couple verbally agreed to the contrary.

CAN A PREMARITAL AGREEMENT PROTECT YOU?

A premarital agreement (or, prenuptial agreement, premarital contract, antenuptial agreement, etc.) is the foundation of any protection against a divorce. The premarital agreement is a written contract between the intended spouses. It specifies the division of property and income upon divorce, including disposition to specific personal property, such as family heirlooms. It also states the responsibilities of each party and their children after divorce. Finally, these agreements lay out responsibilities during marriage, such as what each spouse can expect in financial support or which religion will be used to raise future children. The agreement cannot limit child support.

■ Not Only For The Rich

Premarital agreements are often perceived to be only for the wealthy, but this is not true. The three scenarios above didn't involve rich people, yet all could have benefited from a premarital agreement as these agreements deal both with current and future property. Such agreements help those who eventually acquire significant property as it protects existing assets.

A premarital agreement, in fact, can be more important for the less wealthy spouse entering a second marriage. Why? Because that spouse typically gives-up a major source of income—alimony from the first marriage. A pre-martial agreement can ensure that, if divorce occurs, she will be at least as well-off as before remarriage.

■ Court Enforced

A premarital agreement is properly drafted if it adequately discloses and if other state law requirements are met. Courts will then abide by its terms. With a rock-solid premarital agreement, you can limit surprises in divorce. The court will simply allow you to split property as you both originally agreed. *This not only ensures that you retain property, but also saves you time, aggravation, and attorneys' fees. It can avoid a difficult process and a nasty fight.*

WHAT YOUR PREMARITAL AGREEMENT MUST INCLUDE

Each state differs slightly on what is required for an enforceable premarital agreement. But, generally:

1. The agreement must be in writing and signed

Every state requires that a premarital agreement be written and signed. Many also require that it be notarized or witnessed.

TIP: *Notarize your agreement, even if your state does not require it. This adds protection against claims of duress or forgery.*

2. There must be a reasonable disclosure

There must be a fair, accurate and reasonable disclosure of each party's financial condition.

TIP: *Attach financial statements to the agreement and have the spouse affirm knowledge of the other's financial condition.*

3. Each party must be advised by a separate attorney

Many states either require separate legal advice explicitly or use it as a factor in determining whether or not the agreement was fair.

TIP: *Hire separate lawyers and give enough time between the agreement and the wedding to avoid any appearance of duress. Courts frown on last-second premarital agreements.*

4. The agreement must be unconscionable

Courts will not enforce a one-sided agreement. Also, the contract must not be structured to encourage divorce. For example, by stating that one spouse has no rights to property except upon divorce.

TIP: *Avoid extremely one-sided agreements. It need not be a 50/50 split, but should provide a fair balance.*

5. The couple must follow the agreement during the marriage

Courts disregard premarital agreements when the spouses blatantly disregarded it during their marriage, such as when property designated as the husband's separate property is re-titled to the wife.

TIP: *Treat designated separate property as separate. If loans are made from one spouse's separate property to the marital unit, then those funds should not be commingled when repaid.*

HOW TO DISCUSS A PREMARITAL AGREEMENT WITH A PROSPECTIVE SPOUSE

The greatest barrier to a premarital agreement is the fear of broaching the subject of money and divorce when the couple has yet to marry. People think this discussion shows a lack of trust in the relationship, or that it is too unromantic, or that they will never divorce. While these concerns may be genuine, the best approach to "sell" a prospective spouse on a premarital agreement is openness and honesty.

You may treat the discussion as one about estate planning. The concerns are precisely the same—who gets what if the two of you are no longer together, and what will be the responsibilities to children and other family members. This naturally leads to the topic of a premarital agreement in the most palatable way.

Or, put the responsibility on a friend, family member, or trusted adviser. Perhaps they convinced you that such an agreement is a good idea. This is often so with first marriages, where older family members pressure younger members toward such agreements—especially when a family business is at risk. If your partner believes that the idea originated elsewhere he may accept it easier.

Finally, for second marriages, explain that you want an agreement not because of concerns about this marriage so much as learning from past mistakes. Perhaps you vowed you would never again fight over property. It is better to talk it out now and put the issue behind you.

WHY PREMARITAL AGREEMENTS ARE SO IMPORTANT FOR FAMILY BUSINESS OWNERS

Divorce commonly causes a major disruption to a family-owned business. Commonly, when a child of the founder of the business gets divorced and the ex-spouse sues for half of that child's interest in the business, it forces demands upon the business.

The ex-spouse's demands can lead to lawsuits where discovery consumes family time and money and uncovers information intended to be private—such as salaries for family member, benefits, contracts, etc. Defending such a suit or divorce claim injures the family and the business.

This is why family business owners are increasingly using lawyers to protect against it. The preferred tool to prevent such disaster? . . . the premarital agreement, of course. The *Wall Street Journal* recently reported, *"the number of premarital agreements drafted for members of family-owned businesses has skyrocketed in recent years."* One New York attorney, now drafts close to 300 agreements per year. Ten years ago it was closer to 20.

Protect your business from the destruction which can result from a bitter divorce. *Have every owner of your family business create an agreement (premarital or post-marital) which prevents the in-law from claiming a stake in the business upon divorce. Specify a cash settlement instead. Should a divorce then occur, the ex-spouse will still be fairly treated; but your business remains undisrupted and in the family.*

POST-MARITAL AGREEMENTS CAN BE A PROTECTOR FOR THE ALREADY MARRIED

A post-marital agreement (or *post-nuptial contract,* etc.) is essentially the same as the premarital agreement, only it is created and signed after the couple is married. The post-marital agreement covers two topics: (1) what property each spouse will keep as separate property upon divorce; and (2) the marital property each spouse will receive upon divorce.

However, the enforceability of a post-marital contract is not as clear as with premaritals because some states do not allow a married person to waive rights to property. The theory: the married person is getting nothing in return for giving-up such rights—while the to-be-married person gets the marriage in return. Check with an attorney familiar with your state's laws before contracting.

If the post-marital agreement is recognized in your state, follow the tips outlined for premarital agreements. Because courts evaluate post-marital agreements as they do premarital contracts, it is important that the agreement be in writing, signed, not one-sided, etc. Follow these guidelines and your agreement is more likely to be enforced.

IRREVOCABLE TRUSTS: ALTERNATIVES TO MARITAL AGREEMENTS

Irrevocable trusts are very effective asset protection tools because you no longer own the assets poured into the trust and, you have not retained any benefits of ownership. You have transferred the property with no strings attached. Because you neither own nor control the property, your creditors, including an ex-spouse, cannot claim the property.

Using an irrevocable trust to own assets means giving away those assets forever. This is a serious consequence when protecting against divorce, lawsuit, or other threat. When would such a strategy make sense? When you would inevitably give the assets to certain beneficiaries. For example, the trust might be used for assets which (1) you will leave to your children when you die; and (2) you do not need for your financial security. Consider this case:

Case Study:
Irving's Trust Protects His Summer Home

Irving, an oncologist, bought a summer home on Cape Cod. He and his first wife had three small children. Unfortunately, they divorced about six years later. In the settlement, he received the summer home.

Fifteen years later, Irving was ready to marry again, now in Santa Fe. Both he and his prospective spouse had been married previously and understood divorce. Irving considered a premarital agreement to keep the summer home as his separate property. He had planned to give it to his three children; and, wondered whether working on the home would jeopardize this plan, if he divorced.

After speaking with Irving, we noted three important points: (1) his handiwork on the home might make it marital property; (2) his children and their families used the home throughout the year; and (3) Irving had a lawsuit from a failed real estate venture. It was clear that the best strategy for Irving was to have an irrevocable trust own the summer home, giving beneficial interests to use the home to all three children equally (which already occurred).

Using an irrevocabletrust to own the summer home, Irving protected against possible future divorce and also shielded it from other creditors and lawsuits. By including spendthrift provisions, Irving protected the home from his children's creditors, as well. And, Irving can be a guest at the home often as he likes.

USING OTHER "DIVORCE-PROOFING" LEGAL ENTITIES

Family limited partnerships (FLPs), limited liability companies (LLCs), and corporations can all help you to control certain assets after divorce. Set up the entity and transfer assets into the entity prior to or during the marriage. Assume the controlling position in the entity. For FLPs, be the sole general partner, for LLCs, the sole manager, and for corporations, the sole voting stockowner. Even if total ownership is divided equally, you retain control because of your position.

Divorce courts generally will refrain from dissolving the FLP, LLC, or corporation, especially if third parties, such as children, have an ownership interest. Instead, the court will adjust ownership interests so each ex-spouse has the same percentage. If you were the sole general partner, manager, or voting stockholder before the marriage, you will continue to be so, after the divorce. As such, you will still control and manage assets owned by the entity, even though your ex-spouse has an equal ownership share. You may pay yourself a hefty management salary and refuse dividends, but courts discourage such conduct.

HOW TO AVOID HIDDEN ASSETS

Divorce brings out the worst in people. Spouses, once happily married, turn to unethical and illegal methods to retain marital property. They may hide assets or liquidate them and hide the cash. Even in more cordial divorces, where unseemly tactics are not expected, a lack of knowledge about your marital finances can be dangerous and leave you at a disadvantage in settlement negotiations. Your goal here is to find and preserve all married assets, so they can be equitably distributed.

- List every asset owned by yourself personally, your spouse personally, and the two of you jointly. Record serial numbers and other means of identification. Use videotapes and photographs, if the items are removable.

- Protect all jewelry, artwork, collectibles, cash, stocks, bonds and other small valuable objects in a safe deposit box or storage facility. Completely inventory such items, preferably with a bank or other official witness. Photographs or videotape can also be helpful to show the items and that you are not trying to conceal anything yourself. You may even obtain a restraining order against both yourself and your spouse so that neither of you can access the contents until the divorce has been settled.

- To safeguard jointly-owned stocks and mutual funds, notify your broker in writing not to process any orders without the written consent of both spouses.

- Empty all checking and savings accounts. Transfer funds not needed for daily living to an escrow account or "neutral account," until the divorce is final.

- File a lis pendens (or, *notice of pendency*) on real estate owned by your spouse in his or her name only. You may have rights to such property and, as mentioned, a lis pendens puts the public on notice that a lawsuit is pending which may effect the real estate. This makes the property impossible to sell or mortgage.

- If you and your spouse own joint insurance, draw down its cash value, account for it, and bank it. This prevents mysterious liquidation of the proceeds.

MAINTAINING GOOD CREDIT IN DIVORCE

Good credit is an invaluable asset. With good credit, the world's goods and services are open to you. Without it, it becomes difficult to buy a car, rent an apartment, or even buy necessities. Obviously, you do not want poor or ruined credit. Divorce, typically, damages credit for two reasons:

1. A deadbeat, soon-to-be ex-spouse charges up enormous bills on joint credit cards or charge accounts, without any intention to pay.

2. The financial pressures of divorce becomes too much for the one person to handle effectively.

Safeguarding Assets Against Divorce

To prevent ruined credit during a divorce:

- Contact joint creditors, including joint credit-card companies. Notify them in writing that you want all accounts closed and cards canceled. Explain that you will not be responsible for subsequent charges. Use certified mail to prove receipt.

- Publish disclaimers of liability in the "legal notices" column of a local newspaper.

- Analyze your personal financial situation when a divorce is forthcoming. Decide how much of your monthly expenses will be covered by available cash and credit. If you foresee yourself in a cash-crunch or falling behind in credit payments, contact your creditors. Creditors are more willing to extend payment terms or grant a deferment or forbearance if you are upfront—especially when you explain that the reason for your cash-crunch (the divorce) is temporary. Do not wait until you are months behind in your bills, when creditors are much less patient or willing to give you the time needed to straighten out your financial affairs.

HOW TO AVOID MAJOR TAX PROBLEMS IN DIVORCE

How would you like to lose one-half of your retirement benefits ... and then be hit with a tax bill on your retirement distribution? Unfortunately, this happens in divorces because people fail to properly use a *qualified domestic relations order (QDRO)*. A QDRO is a document which becomes part of the official divorce decree and establishes the ex-spouse's rights to part or all of one spouse's qualified retirement plan benefits.

Most divorce settlements allocate a spouse's retirement benefits. In most situations, the retirement benefits are the husband's and divided with the ex-wife. However, if a QDRO is not filed, the retirement benefits payout from a qualified plan is treated by the IRS as distribution only to the husband. It is as if the distribution were made to the husband who then makes a gift to the ex-spouse. Treated this way, the husband pays taxes on the full amount of the payout, although half the proceeds went to his ex-wife!

Case Study:
Mark Gets Hit With The 1-2 Punch

Mark, a dermatologist, divorced three years ago. In the divorce settlement, Mark gave one-half of his $2 million pension to his ex-wife. However, the actual divorce decree did not specifically assign the ex-wife the rights to the pension benefits, nor did it include her last known address—two essential QDRO requirements. As a result, the entire pension payout was treated by the IRS as a distribution to Mark and he was taxed on the entire $2 million pension, although he received 1/2 of the money.

This mistake cost Mark an extra $396,000 in federal income tax. It could have been avoided with a properly-drafted QDRO.

TIP: *Include a QDRO in the divorce decree if there is to be any distribution of ERISA-qualified retirement plans, such as a pension, stock-option, or profit-sharing plan. (A QDRO is not required for IRA distributions.) Include the assignment of benefits, the name of the plan(s) involved, the addresses of both parties, and all other specific requirements in the form.*

HOW TO REDUCE ATTORNEY'S FEES

Attorney's fees, in a contested divorce, can reach hundreds of thousands of dollars. Even in smaller divorces, attorneys often take a significant portion of the marital net worth with their combined take almost as large as either spouses. What can you do to keep lawyers out of your and your soon-to-be-ex's pockets? The most effective strategy is to have a valid premarital or post-marital agreement. This effectively creates the asset distribution plan and, if you both abide by its terms, eliminates most legal issues in a divorce. With such an agreement, the lawyers see that its terms are obeyed, that new assets are accounted for, and that the divorce formalities are followed.

These guidelines may also reduce attorney's fees:

> **1. Shop around.** Talk to a number of lawyers before you choose one to handle your divorce. To make a more informed decision, compare fees and talk to former clients. You can also change lawyers at any time. If dissatisfied with service or fees, hire another attorney.

2. **Explain your desire to get the divorce over with quickly and make sure your attorney understands your goals.** Attorneys who charge an hourly fee have an inherent conflict of interest. They may want to prolong the divorce to earn more fees. Explain to your lawyer upfront that you will not tolerate a prolonged divorce and want to settle the matter quickly.

3. **Hire an experienced lawyer.** Do not necessarily hire one with the top reputation in your community. Reputation means exorbitant legal fees. An experienced, but not "top-notch," lawyer can usually do just as good as job in most divorces, unless there are tricky issues at stake.

4. **Do not waste money.** Clients run-up their own legal bill by calling their lawyer constantly. Every meeting and phone conference has the clock ticking and the bill increasing. Write down questions and concerns and have one meeting or phone conversation where you address all issues at once.

THE RISKS OF CO-HABITATION

Cohabitation—living with a significant other without marriage is now common. Many people want to live together without marriage. Homosexual couples find this is their only option as gay marriages are generally not recognized. Nevertheless, cohabitation is risky for asset protection purposes. Why? Because the law does not recognize cohabitation as a legally binding arrangement, like marriage. Therefore, if one person dies or the relationship ends, the law usually will not allow one partner rights in the other's assets, even if that was their original intention.

Many people try to formalize their intentions with a cohabitation agreement which is similar to a premarital contract as both distribute property at the end of the relationship. Unfortunately, such agreements are sometimes not enforced by the courts because they do not have the same legal standing as premarital contracts.

TIP: *When cohabiting, use a cohabitation agreement if the distribution of assets concerns you. You will more likely have your intentions followed with such an agreement than without one.*

SUMMARY

- A divorce can be a financially devastating experience, whether you live in a *community property* state or *equitable distribution* state.
- If you have a family business, a divorce can disrupt the business.
- A premarital agreement protects you by establishing what will go to each spouse if there ever is a divorce.
- Your premarital agreement should be written, signed, have reasonable disclosure, not be unconscionable, be followed by the spouses during marriage, and each prospective spouse should be advised by their own attorney.
- There are tactful ways to approach the subject of a premarital agreement.
- Premarital agreements are a must for family business owners.
- Post-marital agreements often are effective protective devices for the already-married—although this depends on state law.
- Irrevocable trusts are protective devices, as are FLPs, LLCs, and corporations.
- Protect marital assets from being hidden by your soon-to-be-ex and take the steps after a divorce to stabilize your finances.
- Protect your credit during divorce. It is an invaluable asset.
- If you transfer ERISA-qualified retirement benefits in divorce, use a QDRO—otherwise, you will suffer a painful tax bill.
- You can reduce your attorney's fees, if you are careful.
- Cohabitation can be financially risky. A cohabitation agreement can ensure your intentions will be followed.

CHAPTER 15:

PRE-BANKRUPTCY PLANNING

We now think differently about bankruptcy. Americans once felt that bankruptcy was an admission of failure—that one had spent beyond one's means. The stigma of bankruptcy was once so severe that many Americans declined bankruptcy, even when their financial situation justified it.

The stigma of bankruptcy has now diminished. As individuals, we realize what American corporations have known for decades—that bankruptcy (1) is often the smartest financial course and (2) is a business, not moral, decision. People understand bankruptcy is often their right move and that there is nothing wrong with it. This explains the over 1.5 million bankruptcies each year.

This chapter explains the basics of bankruptcy, the type bankruptcies, and key consequences of bankruptcy. We also outline the key strategies before bankruptcy without which bankruptcy can be financially devastating. With these strategies, bankruptcy can erase your debts and legally help you to keep most of your hard-earned wealth.

WHAT IS BANKRUPTCY

Bankruptcy is protection our laws provide for debtors. It has deep roots in our legal tradition. The Constitution explicitly recognizes bankruptcy and dismisses a *debtor's prison*. The founding fathers felt it necessary for debtors to have a fresh start, without burdensome debts. Bankruptcy gives this fresh start.

Bankruptcy is a judicial process controlled by federal bankruptcy laws and administered by federal bankruptcy courts. Depending on the type bankruptcy, this process allows debtors to either *discharge* (cancel) their debts or *re-organize* their debts, all under the direction of the court. Although most individuals file discharge bankruptcies, we examine all bankruptcies.

THE 3 TYPES OF BANKRUPTCY

There are three different types of bankruptcy available to an individual debtor; a Chapter 7 liquidation and Chapter 11 or chapter 13 re-organizations. The chapter number corresponds to the chapter in the bankruptcy code which controls the relevant bankruptcy rules. Because each type bankruptcy has different requirements and consequences, you must understand their basics. In many circumstances, you may choose between two bankruptcy options.

■ Chapter 7: The Liquidation Bankruptcy

A Chapter 7 bankruptcy is a liquidation bankruptcy. Non-exempt assets of the debtor are liquidated by the bankruptcy trustee to pay the debtor's creditors. *A Chapter 7 liquidation forces you to lose your non-exempt assets.* What are your non-exempt assets? The answer depends on your state. Each state exempts different property up to different values. Your state exemptions for bankruptcy purposes are those listed in chapter 5 in the sections on state exemptions. *Check your state's exemptions to review what property is exempt under your state laws.*

While the debtor loses all non-exempt property in Chapter 7 bankruptcy, he also loses all debts, except for certain special debts (listed later). A Chapter 7 liquidation is also the most liberating bankruptcy. It gives debtors a fresh start financially. A Chapter 7 bankruptcy is usually thought of as a process by which you lose both your debts and your assets. However, with the proper planning, you can lose most of your debts and *keep most of your assets*. The keys: timing and proper planning.

A debtor may file for Chapter 7 once every seven years. This prevents chronic deadbeats from continually trying to disavow their debts through bankruptcy. Once you've been given a "clean slate" through bankruptcy, you are responsible

Pre-Bankruptcy Planning

for debts accumulated thereafter. If you should get into serious financial trouble during the following seven years, you can file for a re-organization bankruptcy under Chapter 11 or 13. These bankruptcies have no time-period limitation.

■ Chapter 11: The Re-Organization Bankruptcy

Chapter 11 is a re-organization, rather than liquidation. The debtor's debts will not be discharged, but re-organized. The debtor will not lose his assets, as in a liquidation, instead, the bankruptcy court oversees a payment plan for repaying creditors.

First, the debtor's debts are classified, then the debtor submits to the court (through the bankruptcy trustee) a plan to repay the debts—usually over three to five years. The creditors vote on the repayment plan and can make alternative arrangements of how the debts should be repaid. Often, in complex corporate restructuring, this process of wrangling over the repayment plan takes months or years. It is always costly, both in terms of aggravation and attorneys fees. As the debtor, you are never "out of the woods" until the commitments made under the court-approved repayment plan have been met over three to five years.

Nonetheless, because debtors keep their property, a Chapter 11 bankruptcy can make sense for debtors—especially those who can pay their creditors over a few years and have substantial non-exempt assets to lose in a liquidating bankruptcy. A Chapter 11 bankruptcy stops your creditors in their tracks and gives you time to make your commitments. This lets you move ahead without losing any of your hard-earned assets along the way.

■ Chapter 13: "The Wage Earner Bankruptcy"

Bankruptcy under chapter 13, the so-called *Wage Earner Bankruptcy,* is a re-organization process similar to Chapter 11. Wage earner bankruptcy also allows the debtor to keep assets and, like Chapter 11, the debtor submits a repayment plan to the court, based on their financial situation over the next few years.

The principal difference between the two re-organization bankruptcies is who qualifies for them. Chapter 13 is available only to *individuals* with *regular income* who have *noncontigent, liquidated, unsecured debts of less than $100,000 and noncontigent, liquidated, secured debts of less than $350,000.*

In plain English; to file under chapter 13, you must have less than $100,000 in unsecured debt (like credit cards and other loans where there is no collateral) and less than $350,000 in secured debt (like home mortgages, car loans, or other debt where your property is collateral).

If you can qualify for chapter 13, you should generally file under chapter 13, rather than under Chapter 11 because chapter 13 bankruptcies are simpler, more streamlined, and the discharge period is shorter thus keeping attorney fees down.

THE 3 GREAT BENEFITS OF BANKRUPTCY

The following are the three great benefits of filing for bankruptcy:

1. Bankruptcy Stops Your Creditors Cold

The moment you file bankruptcy, under any chapter, your creditors must stop all collection actions. Because of what is called the *bankruptcy stay*, they must refrain from suing you, from seizing property, and even cease calling you or sending harassing letters.

Once a debtor files bankruptcy, the *stay* automatically becomes effective. This *stay* means that all actions of the (bankruptcy-filing) debtor's creditors are stopped or *stayed*. This *stay* is completely automatic. It does not require court action. All legal maneuvers against you on your debts are ineffective from that moment. Further, once creditors are notified of your filing, they cannot contact you to pressure collection.

Most individuals contemplating bankruptcy are hassled by numerous collection agencies, so the bankruptcy stay is a sanity-saver for many debtors. Rather than face the unending stream of anxiety-producing letters and harassing phone calls, the bankruptcy stay ensures that debtors have a safe haven, while their finances are handled by the courts. Many stressed-out debtors find this to be the most important benefit of filing bankruptcy.

2. Bankruptcy Rids You Of Your Debts

You can discharge most debts by filing a liquidation bankruptcy under Chapter 7. Over their heads in debt, debtors find bankruptcy to be a way to erase obligations and to start fresh.

Bankruptcy is not to be taken lightly—there are negative implications. First, your credit will be hurt. While this is becoming less of a problem, because more and more Americans file for bankruptcy each year (so creditors are more forgiving of bankrupt applicants), your credit will certainly suffer. And, it takes ten years for the bankruptcy to be removed from your credit report.

Also, bankruptcy is public. The fact that you filed for bankruptcy may be published in the legal notices of your local newspaper. Further, anyone interested can discover details of your financial life—who and how much you owe, what your assets are worth, what property you transferred within the last year, etc. While few will read the legal notice or examine the public record, be prepared for public exposure of your "dirty laundry."

Of course, if you want bankruptcy to totally rid you of your debts, then don't consider re-organization bankruptcies under chapters 11 or 13. These only re-organize debts, not discharge them.

3. Bankruptcy—The Ultimate Bargaining Tool

Bankruptcy can be an extremely effective bargaining tool for debtors negotiating settlements with creditors. The debtor can threaten bankruptcy if the creditor does not settle. When the debtor threatens a liquidation bankruptcy, the creditor will get nothing. The bargaining position: "Take pennies on the dollar, or get nothing, because I'll file under Chapter 7."

Many debtors with severe debt problems fail to realize how effective this can be. They may be too emotionally involved with their debts or too physically drained by creditor harassment to bargain. We have heard this from many people with creditor problems.

Typically, they want asset protection when the creditors are most aggressive. These people hope asset protection can safeguard them from present liabilities. However, transfers against existing creditors will not be of much help if overturned as fraudulent transfers. Nonetheless, there are legal ways to protect assets even though they may be deemed fraudulent. This protection may occur during the one-year "look back" period, explained later.

Our goal is frequently to avoid bankruptcy, although we threaten it. We want to negotiate "pennies on the dollar" settlements and then protect your wealth from new creditors.

Case Study: *Paul Induces Settlement*

Paul, a psychiatrist, asked us to asset protect him after a hotel investment went bad. While Paul had about $900,000 in net worth, his personal liability on the failed hotel was about $2 million—$1.75 million to a bank and the rest to various suppliers. When he first called, he wanted to protect his exposed wealth from the hotel creditors. We explained fraudulent transfers and that we would not engage in illegal conduct on his behalf. Finally, we called in another asset protection lawyer who specializes in pre-bankruptcy planning.

First, our associate attorney set-up two FLPs to hold most of Paul's exposed assets. Although the transfers might possibly be deemed fraudulent, he knew that this might not be so, if Paul declared bankruptcy after one year from the transfers (the reason why we explained later). Therefore, the transfers were a bargaining tactic and a contingency defense.

Secondly, Paul completed the bankruptcy petition to begin a Chapter 7 bankruptcy. Next, the attorney sent a letter to the bank declaring Paul's tough and ready position, enclosing the unsigned but completed bankruptcy forms: "Our client is seriously considering filing for bankruptcy under Chapter 7 as the enclosed materials make clear," the letter said. "He simply cannot meet his obligations as they stand now ... If we cannot come to a mutually satisfactory settlement of my client's debt to you, he may have no choice but to seek the protection of the bankruptcy court."

He then calculated what the bank would get in liquidation based on the sale proceeds of Paul's non-exempt assets, subtracting attorney's and other fees. The bank would get only 3% of what was owed, if Paul filed under Chapter 7. So, he offered the bank 5% more. In cash, up front.

As a business decision, the bank would realize that a hard line and forcing Paul into bankruptcy would only get them less in the end. Five percent less.

This technique worked for Paul, for the bank, and the other suppliers. Paul's debts were settled for less than 25% and Paul avoided bankruptcy. While Paul did pay over $400,000, he was far better off than if he had declared bankruptcy. Since most of his assets were non-exempt, he would have lost practically all his net worth.

Pre-Bankruptcy Planning

ASSETS YOU WILL LOSE IN A CHAPTER 7 BANKRUPTCY

All non-exempt assets will be lost in a Chapter 7 bankruptcy. This point is important enough to reiterate. *Check your state's exemptions to review property exempt under your state laws. Everything that is not exempt can be taken by creditors.*

DEBTS THAT ARE NON-DISCHARGEABLE

Not all debts can be discharged in Chapter 7 bankruptcy. The following non-dischargeable debts survive a Chapter 7 liquidating bankruptcy:

- Child support and alimony
- Debts not disclosed in your bankruptcy filing
- Restitution ordered because of criminal activity
- Debts incurred due to willful or malicious injury
- Debts that are obtained through fraud or deceit
- Employment withholding taxes
- Income taxes due within three years of the bankruptcy filing
- Tax penalties and fines
- Student loans

3 STRATEGIES TO MAXIMIZE WHAT YOU KEEP IN BANKRUPTCY

The following are the most important pre-bankruptcy planning strategies to ensure that you emerge from a Chapter 7 bankruptcy in the best possible position.

1. Convert Non-Exempt Wealth Into Exempt Wealth

While this generally works in negotiating with creditors at any time, it is especially useful in pre-bankruptcy planning because, to the extent your wealth is not exempt when you file, bankruptcy will cause you to lose it. It's that simple.

What does this mean to you? Much depends upon your state law, the liquidity of your assets, the time frame, and the creativity and experience of your asset protection lawyer. Some examples of this strategy in practice:

- Realizing that he would have to file a Chapter 7 bankruptcy in the next several years, Ken took a second mortgage out on the family's non-homestead vacation home to pay down the mortgage on the primary homestead home. More of Ken's savings were thus invested in an asset which is fully protected by his state's bankruptcy exemption.

- More than a year before she ended-up declaring bankruptcy under Chapter 7, Lee sold her valuable art collection and bought life insurance—an exempt asset under her state laws.

- Doston sold his homestead-protected home for financial reasons just as another creditor sued him. Doston transferred the remaining sale proceeds directly into another exempt asset—annuities. This is an example of the corollary tactic: when selling an exempt asset, direct the funds into another exempt asset.

These are several of the ways you can save unprotected wealth before filing for bankruptcy. Again, timing is everything. To make this strategy effective, you have to plan early and hire an asset protection expert to guide you safely through the often-hazardous waters of pre-bankruptcy planning.

2. Timely Transfer Non-Exempt Property Out Of Your Name

To the uninformed, this seems a simple strategy for defeating creditors in bankruptcy. "Just give everything to your spouse or kids before you file and when it's over, they'll give it back to you." Not only will this tactic be ineffective—as the trustee can undo the transfers, but it may also get you in trouble with the court.

So how can you use this strategy safely? The key is "Timing." Timing is everything in asset protection, and pre-bankruptcy planning in particular. You will see below that transfers made more than one year prior to bankruptcy are usually safe from the trustee's scrutiny. Does this mean that you can give away your property and then wait one year to file for bankruptcy? No.

However, you normally can save much of your wealth if you act early. The best tactic: a series of transfers to specific parties (for example, to children to pay for college or grad school, to a spouse or other family or friends for support, to charities, etc.). Should the trustee examine these transfers, he will see a pattern of regular conduct far in advance of filing bankruptcy, rather than as a last-ditch effort to defeat creditors. So, start early. Transfers made two years prior to filing for bankruptcy are safer than those made one year later.

Pre-Bankruptcy Planning

3. Encumber Assets

This strategy is similar in that it involves transfers of property. You may not think of encumbering assets with mortgages or secured loans as *transfers*, but you should. You are transferring the equity in your assets to a third party. In exchange, you get cash which you can spend or turn into an exempt asset.

Remember Ken who took out a second mortgage on a non-exempt asset and paid down the mortgage on a protected asset. This transferred equity from the vulnerable asset to the protected asset. Encumbering vulnerable assets also does this. In addition, encumbering non-exempt assets makes them less attractive to the bankruptcy trustee.

- An orthodontist with enormous debts mortgaged his vacation condominium to 90% of its value to a friendly lender. He then prepaid various expenses for the next two years. When he filed for a liquidation bankruptcy, the trustee had no interest in pursuing the condominium—not enough value.

- A podiatrist declared bankruptcy under Chapter 7. But, 18 months prior, he had taken loans pledging his stock portfolio as collateral. The cash was spent on such expenses as his children's college tuition and living expenses, and the stocks had lost value.

As with all loan transactions used in asset protection, mortgages must be well documented to hold-up under the scrutiny of the bankruptcy trustee. If you want to protect an asset or have expenses, this is an effective pre-bankruptcy tactic.

WHY TIMING IS CRUCIAL TO SUCCESSFUL PLANNING

Timing is crucial to successfully implement asset protection pre-bankruptcy strategies. Why? In addition to the regular fraudulent transfer rules which always apply, there are specific rules in bankruptcy. *A trustee examining a debtor's finances in a Chapter 7 will routinely ask the debtor about any transfers within one year of the bankruptcy. This is the one-year "look back" period and explains why transfers within that year will be moot. The trustee will know about them and, if there is enough equity involved, will overturn them.*

The trustee can still examine transfers beyond one-year. If the trustee suspects fraudulent conduct or finds inconsistencies in your bankruptcy disclosure statements, the trustee may examine transfers two or three years prior. So, act as soon as possible and delay your filing as long as possible.

BUYING TIME

Most people considering bankruptcy are usually extremely distressed, even panicky. They believe that their creditors will pound down their door at any minute and there is little, if any, time left! In most cases, they are wrong. There is time.

Understand what we call the *behavior pattern of creditors*. This holds true in the overwhelming majority of cases and can be taken advantage of by debtors who know what to expect. This pattern consists of three phases:

Phase 1: Intimidation

Once debts become overdue, the creditor will use every method at its disposal to get payment—letters and phone calls to intimidate you to pay.

Toward the end of this phase most debtors cave in and pay, declare bankruptcy, work out a payment plan, or better yet, come to our office. Understandably, debtors at this stage are extremely worn down, stressed, and generally intimidated. What they don't realize is that eventually this harassment will cease.

Phase 2: Dormancy

No matter what type of creditor you deal with—bank, savings and loan, finance company, supplier, IRS, etc., they all follow similar processes with delinquent accounts. After aggressively pursuing the debtor, they chart their course of action according to how the debtor has responded. If the debtor has tried to pay, they may loosen-up, as long as the debtor continues to pay. If the debtor stops paying, they will again become aggressive.

What happens to debtors who simply pay nothing? Usually, their account becomes a "long run" delinquent account receivable. These debts are often left for months, with no activity whatsoever. We have seen many debts, for millions of dollars, where the creditor does absolutely nothing to the debtor for many months because the creditor has temporarily given up on the account. While they may review the account every three months, and renew attempts to coerce the debtor, for the most part the debtor remains hassle-free.

Phase 3: Completion

Here, the debt is finally disposed of. The creditor may sell the account to a factoring company, write it off as bad debt, force the debtor into bankruptcy, or the debtor himself files for bankruptcy. In any case, the debtor and the creditor's relationship is over.

Pre-Bankruptcy Planning

Since this will be the typical life cycle of your debts, what can you do to take advantage? First, recognize that this pattern exists. This will give you more peace of mind during the intimidation period because you understand it is only temporary. Second, and more importantly, delay bankruptcy filing for as long as possible.

WHY YOU SHOULD DELAY FILING

Most people filing bankruptcy file too soon. By delaying your bankruptcy, you gain three key benefits:

1. You allow yourself the time to make asset-saving transfers

You need at least a year, preferably more, to make the transfers for asset protection. While you should make these transfers earlier, this is not always practical. Still, the sooner, the better. Nonetheless, even if you are completely stressed and it seems that creditors will force you into bankruptcy, do not panic. You are only ending phase 1. You will have more time once your creditor calls your account *long term delinquent*.

2. You allow more overdue taxes to be discharged

Income taxes are dischargeable, only if incurred three years prior to the filing of bankruptcy. Taxes incurred within three years stay with you after bankruptcy. Thus, if you have delinquent income taxes less than three years old, delay filing until you can get rid of your tax bills as well.

3. You give yourself time to pay certain creditors

Perhaps you have one significant creditor to which you cannot make payments, but have other small creditors (credit cards, etc.) which you do want to pay. You can pay them, but not within three months of the bankruptcy (or one year if the creditor is an insider, i.e. a family member). Such payments may be considered *preferences*, and be overturned by the bankruptcy trustee. Thus, the longer you delay bankruptcy, the more you can prefer certain creditors.

WHAT YOU MUST KNOW ABOUT BANKRUPTCY LAWYERS

Lawyers are supposed to have an uncompromising loyalty to you, the client. While you may have doubts about this, the legal ethics is clear: unless the client is about to commit a crime, an attorney's loyalty should be solely to the client. While this is true in most cases, bankruptcy is an exception. Bankruptcy lawyers also have a heightened responsibility to be officers of the court. While this duty exists for all lawyers, it seems even more pronounced for bankruptcy lawyers.

Why is this so important? Because the divided sense of loyalty most bankruptcy attorneys feel may affect the way they serve their clients. Often, these attorneys think their role is simply to assist the client in having their papers completed properly and on time and to ensure that the entire process goes smoothly. In essence, they act as an intermediary between you the client and the court and/or bankruptcy trustee.

What many do not see as their role is to counsel you on how to minimize your losses in bankruptcy. Many bankruptcy lawyers, in fact, won't discuss defensive pre-bankruptcy planning strategies. They consider it a breach of their loyalty to the court. You, as their client, will be "thrown to the wolves" with little, if any, protection if you file bankruptcy under their direction.

Many leading bankruptcy lawyers in this country would think our advice in this chapter is risky or somehow unethical. We, on the other hand, consider it unethical to fail to advise clients about the ways they can *legally* protect themselves from the devastation of bankruptcy. Pre-bankruptcy planning is completely legal and would be fully disclosed in bankruptcy documents or in testimony.

Why are these bankruptcy lawyers not helping their clients this way? The answers are: (a) they are too conservative, (b) they are too concerned with their relationships with local bankruptcy judges and trustees (with whom they must work every day), (c) they do not earn fees this way, and (d) they just do not know how to assist their clients in this way. The important question for you is: "What can I do to make sure I get the pre-bankruptcy advice I need to keep my assets?"

RETAIN AN ASSET PROTECTION LAWYER BEFORE HIRING A BANKRUPTCY LAWYER

Bankruptcy lawyers are generally not good asset protection lawyers. But, do not take our word on it. Speak to the leading bankruptcy lawyers in your community or, better yet, talk to their former clients. You'll probably discover that while these lawyers make the bankruptcy function smoothly, they do not do defensive asset protection. These strategies require planning year(s) ahead of the bankruptcy filing, but these lawyers usually only make fees during the bankruptcy process. So, that is what they focus on. Most bankruptcy lawyers also do not encourage non-bankruptcy solutions (like those outlined earlier) aimed at negotiating settlements without bankruptcy. Why? Because they make their fees in the bankruptcy process.

Clearly then, you do not want a run-of-the-mill bankruptcy attorney (or even a leading bankruptcy lawyer) handling your case alone. You want defensive asset protection, which they probably will not provide. On the other hand, you may want such a lawyer actually handling your bankruptcy, so you can benefit from their uncompromised relationship with the judges and trustees.

To get the best of both worlds, see an asset protection specialist first. Consult with an asset protection attorney as soon as bankruptcy seems a possible option. As noted, the earlier you implement asset protection, the better.

Once your assets and wealth have been shielded, and the plan solidified for at least a year (preferably 18 months to 3 years), then consider bankruptcy. Your bankruptcy attorney will argue hard for your case to the judges and trustees whom he sees every day and you are in a protected position.

SUMMARY

- Bankruptcy is a process by which debtors can either erase their debts or re-organize their finances.
- Chapter 7 bankruptcies are liquidations—erasing most debts, but also erasing all non-exempt property. What is exempt and non-exempt is controlled by state law.
- Bankruptcies under chapters 11 and 13 are both re-organizations—the debtor re-organizes finances according to a court-approved plan. The debtor keeps both his debts and his assets.
- Bankruptcy's three great benefits: it stops your creditors, it cancels your debts, and it is a powerful negotiating tool.
- Certain debts will not be discharged in Chapter 7 bankruptcy.
- Three powerful pre-bankruptcy planning strategies are *Timely Turn Non-Exempt Wealth Into Exempt Wealth; Timely Transfer Non-Exempt Property Out Of Your Name;* and, *Timely Encumber Assets.*
- Timing is crucial because of bankruptcy's one-year look back period. However, you probably have more time than you think to delay creditors.
- Do not rely solely on a bankruptcy lawyer—he or she will not adequately protect you before the bankruptcy begins. Instead, use an asset protection lawyer first and then see a bankruptcy attorney.

CHAPTER 16:

ASSET PROTECTION AND MEDICAID

A serious financial threat faces many Americans—a threat which, for many people, is not detected until it is too late. No, not estate taxes, although this hazard has much in common with estate taxes. In fact, both dangers must be effectively planned against, or they can cause financial ruin to the individual and his or her family. The threat we describe here is the need for long-term medical care, including long-term hospitalization, nursing home care, or long-term at-home assistance. Each year, millions of Americans spend their entire life savings before they qualify for government assistance, such as Medicaid. An entire lifetime of working and savings can be wiped out in a matter of months or even weeks.

How can asset protection strategies help individuals and families cope with the prospect of expensive medical or nursing home care? By protecting an individual's assets so the person can qualify for Medicaid under the government's restrictive qualifying tests without losing their savings to do so. In essence, by protecting your assets, you appear "paper poor" to the Medicaid application reviewer, yet enjoy a healthy standard of living and the ability to pass down your accumulated wealth to younger generations.

> **Note For Physicians**
> *This chapter deals extensively with the Medicaid program, health care, and nursing homes–topics about which you may be considerably more familiar with than most readers. Nevertheless, we write this chapter with a lay person in mind, so your spouse, family member friend, etc., can get as much from it as you will. Therefore, please do not be frustrated if we simplify that which you know to be more complex.*

A SERIOUS THREAT

While this may be obvious to doctors intimately familiar with medical economics, many people do not realize that their life-savings can be wiped out by the costs of long-term medical and nursing home care. For those who do not recognize costs involved here, consider:

- Nursing home care costs upwards of $100,000 per year. The national average: $40,000.

- Assuming a 5% annual inflation, average annual nursing home costs will rise to over $135,000 by 2021.

- Recent studies show that 1 in 3 Americans who lives to 65 will spend 3 months or more in a nursing home; 1 in 4 will spend a year or more; 1 in 11 will spend 5 years or more.

What does this tell you? *They demonstrate how quickly your or one of your family member's savings can be consumed by nursing home care.* What these statistics do not explain is how emotionally draining these expenses can be on the elder or infirmed person's family members. *Even if you are not the patient you often have as much to lose as the parent, or other friend or relative for whom you will provide support.*

In its recent article, "With Elder Care Comes a Professional and Personal Crisis," the *Wall Street Journal* showed the effects elder care can have on the younger "sandwich" generation. The article provided example after example of accomplished business people financially strained and emotionally drained by the challenge of caring for an elderly infirm family member. In a typical example, a successful female executive in the oil

Asset Protection and Medicaid

business foregoes a prominent position to work part-time, after both parents become ill in the same year. She can barely maintain her own career, not to mention enjoy a personal life, while becoming a care-giver and custodian for her parents.

Often, the financial and emotional pressures are even more severe on the younger generation caring for the elderly than on the sick parents themselves. "It's a familiar song," stated an executive at the National Council on Aging. "You can be competent in every part of your life and be blowing this one."

FACT: The Census Bureau projects that seniors over the age of 65 will make up 20% of U.S. population in 2020.

How can you avoid the emotional and financial strain involved in caring for your parents? Have your parents plan for a future medical catastrophe by protecting their savings in a way that allows them to qualify for government benefits, without consuming their assets.

ABOUT MEDICAID

Before you understand how you can structure your financial affairs to qualify for Medicaid, you must first understand what Medicaid is, and how it works.

Medicaid is a jointly financed federal-state program established to provide medical treatment for the poor and indigent. Medicaid only covers someone when savings and income are below threshold levels. Its benefits include prescription drugs, hospital treatment, physician care, and nursing home care—often the most valuable benefit for many people. Because Medicaid is funded and controlled partly by the states, each state has slightly different rules and regulations, both for eligibility requirements and for benefits.

Despite state variances, one powerful criticism of the Medicaid program accurately applies in all 50 states—*Medicaid is a force of destruction of the middle class elderly.* Why? Because only the middle class have their savings to lose (before they can qualify for Medicaid benefits). The rich have ample assets, income, and insurance to cover their health care needs. They do not need to worry about their savings "wasting away." On the other side, the poor automatically qualify for Medicaid benefits. They do not have any savings to worry about.

Who is left? Millions of middle class Americans, who have worked hard and saved over their lifetime, with the hope that they can retire comfortably and leave something to their children. Unfortunately, these are the people hit hardest by the Medicaid laws. They will not qualify, until they have become poor.

Typically, elder care lawyers describe two reactions they see in people losing their savings in order to qualify for Medicaid. Some feel like "chumps" because they worked too hard and saved for too long to have it all taken so quickly. "I should have lived life in the fast lane," many of these Depression-era people say, "rather than skimping and saving for years." Others have an even more troubling reaction, often bursting into tears or rage, feeling that their life's goal—leaving something to their children and grandchildren is literally vanishing before their eyes. Many now feel like failures.

Why does Medicaid create such emotional and financial stress? It largely stems from the way Medicaid laws determines who can qualify for benefits and when.

Here, we will examine one specific type of benefits—Medicaid nursing home benefits. These benefits are a good example for examining the program, because they are somewhat similar throughout the 50 states and, are often the most important benefits for many clients. Today, close to 45% of nursing home costs are paid by Medicaid. (Medicare, though a huge government program, is not a significant player in nursing home benefits.)

HOW YOU QUALIFY FOR MEDICAID NURSING HOME BENEFITS

To qualify for Medicaid nursing home benefits, in most states, you must meet three tests: (1) be eligible because of age or disability, (2) qualify under the income test, and (3) be eligible under the assets test. Only if you qualify under all three parts of the test will you be qualified for Medicaid nursing home benefits. (Some states do not have the income test.)

1. The Age/Disability Test

This is the most straightforward test and the one which makes the most sense. To pass this test, you must either be (1) over 65 years old or (2) physically or mentally disabled.

2. The Income Test

About 1/3 of the states have an income test. This test essentially sets a ceiling for your monthly income, if you are to be awarded Medicaid nursing home benefits. If your income exceeds this ceiling, you fail the test and cannot qualify for the benefits, unless your income subsidizes your nursing home costs.

The income level used in the test is controlled by state eligibility laws and varies greatly among these states. Moreover, it constantly changes with inflation, the economy, and even politics. Nonetheless, a federal law controls the amount of assets a spouse of a married applicant may have (see below) and this indirectly effects the amount of income the spouse may enjoy as well.

3. The Assets Test

If you pass both the age/disability test and the income test, your assets will be analyzed to see whether or not you qualify for Medicaid nursing home benefits. First, Medicaid laws segregate assets into two categories: *countable assets and non-countable assets. Then the laws apply a simple test: to be eligible for Medicaid nursing home benefits, you may not have more than $3,000 worth of countable assets. In essence, you must become poor to qualify.*

■ Non-Countable Assets

Non-countable assets are similar to exempt assets in chapter 5. They are exempt from the government's grasp. As such, Medicaid cannot considers them when determining whether you qualify for benefits. Thus, you can keep these assets and still qualify for Medicaid. Also, like the exemptions described in chapter 5, each state has its own set of non-countable assets and the differences are often significant. Thus, depending on your state's Medicaid laws, non-countable assets may include: *your primary residence, a designated amount of cash-value life insurance, a set-aside amount for a burial plot, household furnishings, one automobile, court-ordered support payments, and "inaccessible" assets.* Of course, there are value limits to many of these assets. So, the remaining equity is vulnerable.

■ Inaccessible Assets

Inaccessible assets are a sub-category of non-countable assets for Medicaid purposes. They are the key to the strategy involving Medicaid trusts discussed later in this chapter. *Inaccessible assets are ordinarily countable assets which, because of how they are titled, are considered by Medicaid to be non-countable.* To be inaccessible, the asset must be titled in such a way that the Medicaid applicant has no access to it now, or in the future. If the Medicaid applicant ever will own a legal interest in the asset or will gain the right to use or dispose of part of the asset, then the asset will become "accessible"—and, its value will be considered toward the $3,000 ceiling for total countable assets.

■ Countable Assets

All assets that are not non-countable are countable. In other words, everything is countable, except for those assets exempted as non-countable or inaccessible. This can include everything from stocks and bonds, vacation real estate, boats, and copyrights. If it is not specifically exempted under the Medicaid laws, then it will be counted towards the $3,000 total.

■ Assets of Spouse

If you're married, you cannot simply give all of your assets to your spouse to qualify for Medicaid, because federal law puts a limit on how much a non-applicant spouse may have in assets if the other is to qualify for benefits. In 1996, the non-applicant spouse was limited to $77,000. And, this is just a ceiling. Many states have their own rules and lower limits. Thus, Medicaid tries to insure that both you and your spouse will be poor before either of you qualify for Medicaid.

4. What This Test Means

In essence, the three-prong test for Medicaid nursing home benefits can be simply explained:

If you are elderly or disabled, if you do not make much money, and if you have less than $3,000 of countable assets, you qualify. If you have more than $3,000 in countable assets, we will only give you assistance after you have spent down your savings to this amount.

ASSET PROTECTION STRATEGY: MAXIMIZING NON-COUNTABLE ASSETS

The asset protection strategy we employ here is identical to those described in chapter 5. To defeat any creditor (other than the IRS or other federal government plaintiffs), a preferred tactic is to turn non-exempt assets into assets exempt under state law. This might include selling ordinary stocks and using the money to purchase a homestead or life insurance or annuities—all depending on which assets your state exempts. To beat the Medicaid application reviewer (or, in other words, the "Medicaid benefits creditor") you use the exact same strategy. Here, turning countable assets into non-countable assets.

Unfortunately, you have less flexibility with this strategy against the Medicaid system than against ordinary creditors using state exemption laws. At least this is true when comparing the exemptions here to that of the most protective states like Florida and Texas. Compared to the protections of the less liberal states, on the other hand, you can do a lot more here to protect your savings and still beat the Medicaid creditor.

Which are the key non-countable assets to use in employing this strategy?

■ The Home

Because the primary residence is considered a non-countable asset under Medicaid analysis in most states, consider pouring as much of your savings into the home as possible. Be creative. Add an addition to the home or make some long-awaited improvements. However, check with a local professional who knows your state's rules regarding the amount of the exemption and the type residence that qualifies. Also, do not pour more cash into the home than you can afford. Your comfortable retirement is the goal of this exercise.

■ Jointly-Owned Assets

Jointly-owned assets can be useful for joint tenants (usually husband and wife) where one tenant is applying for Medicaid and the other is not. This is because Medicaid generally treats jointly-owned assets as if each tenant (spouse) owns one-half the asset, unless the non-applicant spouse can show that his/her contribution to the asset was more than one-half. If so, only the remaining portion will be counted as the applicant's. Thus, at most only one-half of the value of jointly-owned stocks, real estate, etc. will be considered a countable asset for the assets test.

One exception to this rule: Jointly-owned bank accounts are all presumed to be owned by the Medicaid applicant, unless the non-applicant can demonstrate his/her contribution to the account. If so, his/her contribution share of the account will not be counted in the assets test.

■ Inaccessible Assets

Inaccessible assets are assets which would ordinarily be considered countable, but are considered non-countable because of how they are owned. Because the Medicaid applicant cannot get to the asset itself, neither can the Medicaid program. Yet, for our purposes, do not simply give away the asset. This is not an ideal asset protection strategy. Instead, benefit from the asset by being able to take income from it while still having it designated *inaccessible*. How do we create this? With the *Irrevocable Medicaid Trust*, described later.

TIMING IS ALSO CRUCIAL IN MEDICAID PLANNING

Throughout this book, we continually emphasized the importance of implementing asset protection strategies early. Nowhere is this more true than in asset protection planning against Medicaid. Early planning is especially important when it comes to Medicaid because the federal Medicaid laws have specific periods. Rather than a more flexible court analysis of "probable" versus "possible" creditor which occurs in run-of-the mill fraudulent transfer claims, planning for Medicaid must satisfy particular statutes or it is completely ineffective.

The Medicaid program has a "look back" period of 36 months. The Medicaid application reviewer will look back 36 months to see what assets an applicant owned over that time period. If the applicant transferred assets during that time period, these assets previously owned but transferred will be added back into the applicant's balance sheet for purposes of the assets test. In some states, the look back is longer for assets which were once owned by the applicant and are now owned by a trust (for example, Medi-Cal rules at work in California designate a 60-month look back period in such situations). Have a professional consult your state rules for Medicaid planning.

What does the 36-month look back period mean to asset protection strategies? That the individual looking ahead at diminishing savings and a need for nursing home care has two choices. Either:

Asset Protection and Medicaid

(1) To keep enough in savings and other countable assets to pay for 36 months worth of private pay medical care and then apply for Medicaid benefits; or
(2) Protect the assets and savings at least 36 months in advance and obtain Medicaid benefits as well.

The best strategy is (2). Protect yourself in advance and then receive the same benefits you would under scenario (1) without losing any hard-earned savings just to qualify. As mentioned, 36 months of private pay can easily be enough to wipe out even large savings. If you or your family members are between poor and wealthy, you cannot afford to ignore asset protection planning. It can literally save your life's savings.

THE MEDICAID TRUST

Chapter 10 discussed irrevocable trusts. Like all trusts, the irrevocable trust is created by a settlor and administered by a trustee who has *legal title* to trust assets and who runs the trust for the benefit of beneficiaries. The beneficiaries have "equitable title" to trust assets. Irrevocable trusts are useful for asset protection purposes because the settlor cannot undo or modify the trust, so the settlor's creditors cannot. The Medicaid trust is simply another type of irrevocable trust specifically designed to shield a person's assets from the grasp of the Medicaid program.

■ ABC's Of The Medicaid Trust

The Medicaid Trust is like any other irrevocable trust, created to protect trust assets from creditors, with one significant exception. Where other asset-protecting irrevocable trusts could not allow the grantor to be a trust beneficiary, the Medicaid Trust is designed so the grantor is the income beneficiary of the trust. However, there are usually restrictions on the amount of income which the grantor can take and when such income payments shall cease.

■ How Medicaid Trusts Are Structured

For the most effective way to structure a Medicaid Trust, observe the following case:

Case Study: *Medicaid Trust Helps Charlotte*

Charlotte and Izzy are the parents of Michael, a chiropractor near Portland, Oregon. After hearing about Medicaid trusts, Michael thought his parents should create one. Neither had serious health problems now, but they were not getting younger and they had little in the way of savings. Their house was paid off, but the market was weak where they lived. Their main income came from a stock portfolio and social security.

After Michael convinced them to consult an elder-care lawyer, Charlotte and Izzy set-up a Medicaid Trust, naming Michael the trustee. They named themselves as the two beneficiaries while one was alive and named their living trust the beneficiary when the surviving spouse died. They would then pass their savings down just as they would without a Medicaid Trust.

Charlotte and Izzy funded the trust with their stock portfolio. The trust agreement gave Michael discretion of how much income to pay to either of them when neither was applying for Medicaid benefits. In the event that either applied for Medicaid, Michael was instructed to pay no income to that parent. All income payments would be made to the non-applicant spouse. If both applied to Medicaid, no income payments were to be made—the income would carry over, leaving more savings to their grandchildren when both died, through their living trust.

After 36 months, the stocks were no longer countable under the Medicaid test. When Izzy eventually applied to the program five years later, the stocks were designated inaccessible. Thus, Izzy could qualify for benefits without spending down the value of the stocks. Also, Michael could pay the excess income each month to Charlotte. By using a Medicaid Trust, Izzy and Charlotte protected their savings and maintained their total income while Izzy qualified for Medicaid.

An alternative Medicaid Trust structure involves allowing the beneficiary/grantor to receive income without discretion by the trustee. However, here the income amount must be low enough that it does not prevent the

Asset Protection and Medicaid

beneficiary from failing the Medicaid income test. While this structure is limited as to the amount of income it can provide, it does protect the assets of the applicant and is often used when the grantor does not have a spouse who can 'shield' the extra income.

THREE IMPORTANT CLAUSES FOR YOUR MEDICAID TRUST

A good Medicaid Trust has these provisions:

1. No Principal to Income Beneficiaries — The income beneficiaries are the grantors and future Medicaid applicants. They cannot have any right to the principal of the trust assets; only the income. If they reach principal, then the assets will not be considered *inaccessible*, and Medicaid will count their value in their assets test.

2. Irrevocability — As with all asset protection trusts, this one must be irrevocable. If the trust is revocable, such as a living trust or *loving trust*, then assets owned by the trust will not be deemed inaccessible. Remember, if you can undo the trust, so can creditors and the Medicaid program.

3. The Use Of Trust Assets For Medical Care Prohibited — This is similar to the clause recommended for foreign asset protection trusts, which expressly excludes creditors as beneficiaries. The theory is the same: prevent a court/Medicaid evaluation from concluding that the trustee can transfer assets to the beneficiary to pay for medical debts. This clause only secures the fact that trust assets will not be viewed as available for medical expenses.

TWO LEGAL DEVICES EVERY ELDERLY PERSON SHOULD HAVE

Every year, millions of elderly Americans suffer illnesses that leave them incapacitated. While this is difficult enough on family and loved ones, even more frustrating can be the legal and financial problems that occur when others are trying to get the sick person's affairs in order. To help ease these burdens and make the life of family members and loved ones easier, the elderly people in your family (including yourself at some point) should have two legal devices before they become incapacitated:

1. A Durable Power Of Attorney

This legal document gives another the right to make decisions for you. Such power can be restricted to certain functions (a durable power of attorney for health care decisions or only for property decisions). If you have a trusted person in mind, such as a spouse or child, then he should be given a power of attorney for both health care and financial/legal affairs. That way, if you are ever incapacitated, you know that your wishes will be carried out.

2. A Living Will

This legal document directs a certain course of medical action if you can no longer make decisions or communicate them to others. The main drawback here is that you must be a "qualified patient" before it is activated and there usually must be a diagnosis by multiple physicians that your illness is terminal before treatment will be discontinued.

Asset Protection and Medicaid

SUMMARY

- The threat that a family member's savings will be wiped out by catastrophic illness or long-term nursing home care is very real and as dangerous as any lawsuit.
- Even if your medical care is taken care of, caring for a loved one brings severe financial and emotional strain.
- Medicaid, because of the way it tests applicants, forces middle-income Americans to consume their life savings, before they can receive the medical benefits they need.
- An applicant must pass the age/disability, income, and asset tests, before they can qualify for benefits.
- Medicaid will only consider "countable" assets in the asset test, not "non-countable" or "inaccessible" assets.
- The asset protection strategy at work here: Maximize Your Non-Countable Assets. Key assets for this strategy include the home, other jointly-owned assets, and inaccessible assets.
- Timing is crucial here because of Medicaid's "look back" period.
- The Medicaid Trust, an irrevocable trust, is a key asset protection tool in this type planning.
- Your Medicaid Trust must be irrevocable. It must allow the applicant only to get at income (no principal), and should ban the use of trust assets for medical care.
- Every person should eventually establish a durable power of attorney and a living will, before becoming incapacitated.

CHAPTER 17:

THE TYPICAL PHYSICIAN'S ASSET PROTECTION PLAN

Congratulations! You have read some dry (although we tried to make it interesting) material, covering many topics and legal principles, all with one goal—preserving your financial security. We know that, as a doctor, you are busy. Therefore, to sacrifice your time and energy deserves a warm and hearty congratulations. You earned it.

Still, you have not completed your mission. In fact, you have only taken the first step toward your secure financial future. You still need to complete this first step, and then a few more. This chapter explains the final steps and how you can easily carry them out.

Here, you learn how we typically structure most of our physician clients. While your situation may differ from our "Doctor Jones" example, in our joint experiences, we have found that most physicians can be adequately protected with the planning we outline in this chapter.

We encourage you to read this chapter, to use the "Financial Assessment Worksheets" in the appendices, and to determine your vulnerability to lawsuits and other threats.

Dr. Jones: Our Typical Physician Client

Here we illustrate what kind of planning most of our physician clients use when they come to us for assistance. We also provide an example of what the various entities and planning cost. To demonstrate our planning, we use the example of Dr. Jones. Let's assume Dr. Jones is a 52-year-old cardiologist in a practice with 4 partners and 6 employees. He has a spouse (50) and 2 kids (15, and 17).

Dr. Jones' Lawsuit Concerns:
- Malpractice liability (he has insurance but concerned about judgments in excess of coverage limits)
- Non-malpractice claims (he has his own practice with some employees)
- Personal lawsuits (he has teenage drivers, some rental real estate, etc.)

Dr. and Mrs. Jones' Assets:
- Home ($300,000 equity) owned jointly (no tenancy by the entirety)
- Vacation condominium ($150,000 equity) owned jointly
- Profit sharing plan (in his practice) $800,000
- IRA $350,000
- Cash, CDs, bank accounts $75,000
- Life insurance - $1 million policy on him ($20,000 cash value), owned by her
- Cars and various other lower-equity assets

Jones Family Goals:
1. Protect as much of their assets from lawsuits without losing control
2. Create a thorough tax-saving estate plan
3. Avoid any common planning pitfalls

Jones & Partners' Practice Tax Goals:
- Purchase benefits for the partners with pre-tax dollars (deductions)
- Put more away for their retirement in tax-favored dollars (deductions)

Certainly, not all of our doctors fit this exact profile. Many are not married or are in their second marriage and our planning needs to be slightly different. Also, many of our clients have either more or less in assets than does our fictional Dr. Jones. As necessary, we create fewer or additional structures to shield the build-up of wealth as the physician continues through his/her career.

The Typical Physician's Asset Protection Plan

■ Step 1: We Protect Your Assets

Our first mission for clients who come to us for asset protection–as opposed to those who come primarily for estate planning–is to shield their assets from all types of outside threats. For the Jones family, we would recommend the following:

• **HOME**: We check the homestead exemption in the client's state. Assuming that the protection is inadequate (as it is in 48 of 50 states), we employ further protections. This may include using a QPRT– an irrevocable trust which protects the home, but allows Dr. and Mrs. Jones to live in the house for 20+ years. After that period, the house goes to the children, but they still live there, by paying rent. This protects the home from all lawsuits, and saves all estate taxes on the home.

Depending on the circumstances, we might also use an FLP to own the home. This has certain tax disadvantages. But, if a lawsuit threat is more menacing, we use a very protective device, a QPRT.

• **VACATION CONDO:** This piece of property will definitely be transferred to a stand-alone entity, either an FLP or LLC. This will (1) immunize all of the other Jones family wealth from any lawsuits from the condo, (2) protect the condo from any lawsuits from Dr. Jones' practice and other outside lawsuits, and (3) reduce income and estate taxes. Of course, Dr. and Mrs. Jones maintain 100% control of the condo at all times.

• **PROFIT-SHARING PLAN:** We will analyze whether or not the plan is ERISA-qualified. If it is, and the Joneses do not have an IRS problem, we may leave the plan alone, as it is protected by ERISA. If it is not, we have a number of choices. We might want to amend the plan to have it qualify for ERISA protection. We might also explore transferring the funds to an offshore trust to purchase tax-deferred investments (like annuities). While a tax is paid upon purchase, if the main concern is protecting against an imminent lawsuit, the cost is well justified.

We might also want to use a closely-held insurance company (CIC) as a substitute tax-favored retirement vehicle. As discussed in the special bonus chapter 18, the CIC is asset protected and allows significant tax benefits as well.

If there is no lurking creditor problem, we may leave the plan alone. However, we will continually communicate with the physicians and make the proper planning choices if circumstances change.

- **IRA:** Again, we examine the exemption in the client's state. If the protection is weak, as it typically is, we may want to shield these funds. This might include transferring the funds into an FLP or LLC, an offshore trust, or a domestic profit-sharing plan which keeps tax-deferral and qualifies for ERISA. We often create such a plan for the physician who has other part-time work (consulting, moonlighting, etc.).

- **LIFE INSURANCE:** Owned in either of their names personally, the cash value of the policy and proceeds themselves are exposed to lawsuits and creditor claims. For these reasons, the policy should be transferred to an ILIT. However, even more important, are the estate tax concerns discussed below.

- **OTHER ASSETS:** If the equity of the other assets is significant, it might make sense to own them in other FLPs or LLCs. These, of course, maintain 100% control with Dr. and Mrs. Jones. They also protect the assets themselves and isolate their liability risks. This may be especially important for cars or boats which the children may operate.

■ Step 2: Create a Tax-Saving, Pitfall-Free Estate Plan/Avoid Common Errors

The second goal for most of our clients is to create a thorough estate plan which avoids all common pitfalls. After all, what is the good in shielding your hard-earned wealth if you end-up leaving most of it to the courts, lawyers, and the IRS? While many clients come to us without basic estate planning documents (i.e., wills or living trusts), they generally recognize the need for such planning.

In the Jones family's case, we would recommend the following:

- **Living trust/pour-over will**

These are the basic estate-planning documents. They save the family thousands of dollars in probate fees, and create significant estate tax savings. As the Joneses have built a taxable estate (greater than $1.25 million as of 1998), they require estate tax planning. Even with normal inflationary growth, their estate tax bill runs into thousands of dollars, when their joint life expectancy ends. With a properly drafted living trust (with A-B provisions), they may save over $250,000 in estate taxes.

The living trust also allows their family to avoid the delay and publicity of probate.

• Powers of attorney for healthcare & financial affairs

These documents are essential for an orderly administration of one's affairs, if one becomes incapacitated. These are simple documents which we typically package with the living trust and will. In our example, Dr. and Mrs. Jones should also execute these documents.

• Irrevocable life insurance trust (ILIT)

The irrevocable life insurance trust (ILIT) is the most overlooked estate planning document in the plans of the physicians we see as clients. In fact, one of the most common pitfalls we see among new clients is that they have a cash value life insurance policy owned in the physician or spouse's name. This has three problems: (1) any cash value is vulnerable to lawsuits (unless it's protected by state exemptions); (2) when the second spouse dies, the proceeds will be subject to estate tax; (3) the proceeds are paid out and can be subject to the kids' creditors.

A properly-structured ILIT solves all of these problems. It protects the cash value from all creditors of both spouses, it eliminates all estate taxes on the proceeds, and it allows the family more flexibility on how the proceeds are eventually paid to children and grandchildren, often paying them amounts over time (i.e., at age 25, 30, 35) with spendthrift provisions that protect all funds from their creditors in the future.

In the Jones family example, because they have an estate in excess of the exemption amount, when the last of Dr. and Mrs. Jones dies, half of the $1 million proceeds goes to the IRS. That means $500,000 straight to the IRS. Why should the Joneses be paying premiums when only half of the benefit of their investment goes to their family? By using an ILIT to own the policy, the Joneses give $500,000 more to their children or grandchildren. The only cost–about $2,000 for an effective ILIT and supervision by an attorney.

Further, by using the ILIT, the $20,000 cash value is protected from creditors and the Joneses have more control on how the proceeds are used after they are gone. Given these benefits, who wouldn't spend a couple thousand dollars to establish and fund the ILIT? Obviously, we would recommend the ILIT to Dr. and Mrs. Jones.

■ Step 3: Create a Tax-Saving Plan for Dr. Jones' Practice

A. Allow the Practice to Provide Pre-tax Benefits to Physicians Only

Many physicians, like Dr. Jones, would like to take more benefits out of their practice in a tax-favored way without providing those same benefits to their employees. With ERISA pension and profit-sharing plans, employees must be included. However, with a unique planning vehicle called a VEBA, Dr. Jones and his partners could purchase life insurance and disability benefits with tax-favored dollars -- and not offer equal benefits to their employees.

We would definitely recommend Dr. Jones and his partners investigate a VEBA for their practice. For more about VEBAs, see chapter 18.

B. Allow the Practice to Add Another Asset-Protected "Pension" through a CIC

Dr. Jones and his partners have desired to put away more money into retirement plans through deduction from their practice. However, they have maximized contributions to their profit-sharing plan. The CIC could allow them to put significant amounts away every year into a tax-deferred vehicle and get a deduction in the process. Further, these funds would be asset protected against any creditor.

We would recommend the CIC to Dr. Jones and his partners. See more about the CIC in chapter 18.

IF YOU ALREADY HAVE A PLAN

Many of our clients already have some or all of these documents in place. They may have complex estate plans and even asset protection entities created by other attorneys. Often, these clients want us to review their documents–either they seek a second opinion regarding the effectiveness of their plan or they know that their documents are old and that recent tax changes require that they be updated.

If the concerns are asset protection or federal estate tax planning, our firms can adequately handle such review for clients throughout the nation. In addition, we work with local attorneys to handle matters of state law, primarily probate. Very often, a review of existing documents and certain amendments to those documents are what is required to go from an incomplete or outdated plan to one that is up-to-date and comprehensive.

SPECIAL BONUS:

FINANCIAL RISKS EVERY DOCTOR MUST AVOID

As a physician, you certainly consider all your patient's symptoms as well as his individual and family medical history before making a diagnosis. Additionally, when dealing with the diagnosed condition, there are numerous possible treatments, each useful in different ways.

You must handle your finances as you handle your patients—comprehensively. Why address only one symptom of uncertainty—lawsuits—when other dangers also threaten your financial security? What are these dangers? Poor investments, income and estate taxes, inflation, interest rate fluctuation, accidental death, disability, and depreciation, to name a few.

Only when you understand all potential threats, can you adequately protect yourself from them. An integrated plan that protects against all risks will allow you to sleep well, knowing that in the morning, and each morning thereafter, your savings remain safe. From this section, you will learn to diagnose the key threats to your family's finances. More importantly, you will understand the many tools available to better protect you from such threats.

RISK #1—Bad Investments & Stock Market Crashes

Of all the financial risks, this is the most obvious. It is so with many prospective clients who seek our advice. Now that many more people are in the market— investing in stocks and mutual funds— this risk has also taken on more importance on a global level.

Stock Markets: An Obedient Pet or Wild Beast?

Before we detail how to reduce the downside risk of investing in stocks, consider an analogy. Consider an investment in the stock market like having a wild animal for a pet. You may love your pet for the benefits the pet offers, including the novelty and security you enjoy from walking around your neighborhood with a pet lion on a leash. No matter how much you and your pet bond, something lurks in the back of your mind. You can take the animal out of the wild, but can you ever take the wild out of the animal? At any moment, your once-wonderful pet could turn into your worst nightmare.

In many ways, this is the same as investing in the stock markets. You may have done well with your investments over the past 5-10 years, but the market has hardly been tamed. American investors with recent success have developed potentially destructive attitudes about the stock market. As so many investments have returned great results in the past decade, many investors have forgotten the potential downside. Many investors, especially baby boomers, think that the market will continue to rise ... always. Inquisitive clients ask, "Why shouldn't it continue?" Let us provide an answer.

Supply, Demand & The Baby Boomers

The success of the stock market (and mutual funds market, of course) over the past 20 years has chiefly been driven by supply-demand economics and U.S. demographics. The economic theory of supply and demand, so often applied to a product and its price, applies also to the stock market.

We would say that when there are more buyers than sellers for a specific stock, and the supply of that stock remains constant, its price will increase. Similarly, when more people are saving (buying stocks) than spending (selling stocks), the stock market (measured by the S&P 500) will also increase.

The baby boomer generation, including 75.8 million Americans born between 1946 and 1964, now represents over 70 million of America's population of 265 million (see table).

Age Group	Population
35-53 (baby boomers)	70 million
54-64	24 million
65+	34 million

So, 94 million (70 million + 24 million) Americans are in their prime earning and saving periods, with only 34 million in spending mode (retirement). This demographic anomaly has created a magnificent inflow of capital to 401(k) plans, pension plans, profit-sharing plans, IRAs, mutual funds, annuities, brokerage accounts and other vehicles which distribute the funds primarily into stock investments. The supply of investment capital has then grown significantly, while the demand for capital (those withdrawing capital to live in retirement) has been very small in comparison. As we would expect, the price of stocks—as measured by the S&P 500—has increased terrifically.

Though this has been great for investing, you must consider the potential downside for future investors. Since 70 million people are 35-53 and only 58 million are 54 or older, we will probably see a continued rise in the S&P 500 for another few years. The baby boomers cannot take money out of their qualified plans until they turn 59½. This could begin in 6 years, though the average boomer won't retire for 15 years. As they retire, their deposits will end and large withdrawals will begin. Without some major increases in savings rates of Generation Xers in the U.S. to offset these huge withdrawals, the stock markets should severely decline. When this will happen and how much the stock market will slide is unknown.

Ten years ago, we predicted that this fall wouldn't really begin until the baby boomers turned 65 or 70. However, companies are enforcing mandatory retirement ages and giving incentives for early retirement, so the average retirement age is getting younger.

Whether it begins in the next five or fifteen years, the retiring baby boomers will cause the following: less cash to be available for investments, a market drop, and more failed companies. The supply-demand formula will work in reverse—with the S&P dropping at least as rapidly as it has grown over the past decade.

Can you reduce your risk in stock investments?

Many investment advisers talk about diversification and how it protects you from investment risks. To analyze their assertions, you must first understand the three types of risk in any stock investment:

Firm-specific risk
Industry risk
Market risk

The truth is that diversifying your portfolio, while extremely important, protects you only against firm-specific risk and industry risk. Let's look at an example:

> Dr. Correa is considering where to invest his hard earned money. From his research, he becomes impressed with Flyaway Air, its low cost strategy, and its new CEO. If he invests in Flyaway, his firm-specific risks include: its employees going on strike, the CEO quitting, a problem with its scheduling software, a crash on one of its flights, or other bad luck the company may encounter. If Dr. Correa invests in an airline sector mutual fund, rather than Flyaway, a drop in Flyaway share will not greatly effect his total investment. Thus, he has diversified out of firm-specific risk.

However, the doctor still has industry risk. The air traffic controllers could strike again; fuel prices could skyrocket, air crashes could scare people from flying for a while—all which could effect the airline industry. Though investing in a sector fund is less risky than investing in a single stock, the risk is still too great for the expected return. To reduce risk, Dr. Correa could spread his money across many industries. For example, a diversified S&P Index fund would protect against both firm and industry risk and insulate him from industry-specific risk. A downturn in one or two industries would not significantly threaten overall performance.

Is the doctor's investment then protected against all risks? *NO*. We still have *market risk,* or risk that the entire market will decline in value.

When advisers discuss *diversification* or *asset allocation* to reduce risk, they are concerned with firm and industry risk, not market risk—the risk that the entire market will drop. The best they can do is spread your wealth between different assets—stocks, bonds and real estate. Let's examine each separately.

Real estate may not be an attractive alternative. The market could be inflated, interest rates could be high, or you just may not be comfortable betting your retirement on an investment about which you know nothing. Further, real estate is an active investment, requiring the landowner/landlord's time and energy for a decent return. For example, one client recently complained that he spent Christmas taking care of a broken heating unit in a rental property. This commitment may not fit with your time demands, interests, and life goals.

What about **corporate and government bonds** and **money market securities**? Later, we discuss inflation risk. But, these investments have returned only 5% per year since 1926, compared to 12% for stocks. Consider these investments on an inflation-adjusted basis, and you will see that you may actually lose *real* money by investing in these classes of investments.

How to eliminate market risk and enjoy stock market returns

You may now feel caught in a Catch-22. You must invest in stocks to build a nest egg to retire, but the market risk looms large as the baby boomers retire. Can you take advantage of the stock market without subjecting your retirement to substantial market risks? Yes—with one investment class we found after extensive research done in preparation of another investment book. These investments are called *Insured Mutual Fund Management Plans (IMFMPs)*.

IMFMPs are mutual fund stock investments that are insured against loss of principal by a third party insurance company, if held by the investor for a minimum number of years. IMFMPs are *managed* mutual fund plans. A money manager uses mutual funds to maximize investor return. The most successful plans use a combination of index funds, which reduce transaction costs and management fees, increasing the investor's net returns. One IMFMP using index funds which we recommend returned over 60% in 1998 without investor risk.

IMFMPs are not easy to find. Fewer than a dozen *Registered Investment Advisers (RIAs)* have insurance coverage on their managed mutual fund accounts. This is not surprising because an adviser must register with the SEC and have an exemplary mutual fund risk management record for at least five years to qualify for insurance. He must then convince an insurer that his method of managing funds, a definable and quantifiable strategy, is worthy of their guarantee ... no small task.

How does the IMFMP work for the physician?

Most IMFMP managers require minimum investments of $25,000, though investments are commonly $100,000 to $1,000,000 and can be made within a pension or retirement plans, brokerage account, annuity or life insurance policy. These funds are insured if you allow the money manager to invest your funds for a continuous five year period.

The funds are available to the investor at any time during the five-year period without any load or surrender charge. However, the insurance is only valid if the money is left with the advisor for five years. During that five year period, you may withdraw 10% of your investment every year without disqualifying the insurance. The insurance contract is then modified to reflect your reduction in principal.

Perhaps the most attractive feature of the insured funds is that you can "lock-in" your gains. If, at any time, during the five year contract the investor wants to lock in the appreciated amount, he can do so by beginning a new contract which will start on the new date with the appreciated investment as the "new" principal. Let's look at an example:

> Dr. Peng invests $500,000 in an IMFMP from his existing pension—a 401k, IRA or other retirement account. On March 15, 1999, the warranty is that Dr. Peng will receive the larger of: (1) the appreciated value of the fund or (2) his original $500,000 investment on March 15, 2004.

Dr. Peng doesn't worry about his investment over the next year because the principal is insured. However, on January 25, 2000, the value of his account is $650,000, a 30% gain over the last 10 months. *Dr. Peng then utilizes an additional benefit of his IMFMP, and extends his contract another year. His modified contract now insures his $650,000 against loss through January 15, 2006.* If the investment is through a retirement account and cannot be withdrawn until age 59½, there is no reason why Dr. Peng shouldn't extend his contract each year the investment appreciates. He then enjoys the upside of stock market investing without risk of lost principal.

Unlike mutual funds which charge fees for stock-picking that is generally inferior to index fund investing, IMFMPs like those we recommend charge similar fees as mutual fund investments, and are insured against loss. For the same management fees charged by index funds, you enjoy stock market gains while insuring against FIRM, INDUSTRY, and MARKET RISK. This unique strategy truly reduces your risk in stock investments.

Risk #2—Taxes

There are only two certainties, death and taxes. To combat this truism, there are some tax benefits from many asset protection tools noted earlier in the book, namely limited partnerships and trusts. But, there are more effective ways to reduce or eliminate capital gains and estate taxes. To see why this is so important, consider how much Uncle Sam is really taking from you. First, a percentage of your earnings through income taxes.

1999 INCOME TAX RATE SCHEDULES

SINGLE					
Taxable Income is Over	But Not Over	The Tax is	Plus	Of the Amount Over
$0	25,750	-	15%	$0
25,750	62,450	$3,862.50	28	25,750
62,450	130,250	14,138.50	31	62,450
130,250	283,150	35,156.50	36	130,250
283,150	—	90,200.50	39.6	283,150

MARRIED FILING JOINTLY & QUALIFYING WIDOW(ER)				
Taxable Income is Over	But Not Over	The Tax is	Plus	Of the Amount Over
$0	$43,050	-	15%	$0
43,050	104,050	$6,457.50	28	43,050
104,050	158,550	23,537.50	31	104,050
158,550	283,150	40,432.50	36	158,550
283.150	-	85,288.50	39.6	283,150

HEAD OF HOUSEHOLD

Taxable Income is Over	But Not Over	The Tax is	Plus	Of the Amount Over
$0	$34,550	-	15%	$0
34,550	89,150	$5,182.50	28	34,550
89,150	144,400	20,470.50	31	89,150
144,400	283,150	37,598.00	36	144,400
283,150	-	87,548.00	39.6	283,150

MARRIED FILING SEPARATELY

Taxable Income is Over	But Not Over	The Tax is	Plus	Of the Amount Over
$0	$21,525	-	15%	$0
$21,525	52,025	$3,228.75	28	$21,525
52,025	79,275	11,768.75	31	52,025
79,275	141,575	20,216.25	36	79,275
141,575	-	42,644.25	39.6	141,575

Let's assume you invest your hard-earned after-tax dollars in stocks, bonds or real estate. If these investments appreciate, Uncle Sam takes another piece in capital gains taxes.

CAPITAL GAINS TAX RATE SCHEDULES, EFF. MAY 7, 1997

If your income tax rate it	Your capital gains tax rate is
15%	10%
28%-39.6%	20%

If your income tax rate is 15%, then your capital gains tax rate will be 10%. In all other tax brackets, you will pay 20%. Now, you pay taxes on money earned, and taxes on appreciated after-tax investments. Uncle Sam isn't finished. If you die with substantive assets, he dips in again with estate taxes.

ESTATE TAX RATE SCHEDULES, EFF. MAY 7, 1997

Value of Estate or Gift Above	But Less Than	Total Estate Tax Due	Tax Rate on Excess
$650,000	$750,000	$155,800	37%
750,000	1,000,000	248,300	39%
1,000,000	1,250,000	345,800	41%
1,250,000	1,500,000	448,300	43%
1,500,000	2,000,000	555,800	45%
2,000,000	2,500,000	780,800	49%
2,500,000	3,000,000	1,025,800	53%
3,000,000	10,000,000	1,290,800	55%
10,000,000	21,040,000	5,140,800	60%
21,040,000	-	-	55%

As an example of how these taxes could affect you, consider $100,000 of earnings you make at age 35. If you invest in an S&P index fund that returns 12% per year which you sell at 70 and live off the interest until you die at 85, you will incur the following tax liability.

First, your $100,000 of earnings are taxed approximately 35% (federal and state income taxes). $35,000 goes to the government, leaving you $65,000.

If you invest in stocks with your $65,000 for a return of 12% for 35 years before retiring, you have $3,431,975. Sound great? Unfortunately, when you sell this to purchase an income producing investment, you owe $686,395 in capital gains taxes.

However you still have $2,745,580 for your retirement. A more conservative investment yielding 7% on your $2.5 million gives you $192,191 each year. Income taxes of $76,876 on this income leave you $115,314 annually. Not bad. You get $115,314 per year after the IRS takes their unfair share. But, you still pay taxes on that original $100,000.

When you die, with $2,745,580, estate taxes will vary based on your total estate. Approximately 50% of your estate (or $1,372,790) will be due, in cash, nine months after your death.

IRS Taxes Received From Your $100,000 of Earnings

Income Tax	$100,000 x 35%	$35,000
Capital Gains Tax	$3,431,975 x 20%	$686,395
Income Tax on Retirement Disbursements	$192,191 x 40% x 15 years	$1,153,144
Estate Tax	$2,745,580 x 50%	$1,372,790
Total Taxes Paid		$3,247,329

Why sit back and take what the IRS gives you? You have the right to legally reduce your taxes, the legendary judge Learned Hand, said: "Anyone may so arrange his affairs so that his taxes shall be as low as possible. He is not bound to choose that pattern which best pays the treasury. There is not even a patriotic duty to increase one's taxes." Let's take a look at the best tax tools available.

HOW PHYSICIANS CAN REDUCE THEIR TAXES

One of the top asset protection tools is also one of the best tax-planning tools—the *closely-held insurance company (CIC)*, briefly discussed in chapter 11. This essential planning vehicle is explained through the following article recently published, presented with permission here:

Benefits of Insurance Company Ownership For Physicians

As frequent speakers to physicians on asset protection and tax-favored wealth planning, we are often asked about captive insurance companies and how physicians can use them for both types of planning. This article addresses the use of so-called "captives," or tax-exempt closely-held insurance companies (CICs). Certainly, CICs may be ideal tools, if established and maintained properly, and if suited to the individual physician's or group's economic need. In this article, we examine the benefits and costs of CICs and then demonstrate a case study of an physician using one.

What is a CIC

The CIC is a legitimate insurance company, licensed to write insurance in the U.S., registered with the IRS, but typically based in an offshore jurisdiction, such as Bermuda or the British Virgin Islands. Most CICs are established in these countries because they require a smaller capitalization and they have favorable insurance laws and tax treatment. Although funds in the CICs can be maintained and managed in the U.S., offshore CICs have grown to over 4,000 companies, writing an estimated $60 billion in premium per year, or more than a third of the total commercial insurance sold in the United States. While Fortune 500 companies have long used CICs to protect assets and gain tax advantages, only in the last decade have individuals, business owners, and professionals begun to take advantage of them as well.

The physician/group's CIC can insure all, or portions of, the medical practice's significant risks, such as malpractice. Also, you can insure yourself for high liability, non-malpractice risks like wrongful termination or sexual harassment (see following discussion of CIC as asset protector) for which you typically will not have insurance.

If you were to be sued successfully, you would have to pay these claims out of your "after-tax" savings. By insuring yourself for these otherwise "uninsurable" risks, you get a present year tax deduction and, if you have to, will pay the claims with pre-tax dollars out of the CIC's loss reserves. Lastly, the CIC may insure relatively low liability risks like Y2K problems or weather-related damage to the office. Further, the CIC can transfer any of its risk to another reinsurer, leaving as little economic risk to the physician as he/she chooses, while still allowing for the tax benefits described below.

CIC As A Tax Planning Tool

The CIC is a powerful tool to build wealth through tax-deductible contributions from a medical practice, because premiums paid by the practice to the insurance company are deductible as ordinary business expenses under the tax code. Deductions for premiums can be over $1 million per year.

Beyond the yearly income tax savings for the practice, there are other tax benefits with the CIC: (1) capital gain postponements on appreciated assets, (2) tax-free growth, and (3) reduction or elimination of estate tax on property transferred to children. While the specifics of these tax benefits are beyond the scope of this article, such benefits are clearly supported in the Internal Revenue Code and tax cases. In fact, Congress has allowed substantial tax incentives to small insurance companies for over a century.

Thus, with a CIC, an individual physician or group could take a significant deduction from the practice each year and grow the funds in the CIC completely tax-free. If the physician chooses, he can take the funds back and pay only long-term capital gains tax. This three-tier tax advantage is not found in pensions, IRAs, or other commonly-used retirement vehicles.

Tax Benefits of Traditional Planning vs. The CIC

	Pension/Profit Sharing	**IRA**	**Physician or Group CIC**
Annual contributions are deductible	YES	NO	YES. Premiums paid to the CIC are deductible
Limitations on annual contributions	Between $10,000 and $30,000 per year	$2,000 per year for individuals	$1.2 million per year in annual deductible premiums
Employees generally must be included	YES	NO	NO
Tax treatment of distributions	ORDINARY INCOME (up to 39.6%)	TAX-FREE	TAX-FREE
Funds may be managed in the U.S. or offshore	NO. Only in the U.S.	NO. Only in the U.S.	YES. CIC reserves may be housed and managed in the U.S. or abroad
Tax treatment of distributions	ORDINARY INCOME (up to 39.6%)	ORDINARY INCOME (up to 39.6%)	LONG-TERM CAPITAL GAIN POTENTIAL
Penalties on early distributions?	YES	YES	NO
Tax treatment of funds remaining at physician's death	ORDINARY INCOME (up to 39.6%) + ESTATE TAX (up to 55%) TOTAL: 75-90%	ORDINARY INCOME (up to 39.6%) + ESTATE TAX (up to 55%) TOTAL: 75-90%	100% TAX-FREE. Funds in CIC may pass to owners (heirs) free of income/estate tax

CIC As An Asset Protection Tool

In addition to its tax benefits, the CIC offers asset protection advantages as well. Physicians can have the CIC to supplement their existing malpractice policy. Such "excess" malpractice protection gives the physician the security he will not be wiped out by a lawsuit award above traditional coverage limits. As physicians see more and more outlandish jury awards in medical malpractice cases, this protection can be significant. Further, the CIC may allow the doctor to reduce existing insurance, as the CIC policy provides additional coverage, if needed.

Also, a physician-owned CIC gives the physician the flexibility to customize policies not available with large third-party insurers. For example, many physicians prefer a malpractice policy that pays the doctor's legal fees (and allow you a full choice of attorneys), but not pay creditors or claimants (what we call "Shallow Pockets" policies). This prevents the physician from appearing as a "Deep Pocket"—a necessary asset protection strategy today.

In addition, the physician's CIC has the flexibility to add coverage for liabilities unavailable through traditional malpractice policies. Wrongful termination, harassment, or even HCFA violations are examples. Awards in these areas can be over $1 million so physicians should have a CIC for this reason alone.

Although physicians can sometimes purchase policies like the ones described above from traditional 3rd party insurers, they would not enjoy the powerful tax advantages described above. In essence, the question for the doctor becomes: If you are going to use insurance to protect your assets, why give away the potential profits and tax benefits to the insurance company, when you could own the company yourself? Let's examine this more closely.

Compared With Self-Insuring: Annual Deductions & Superior Asset Protection

Because our society has become so litigious, many physicians are "self-insuring" against potential losses like the ones named above. These doctors have saved funds to be used to pay any lawsuit expenses which arise. While this planning may prove wise, the doctor would be better off using a CIC to insure against such risk. That is because—as discussed earlier—premiums paid to the CIC are fully tax deductible, while amounts saved to self-insure are not. The CIC in other words, allows doctors to get a full deduction each year—protecting against the same risks they previously self-insured against.

Moreover, when the physician self-insures, the funds stay in his/her name, or the name of the practice. Thus, they are available to any lawsuit claimants, creditors, divorce proceeding, bankruptcy trustees, etc. who may attack the doctor's assets. Simply put, there is no asset protection tool shielding the self-insured funds. Conversely, using the CIC, the physician has transferred such funds to an independent operating, fully-licensed insurance company. Any lawsuit, claim, divorce, tax or other action against the physician or his/her practice is completely separate from the CIC. Thus, the funds in the CIC are ideally asset-protected against any litigation risks of the physician.

Protection From Practice Risks: The Physician's Options

	3rd Party Malpractice Ins.	Self-Insuring	Ind. or Group CIC
Limits on amount of coverage	Typically $1/$3 million policies only. No shield against awards in excess of these limits	As much as the physician can save.	Flexible. The CIC may policies beyond $1/$3 coverage, or even replace those policies.
Limits on scope of coverage	Typically provides little shield against harassment, wrongful firing, or other employee claims	Saved funds may be used to pay any type of claim.	Policies are completey flexible--may be written as physician wants.
"Shallow Pockets" policies available?	No. Policy proceeds can be claimed by successful lawsuit plaintiffs.	No funds may be claimed by successful lawsuit plaintiffs.	Yes. Completely flexible policies--they may pay for defense fees, but not to lawsuit plaintiffs.
Tax treatment of funds used	Practice gets full income deduction each year for paying policy premium.	No deduction for saving funds.	Practice gets full income deduction each year for paying policy premium.
Physician's company earns profits	No. Third party insurance company enjoys profits.	No profits to be made.	Yes, CIC enjoys profits. May share with re-insurer.
Physician's co. gets favorable tax treatment	No. Third pary insurance company gets favorable tax treatment.	N/A	Yes. CIC gets favorable tax treatment.
Unpaid reserves may ultimately benefits physician & family	No	Yes. If saved funds not paid out, physician and family have them.	Yes. If CIC reserves not paid out, they may be paid to physican and/or family members.

No Loss Of Control

When investigating the merits of a CIC, many physicians are concerned with losing control of the funds paid to the CIC. While the physicians' concerns are certainly justified, the proper CIC structure allows for complete and discloseable control by the physician. There is no need for the physician to trust any other person or entity with their assets—a drawback of some of the other asset protection structures we use, such as irrevocable trusts. Further, while the CIC is typically established outside the U.S. to keep administrative costs low, the physician's funds can remain in the U.S., in American stocks, mutual funds, money management accounts, etc.

Avoiding Land Mines

As mentioned, the CIC structure must be properly created and maintained. If not, not only may all asset protection and tax benefits be lost, but the doctor may suffer serious tax penalties.

For these reasons, using professionals with expertise in establishing CICs for physicians is critical—especially the accountants and attorneys involved. Any structure they advise should be based on *substantial tax authority*, and disclosed to the IRS. Further, the CIC should not be a straw corporation, lacking the necessary parties involved to run an insurance operation, such as actuaries and underwriters. While using such experts and a real CIC structure may be more expensive than some of the cheaper alternatives being touted on the internet or at fly-by-night seminars, this is one area where "doing it right" is the only way to enjoy the CIC's benefits and stay out of trouble with the IRS.

Can You Afford a CIC?

Setting up a CIC requires particular expertise, as explained above. Thus, as might be expected, the professionals most experienced in these matters charge significant fees for both the creation and maintenance of CICs. Setup costs are typically around $50,000 and annual maintenance costs another $35,000, although CICs can often be established for a group of physicians (where all funds are segregated for each doctor) for about $15,000 per doctor. While these fees are significant, given the CIC's potential tax and asset protection benefits, they are viable options for many physicians and/or groups practicing in high-income high-liability specialties.

Case Study: Dr. Steve

Dr. Steve is a successful Southern California surgeon who was concerned about protecting his assets from a judgment beyond his $1 million/$3 million policy and wanted to build tax-favored wealth beyond his profit-sharing plan. He established a CIC individually. Let's take a look at the benefit Dr. Steve enjoyed from his CIC in just year 1. Also, let's take a look at how the CIC will continue to build a tax-favored nest egg for Steve in the future.

Dr. Steve & his CIC: Effects on His Practice's Bottom Line

	Before the CIC	Year 1 with CIC
Malpractice protection	Traditional $1/$3 million coverage	Traditional coverage plus additional $2 million in
Practice income (net)	$300,000	$300,000
CIC premium paid	$0	$100,000
Personal income: stock transactions	$75,000	N/A
CIC income: stock transactions	N/A	$75,000
Taxable income	$375,000	$200,000
Federal & state income taxes (assume 45%)	$168,750	$90,000
Adjusted after-tax wealth	$206,250	$285,000
Benefit to Steve's bottom line		$78,750

Dr. Steve and his CIC: Building His Tax-Free Nest Egg

	Before CIC	Year 1 (After CIC)	Year 2	Year 10
Annual premium paid to CIC	N/A	$100,000	$100,000	$100,000
CIC income: return on prior reserves	N/A	$10,000 *(assume 10% return on investment. CIC pays no tax on earnings)*	$21,000	$159,374
CIC reserves	N/A	$11,000	$221,000	**$1,753,117**

Special Benefits of CICs

Physicians can utilize the CIC structure in a number of other ways beyond the annual deduction/retirement savings vehicle we described above. The two most common physician uses of the CIC are the following:

1. Using the CIC to Save Taxes Upon Sale of a Practice

As managed care's presence grows throughout the country, larger and larger practice groups are continually emerging to compete for the managed care contracts.

As part of this consolidation, an increasing number of physicians are selling their practices to larger groups and networks. While these deals differ greatly in amount and terms, any physician selling his/her practice would like to do so with the smallest tax hit as possible – with the largest economic gain to the physician personally. In our practice, we have helped many physicians sell their practices in a tax-favored way. Often, this involves utilizing a CIC.

While the specifics of the strategy depend on the facts of the case, the foundation of the planning is to have the ownership of the practice be transferred — in whole or in part – to a CIC prior to the sale of the practice. This could be done by taking the shares of the professional corporation and capitalizing the CIC with that stock. For reasons beyond the scope of this discussion, if this transaction is structured properly, there will be no tax on this transfer.

Once the CIC owns the entity running the practice, the buyer will purchase the practice from the CIC. Again, if structured properly, this purchase price amount could be paid to the CIC where the CIC would have no tax due on the sale. When compared with a traditional sale of stock, where the physician(s) will pay at least a 20% capital gains tax, such a strategy can easily save the doctors well into the six-figures in taxes. Once the CIC is funded, the doctor will have the same options described above to invest those funds and to get the funds back in his/her name.

A key in the planning here is to consult with the CIC experts in advance of the transaction. If the physicians can get input prior to agreeing on the terms of the deal, the doctor can often negotiate a transaction which allows greater tax benefits, with little or no negative affect on the buyer. In fact, the buyer may often realize a better deal by letting the doctor structure the sale this way, as the funds net to the doctor could actually be higher when the buyer pays less – all because the transaction took the IRS out of the deal.

This essential strategy – transferring ownership of the practice to the CIC prior to selling it – can be used with any highly-appreciated asset, including real estate, stocks, mutual funds, etc. For more information, please contact Christopher Jarvis at (888) 317-9895.

2. Using the CIC to Shield Royalty Streams

Many physicians have participated in the technological boom over the past twenty years, both as users and as inventors. We have many physician clients, in fact, who realize significant income from the royalty streams that have developed out of their products. Breast implants, surgical instruments, and dermatological products are just some of the examples we have seen our clients create and then bear fruit.

If the goal for the physician is to put more of the royalty stream in his/her pocket, while also working to asset-protect the funds, then the CIC is a tool to be considered. Depending on the nature of the product and the royalty stream generated, the CIC can be structured to shield 100% of the income from taxes and protect the funds from all of the physician's creditors.

For example, we had a plastic surgeon client who was to receive a breast implant royalty stream of between $250,000 and $500,000 per year. We set up a structure where the CIC was capitalized with the royalty rights. The CIC was then owned by an offshore LLC. This allowed the physician to control the CIC and its funds, while protecting them form any of the physician's creditors. Furthermore, the royalties accrued to the CIC completely tax-free and grew in the CIC tax-free as well, while invested in U.S. mutual funds. Over a 5 year period, the tax savings will be well over $1 million.

Conclusion

Because the CIC tool is so flexible, there are many ways to use it for tax and asset protection planning. Consider it an ideal tool in your overall plan.

Risk #3—Inflation

How much did you pay for your first new car? $1,000? $2,500? $5,000? $5,000 today won't pay for a service contract on your new car. An annual inflation of 6% will make one of today's dollars worth 17 cents in 30 years. Thus, when you consider investments, evaluate the inflation-adjusted returns of those investments. Your payoff is only as valuable as its purchasing power.

The annual rate of inflation over the past 72 years was 3.1%. So, why do people invest in government or corporate bonds, with average returns of just over 5% since 1926 -- when the appreciation is almost completely offset by inflation? They have marginally increased their buying power, if at all, as reflected in the following chart:

Asset Class	Nominal Return	Inflation Rate	Real Return
Stocks (S&P Index)	12.0%	3.1%	+8.6%
Bonds	5.1%	3.1%	+1.9%
US T-Bills	3.7%	3.1%	+0.6%

Staying ahead of inflation

If inflation is your concern, invest in inflation-index bond funds, precious metals, or real estate. Bond funds and metals probably give a 1%-2% inflation-adjusted return over the long haul. Real estate prices generally follow inflation closely, these investments are immune to inflation. We cannot predict the ultimate gain from in real estate, but you will have many additional risks and costs. Property taxes, landlord headaches, lack of liquidity, and maintenance may outweigh the inflation-hedge benefit. Real estate may be a portion, not the majority, of your entire investment portfolio.

To stay ahead of inflation, you may invest in the stock market. Though the stock market has had no correlation to inflation, the inflation-adjusted return of the market has been +8.6%. Stock investing may not be a true hedge against inflation, but over long a period, it should give you a better inflation-adjusted return than other investments. Investing in stocks and real estate, rather than bonds and money markets, will give you the greatest probability of a significantly positive inflation-adjusted return.

Risk #4—Losing Your Retirement to Taxes or Bad Investments

If your assets total $1 million, or you plan to live on the interest during retirement, your family may face two financial nightmares: First, you may outlive your retirement funds if you make poor investment choices. Second, your family may lose about half of your estate to estate taxes.

Let's look at how valuable $1 million is to you during retirement and to your heirs after you die.

> $1,000,000 generates $70,000, assuming 7% interest
> $1,000,000 is worth $500,000 to your heirs, assuming a 50% estate tax rate.

Balancing retirement risks

If you need $70,000 per year to retire, this plan may be adequate. However, if you consider inflation and stock market downturn risks, you may not want to risk your entire retirement on the gamble of low inflation and stock market appreciation.

Unless you spend your last dollar on your last cup of coffee—and, who has that timing?— you will either (1) outlive your retirement, or (2) pass away with some wealth. Since we don't know when we shall die, we don't know how long our retirement will last. However, with forced (early) retirement and rising life expectancies, you may expect to spend more years in retirement than did your parents. Having enough money for your (and your spouse's) retirement is increasingly difficult.

Many of our clients also want to minimize estate taxes and leave more for their children/grandchildren/charity. How do you balance these goals comfortably? An ideal approach can be achieved using a combination of annuities and life insurance.

Annuity & Insurance: Security for You and Your Heirs

Using the above example, assume you and your spouse are both 55 and have $1 million in retirement savings and want to quit working at 65. **You could take $800,000 and purchase a $70,000/year annuity that begins paying you in 10 years and grows according to the CPI index, which measures inflation.** This will protect you against outliving your retirement. With the remaining $200,000, you could purchase $2 million dollars in life insurance. With the insurance policy in an irrevocable life insurance trust (*about $2,000*), the entire $2 million passes to your beneficiaries without estate taxes. You and your spouse then have secure retirement income, you've left plenty to your heirs, and nothing to the IRS.

Since stocks return about 12% per year, and you need a 7% return, you may wonder if it is possible to live on the interest, and leave more to your heirs than the annuity and insurance strategy. Anything is possible. However it is unlikely. Consider:

- You need an income for retirement of $70,000 per year, so your $1,000,000 must pay interest of at least 7% annually;
- Because of 55% estate taxes, your $1 million must appreciate to $4.4 million before you die if you are to leave your heirs $2 million.

If you assume that the average stock market return is 12% per year, living on the interest begins to be more profitable after your 29th year of retirement. For your investments to outperform annuity and insurance, you would need:

- The stock market to continue at a growth rate of 12% per year for 29 more years
- Inflation must stay below 3% for 29 years
- You must outlive your life expectancy by 10 years (29 vs. 19)
- You must not suffer any major medical condition before your death at age 85

Risk #5—Accidental/Premature Death

This hits close to home as it happened to Chris' family. When Chris' successful stepfather, Tom, died prematurely at 39, it devastated his mother emotionally and financially. Though she was left with some cash and real estate, the drop in the real estate market left her investments worthless. As bills piled up over the next five years and the real estate market failed to climb, she eventually filed for bankruptcy, lost her home and had to start over.

Before you die, there are three things you must do for your family: (1) Cover their living expenses; (2) Make available funds for estate taxes, due in cash 9 months after your death; and, (3) Cover education expenses for your children.

Protecting your family with insurance

You need about 10 times your salary in life insurance if you leave a spouse and children. This won't cover education costs. You need an additional $100,000 of today's dollars for each child who will attend college.

> For example: Joe and Mary have three kids, ages 2, 4, 6. Joe makes $60,000 and Mary works part time earning $10,000. If Joe passed away, he would need to leave $60,000 x 10 = $600,000 of life insurance to cover his families expenses until his children graduate from college. He would also need $100,000 x 3 = $300,000 of insurance to cover their college costs. Total need = $900,000. Joe's employer offers him 3x his salary in life insurance $60,000 x 3 = $180,000. $900,000 needed - $180,000 provided = $720,000. Of course, the more planning you do now for their education in the form of trusts and educational IRAs, the lower your future insurance needs. Plan ahead to lower your insurance needs and reduce insurance costs. Each ten years you wait, doubles the cost of insurance.

If you don't plan properly, between 37% and 60% of the gross estate left to your heirs may go to Uncle Sam.

Shielding a business

If you own a business or professional practice, you have another concern—business succession. 90% percent of businesses fail to make it to the second generation. Why? The families often lack money for estate taxes (due in 9 months in cash). Thus, the business must be sold to pay taxes on the transfer of that business. To combat this problem, every business needs a buy-sell agreement with life insurance on all partners/owners. This allows the surviving partners to buy out the decedent's survivors and continue the business. If it is a sole proprietorship, the insurance allows the family to pay the estate tax bill without liquidating the company. These expenses can be deducted for tax purposes.

Another interesting tool to purchase the insurance in a tax-favored way is a *Voluntary Employee Beneficiary Association (VEBA)*. VEBAs are tax-exempt organizations that provide death benefits to the families of employees and owners of small businesses, including medical practices. Payments into these funds are tax deductible. VEBAs are covered in detail later in the chapter.

Risk #6—Disability

When you talk about asset protection, consider your single greatest asset—your earning potential. With both premature death and disability, this asset is lost.

With a disability, your ability to earn for your family is gone *and* you may need time and money. This can mean trouble, and disability is much more common than early death. What is the probability you will suffer at least one disability which lasts for three months or longer before age 65?

Age	Probability
25	44%
35	41%
45	36%
55	27%

Of the disabilities that last at least three months, many become lifetime disability, as the following table shows.

Age	Lifetime Disability
25	25%
35	28%
45	33%
55	40%

Sustaining a disability is very common. Why do people carry homeowner's insurance when the odds of a fire are 1 in 1,200 and the federal government doesn't require disability insurance when at least 1 in 3 people will be disabled?

Consider the following case:

> Lee, a surgeon, had contracts with a number of hospitals and health maintenance organizations, but was not their employee. In a car accident, Lee lost two fingers and severely damaged his nerves in both hands. Lee's days as a surgeon were over. Unfortunately, his disability insurance only covered him for accidents while performing under his contract with the organization. Since driving his car on a Saturday night out was not covered, he received no compensation.

Not only did Lee's family lose his $150,000 income per year, but they also had to pay another $36,000/year for home-based services. This tragic accident cost Lee's family more than lost income.

Three different types of disability policies protect against possible disability:

A. exactly same profession;
B. similar training/education profession;
C. any gainful profession.

Of course, choice "A" is the most comprehensive and "C" the least. While all types exist, many insurers no longer issue "A" for physicians because they found a great deal of insurance fraud. You can purchase only "B" or "C," but we exemplify all three to show the differences.

> Clayton, a surgeon, earns $150,000 per year. Clayton came down with arthritis from years of practice, and could not longer practice. If Clayton had disability policy of type (A) above, he would receive $12,500 (or the policy maximum) per month. If Clayton worked as a professor of surgery at the local university making $102,000 per year, he would still receive $12,500 per month. If Clayton had disability policy (b) he would only receive $4,000 per month, or the difference between his previous job and his new job which required similar training and education. If Clayton purchased the least expensive disability insurance, he would receive nothing. In fact, if Clayton got a job telemarketing, he would still receive no benefit under policy type (C). Type (C) is the most affordable policy, but it's only good if you don't mind an $8/hour job.

There are a few legitimate ways to purchase disability benefits with pre-tax dollars -- including VEBAs, discussed later. Ask us about ways to purchase disability insurance with tax-deductible funds.

Risk #7—Reverse Parenting & Long-Term Care

You know your responsibility to your children, but what about taking care of your parents or in-laws? Will you have enough money to help them if they need it? As our parents live longer, there is more chance that they too will outlive their assets and require assistance from their children.

We cannot rely on social programs to take care of our parents. For example, Medicaid nursing home benefits don't start until the individual who needs care has reduced his net worth to below $2,500! Unfortunately, most Americans believe their health and disability insurance will cover this if Medicare doesn't. The qualifications for Medicare are very strict, and the expenses of long-term care (either home health care or nursing home care) are not covered by Medicare or health and disability insurance.

The odds aren't good

The chances someone will need long-term care depends on age. If you reach age 55, there's a 1 in 10 (10%) chance that you will spend time in a nursing home. At 65, there's a 43%. At 75, you have a 60% chance. Over 70% of America's couples, over 65, will have at least one spouse enter a nursing home.

One in 12 of us will get in a car accident every year, and fewer than one in 1,000 homes will catch fire. Yet, everyone has automobile and homeowners coverage. Why do so few people have long-term care insurance when 7 out of 10 couples over age 65 will have one spouse in a nursing home?

The costs are staggering

How expensive are nursing homes? More than you might think. Costs vary, but the average is about $5,000 per month, or $60,000 per year, depending on the type of care. By year 2010, that number will more than double to over $120,000 per year. According to the *New England Journal of Medicine*, the average length of a nursing home stay is two and a half years. $150,000 will be necessary to support you and/or your spouse (or your parents or in-laws). Eighty-five percent of all Americans over 65 exhaust their assets within one year of entering a nursing home.

Your options

Purchasing a long-term care insurance policy can reduce or eliminate the financial risks of long-term illness or disability. Look into this as part of your complete financial analysis.

Minimizing your parents' estate and having them qualify for Medicaid is also an important strategy. By utilizing estate planning strategies discussed earlier, you can reduce assets of long-term care candidates (i.e., your parents), and help your family keep its wealth while getting government assistance for serious health problems.

Talk to an attorney who specializes in asset protection and estate planning to review your situation. While putting a loved one in a nursing home is very difficult, (and we can't help you with the emotional aspects), we can help you alleviate the financial risks.

Risk #8—Staying Benefit-Poor While Working Hard

You may work harder today than ever before, but doing poorer financially. The problem may be reduced reimbursements, or that you don't use your practice to benefit you personally as much as you would like.

If you have your own medical practice and want to pay for benefits with pre-tax dollars, there are restrictions. ERISA, the IRS, and other rules forbid you from providing yourself benefits without similar benefits for your employees. This is frustrating, not only for physicians, but for owners of all closely-held businesses or professional practices. Two possible solutions are available: 1.) a *Split Dollar Plan*, and 2.) a V*oluntary Employee Benefit Association (VEBA)*. Both give you excellent life and disability benefits with pre-tax dollars, without forcing you to spend too much on your employees.

What is a Split-Dollar Plan?

Split dollar isn't special life insurance. It is a special way to buy life insurance. This method is used to fund buy-sell agreements and to give key employees additional benefits. Split dollar insurance is an insurance contract where two parties, usually an employee and an employer, split the premiums and the benefits. I.R.S. Revenue Ruling 64-328 states that: "Split-dollar is an arrangement whereby the party with the need and the party with the ability to pay premiums join in purchasing an insurance contract in which there is a substantial investment element."

How a split-dollar plan helps you to retain key employees and fund a business buyout.

> Example 1 - Dave and Charlie, partners in a plastic surgery practice, employ another surgeon, two nurses, and two administrative people. They enjoy their work and find it very profitable. They hired Dan, a skilled young surgeon, whom they would like to retain. However, they don't want an elaborate benefits program for all five of their employees. After considering numerous alternatives, they chose a split-dollar plan. Dan's family gets a sizable death benefit and the cash values grow significantly until age 65, as long as Dan continues working for Dave and Charlie (a nice "golden handcuffs").

Example 2—What happens if Dave (or Charlie) dies? If their practice is worth $3 million at Dave's death, there are two problems. First, Dave's heirs will step into his shoes and take half the practice. If Charlie doesn't get along with Dave's spouse, this is not a good alternative. Second, Dave's heirs will owe the IRS about $750,000 for the $1.5 million share of the business they received at Dave's death. Dave's spouse may want, or need, to sell assets of the business to pay the taxes. This is not good for Charlie. Since Charlie doesn't have $1.5 million to buy out Dave's spouse, what can he do?

The practice could purchase two split-dollar insurance policies; one on Dave's life and one on Charlie's with funds paid primarily by the company. Dave and Charlie may continue their practice after the death of the other partner as the surviving families get cash, rather than shares of a practice, when liquid assets are vital to pay estate taxes.

The split dollar plan helped retain the young surgeon and continue the surgical practice after the death of one partner; achieved almost completely with the practice's pre-tax income.

What is a Voluntary Employee Beneficiary Association?

A *Voluntary Employee Beneficiary Association* (VEBA) for many years were only available to large employers. In 1986, Congress allowed smaller employers to participate in VEBAs through multiple employer trusts.

The main purpose of VEBAs is to pay life and accident insurance and medical benefits to members, their dependents, and beneficiaries. Educational benefits, medical reimbursement, salary continuation benefits, severance pay and long term care benefits can also be offered.

VEBAs are powerful planning tools because physicians may purchase their own benefits with pretax dollars without paying benefits for employees. With a VEBA, you can:

- Make sizable tax-deductible contributions in peak earning years and minimal contributions in lean years;
- Grow contributions on a tax-deferred basis;
- Fund the plan without risking over-funding;
- Take early distributions without penalties;
- Provide no vesting to employees who are terminated or resign;
- Provide for estate taxes with pre-tax funds;

- Work beyond an artificially imposed retirement age without the problems of pension plans.

The VEBA benefits are also asset-protected, unlike many other benefit plans. An example:

> Carl, an opthalmologist, wants to purchase life and disability insurance to protect his family. Because he is very successful and in a 39.6% federal tax bracket, he prefers to pay with pretax dollars. However, he believes that he will have to set up a benefits program for all five of his employees. He wants the tax deduction, but doesn't want to pay expensive benefits for five people.

Carl can join an existing VEBA which qualifies the payments as tax deductible. He can purchase benefits for everyone in the company with pretax dollars. To qualify for the 501C not for profit status, you must offer similar benefits for everyone. But, you can purchase greater benefits for yourself than for your employees by purchasing a whole life policy for yourself and term insurance for your employees. The benefit is the same, relative to salary, but your coverage lasts until you die. This is a great solution, but since the rules are complex, talk to an expert.

While this can be a great tool for physicians, investment in a defective VEBA may cause you to lose the tax-deductibility of your contributions and its tax-deferral of the growth. Deal only with legitimate multiple employer VEBAs. If you are unsure of a prospective VEBA, please call our office.

If you want to pay for benefits with pre-tax dollars and retain your key employees, a variation on a VEBA is for you. 419 plans provide death and severance benefits for you and your employees. No benefits are paid to employees who voluntary leave your employ and these plans let you implement vesting schedules. They are very attractive for a business owner or physician whose income is at least 50% of his firm's total after-tax income.

Risk #9—Costs of Parenting

If you have children, you know how expensive they can be! Each child costs the parents $1,000,000 in food, clothing, education and miscellaneous expenses before the child turns 21.

The strategy is not to save $5 here and $10 there. You can invest for your children's education and never pay tax on that investment's dividends or capital gains through an Education IRA.

The Education IRA lets you place $500 per year (a married couple can donate $1000 per child/per year) into an account for the benefit of a child's education. Unlike other forms of funding a child's education, the Education IRA account is not subject to gift tax, capital gains tax, or income tax.

Let's consider three alternatives: 1.) Donald starts an Education IRA for his daughter Dana; 2.) Mary sets up a trust with her son Michael as the beneficiary; or 3.) Paul plans to use funds from his brokerage account to pay for his granddaughter Patricia's education.

If you consider that Dana, Michael and Patricia are all 5 years of age, here are the financial consequences of the three plans.

Costs	Education IRA	Trust	Gift
Setup Fees	$15-$50	$1500-$4,000	$0 (no formal structure)
Annual Administrative	$15-$25	1/2-1% trustee fees	$0 + brokerage fee
Income Taxes Due	None	Yes, on all dividends	Yes, on all dividends
Capital Gains Due	None	Yes	Yes
Gift Taxes Due	None	Yes, if over $10,000	Yes, if over $10,00

Annually during accumulation, the Education IRA pays no income taxes on dividends or interest and no capital gains on sales of securities. Money put into the Education IRA is never subject to tax. Since the account is in the name of the child, it is protected from your creditors. If you start early enough or have relatives who want to donate $500 for your children's education, you may not need any other educational savings program.

If you started late or want to make a large gift to a child for his education, like Mary did for her son Michael, you may set up a trust. Arnie and David discussed trusts at length earlier, but the bottom line is that you lose control -- the assets are transferred to the trust and can only be used for specific purposes, which you designate beforehand. The trust is also protected from your creditors because you have gifted funds to your child or grandchild. However, there are costs for creating the trust one-time legal fees and continuing trustee fees.

These solutions are superior to merely "hoping to pay" for a child's education. A little planning goes a long way to reduce the financial burden of college.

Conclusion

Whether we are doctors, nurses, or business owners, we work hard for our money -- we are not materialistic simply because we want to protect it. That's what this book has been about.

You have seen many different strategies to protecting yourself against lawsuits, taxes, and bad investments. Use this knowledge to build your financial fortress; one that will safely grow and provide for your needs.

"People don't plan to fail. They fail to plan." A cliché, perhaps, but very good advice. If you don't act on your concerns, then this book is not worth its paper. If you do act, this book may pay for itself a thousand times over.

Keep in mind these concepts. Occasionally review the chapters. You will then make sounder financial decisions. Of course, in our national practice we help clients with all their asset protection, retirement, investment, and tax planning needs. If you would like to speak with us, please contact us, at (888) 317-9895.

Thank you for your time. It has been our pleasure to share our knowledge and experiences with you. We hope it helps you in the years ahead!

Appendices

APPENDIX A
"THE LANDLORD'S SOURCES OF LIABILITY"

A landlord today has a multitude of liability sources. He can be sued by his tenants, by his tenants' guests, by sub-lessees, by neighbors, by neighborhood associations, by local government agencies, and even by trespassers. What's even worse is that he can be sued for defects in the land or building about which he knew nothing. Fault is often not part of the equation — the landlord is "strictly liable" whether or not he acted negligently. The following are the most common sources of landlord liability:

1. Liability For Defects in the Premises

When a defective condition causes a tenant to be injured, the landlord will almost always be held liable, even if the landlord did not know of the defect in question. This will also be true if the injured person is a guest of the tenant or, in some cases, a trespasser. The legal justification for such a policy is that the landlord is the better party to pay for injuries than the tenant. If landlords are stuck with the bill enough times, the argument goes, they will, as a group, provide a better and safer premises.

The following are examples of situations where landlords have been held liable for injuries caused by defects in the premises:

- For a tenant's injury when a building handrail gave way
- As a result of a fire which injured 15 tenants when a heater in one apartment was defective
- For tenants' mental distress caused by the building's "slum conditions"
- For a guest's injury when she tripped over a rock on a common stairway
- For a tenant's injury resulting from a fall into a shower door made of untempered glass

2. Liability For Acts of Unruly or Criminal Tenants

Landlords may be held liable for injuries and property damage caused by their tenants. This reality may be abhorrent to many landlords because they have little daily control of their tenants. Outraged landlords ask me, "Why should I be responsible for the tenants' behavior, when the tenants themselves are adult citizens?" While this may sound like a compelling argument, it is not one the courts often give much weight. In fact, every day, landlords are forced to pay judgments when others have caused the injury or damage.

These judgments usually come down because one of the tenants is a nuisance and the landlord has not done enough to get rid of the nuisance. Often, a drug-dealing tenant is the source of the problem. This situation is particularly difficult for the landlord because it is difficult to prove that drug-dealing has taken place and the landlord cannot evict the tenant without some type of proof. In this way, the landlord is damned if he tries to evict the tenant (wrongful eviction lawsuit) or if he doesn't (liability for the nuisance).

3. Liability For Injuries To Others By Outsiders

Under certain circumstances, a landlord may even be forced to pay for property damage or physical injuries to a tenant or guest that result from the acts of non-tenants on the landlord's premises. This means that the landlord's liability even extends to the acts of people with whom he has no relation whatsoever. And this liability can be imposed even if no prior similar acts have occurred! Consider these actual cases of landlord liability which have been decided recently:

- A landlord is held liable when one of her tenants is raped. The theory: she had provided poor lighting in the common areas.
- A landlord is held liable when a tenant is assaulted in the parking lot of the landlord's building.
- A landlord is forced to pay when a tenant's vicious dog bites another tenant's guest. While the landlord had the legal "right" to then sue the dog owner for reimbursement, he knew the dog owner had no money. (That's why the injured lawyer went after the landlord in the first place.)

With this background of reality, it is amazing how many landlords, especially residential landlords, do not utilize asset protection strategies. If you are a residential landlord and you own the property(ies) in your own name, you are sitting on a lawsuit time-bomb. *And don't think that insurance will protect you,* as many homeowner or landlord policies exclude the most common types of lawsuits in the fine print. *Your only solution is to set up an asset protection plan where dangerous assets like rental real estate are owned by a legal entity which isolates them from your other safe property and savings.*

Appendices

APPENDIX B
"FEDERAL BANKRUPTCY AND NON-BANKRUPTCY EXEMPTIONS"

1. FEDERAL BANKRUPTCY EXEMPTIONS

The federal bankruptcy exemptions are only available to you if you are filing for bankruptcy in the following states. If you are filing in these states, compare the federal exemptions to the ones in your particular state (you can call the authors to find the state exemptions) and use whichever allows you to keep more of your property. If you are filing for bankruptcy in states other than those listed here, you must use the state exemptions.

The federal exemptions are available to you if you are filing for bankruptcy in:

Arkansas	Massachusetts	New Mexico	Texas
Connecticut	Michigan	Pennsylvania	Washington
District of Columbia	Minnesota	Rhode Island	Wisconsin
Hawaii	New Jersey	South Carolina	Vermont

The federal bankruptcy exemptions protect the following property and amounts from being taken from a debtor in a bankruptcy proceeding:

HOMESTEAD
Real property, up to $7,500. Unused portion up to $3,750, may be used for other property.

PERSONAL PROPERTY
1. Motor vehicles up to $1,200.
2. Animals, crops, clothing, appliances and furnishings, books, household goods, and musical instruments up to $200 per item, and up to $4,000 total.
3. Jewelry up to $500.
4. Health aids.
5. Wrongful death recovery for person you depended on.
6. Personal injury recovery up to $7,500, except for pain and suffering or for pecuniary loss.
7. Lost earnings payments.

PENSIONS
ERISA-qualified benefits needed for support.

PUBLIC BENEFITS
1. Public assistance, social security, veteran's benefits, unemployment compensation.
2. Crime victim's compensation.

TOOLS OF THE TRADE
Implements, books, and tools of the trade, up to $750.

ALIMONY AND CHILD SUPPORT
Alimony and child support needed for support.

INSURANCE
1. Unmatured life insurance policy.
2. Life insurance policy with loan value up to $4,000.
3. Disability, unemployment, or illness benefits.
4. Life insurance payments for a person whom you depended on, which you need for support.

MISCELLANEOUS
$400 of any property, and unused portion of the homestead exemption, up to $3,750

2. FEDERAL NON-BANKRUPTCY EXEMPTIONS
These exemptions can be used if you are filing for bankruptcy in a state not listed above. They can be used in addition to the state exemptions found in your *State Exemption Report*. These exemptions are as follows:

RETIREMENT BENEFITS
1. CIA employees.
2. Civil service employees.
3. Foreign service employees.
4. Military service employees
5. Railroad workers.
6. Social security benefits.
7. Veteran's benefits.

SURVIVOR'S BENEFITS
1. Military service
2. Judges, U.S. court directors.

3. Lighthouse workers.

DEATH AND DISABILITY BENEFITS
1. U.S. government employees.
2. Longshoremen, harbor workers.
3. Military service.

MISCELLANEOUS
1. Military deposits to savings accounts.
2. 75% of earned but unpaid wages (judge may approve more — see chapter 5)
3. Klamath Indian tribe benefits.
4. Military group life insurance.

Appendices

APPENDIX C
"STATE TENANCY BY THE ENTIRETY LAWS"

The following chart explains:
1. whether or not your state allows Tenancy by the Entirety ("T/E") as an ownership form;
2. whether or not T/E is allowed for personal property (all states that have T/E allow it for real estate); and
3. whether or not the assets owned by T/E are exempt from creditors as explained it chapter 6.

> **READ THIS DISCLAIMER:**
> Some details of these laws have been left out — to make the chart more readable. Also, state laws do change. Therefore, it is crucial that you check with an attorney familiar with your present state laws, in all their detail. Use these charts to give you a general understanding of what exemptions exist in your state. However, to implement them in your plan, you must check with an attorney!

STATE	T/E Allowed	PERSONAL PROP.	EXEMPT
Alabama	Unclear	?	?
Alaska	Yes	Yes	No
Arizona	Unclear	?	?
Arkansas	Yes	Yes	No
California	No	N/A	N/A
Colorado	Unclear	?	?
Connecticut	No	N/A	N/A
Delaware	Yes	Yes	Yes
D.C.	Yes	Yes	Yes
Florida	Yes	Yes	Yes
Georgia	Unclear	?	?
Hawaii	Yes	Yes	Yes?
Idaho	Unclear	?	?
Illinois	Unclear	?	?
Indiana	Yes	No	Yes
Iowa	Unclear	?	?
Kansas	Unclear	?	?

STATE	T/E Allowed	PERSONAL PROP.	EXEMPT
Kentucky	Unclear	?	?
Louisiana	No	N/A	N/A
Maine	No	N/A	N/A
Maryland	Yes	Yes	Yes
Massachusetts	Yes	Yes	?
Michigan	Yes	No	Yes
Minnesota	No	N/A	N/A
Mississippi	Yes	Yes	?
Missouri	Yes	Yes	Yes
Montana	Unclear	?	?
Nebraska	Unclear	?	?
Nevada	No	N/A	N/A
New Hamp.	No	N/A	N/A
New Jersey	Yes	No	No
New Mexico	No	N/A	N/A
New York	Yes	No	No
North Carolina	Yes	No	No
North Dakota	No	N/A	N/A
Ohio	Yes	Yes	?
Oklahoma	Yes	Yes	?
Oregon	Yes	Yes	?
Pennsylvania	Yes	Yes	Yes
Rhode Island	Yes	Yes	Yes
South Carolina	Unclear	?	?
South Dakota	No	N/A	N/A
Tennessee	Yes	Yes	?
Texas	Unclear	?	?
Utah	Yes	Yes	?
Vermont	Yes	Yes	Yes
Virginia	Yes	Yes	Yes
Washington	No	N/A	N/A
West Virginia	No	N/A	N/A
Wisconsin	No	N/A	N/A
Wyoming	Yes	Yes	Yes

Appendices

APPENDIX D
INTESTACY: WHAT HAPPENS IF YOU DIE WITHOUT A WILL OR LIVING TRUST

If you die without a valid document disposing of your property — either a will or a pour-over will and living trust — your state will decide exactly how your estate should be divided. Each state has a statute which controls the distribution of a decedent's property in these circumstances. Such a statute is called an "intestacy" law because "intestacy" is the legal term for dying without a valid will (or pour-over will and living trust).

As I stated earlier in the book, dying without a will is the worst estate planning mistake you can make. Not only do you lose estate tax benefits and lose the probate fee savings of a living trust, but *you also lose all control of how your property will be given away when you die.* Instead, you allow the politicians to decide how your property is divided. And they usually make a mess of things — as you might have guessed.

> **READ THIS DISCLAIMER :**
> The following is a general description of how property is divided under California's intestacy laws. Use this description to give you a general understanding of what intestacy laws are all about. Check with an attorney familiar with the laws in your state for particular legal advice. Or, better yet, set up a living trust and a pour-over will and rest easy knowing this law will not apply to you.

Sample Intestacy Law

If you die intestate, your property will be divided as follows:

a. If you have a surviving spouse, but no surviving issue (descendants), parent, brother, sister, or issue of a deceased brother or sister, the surviving spouse gets everything.

b. If you have a surviving spouse, and any of the following are true, the surviving spouse gets one half of the estate:

    1. You also are survived by one child (that child gets the remaining half); or

    2. You also are survived by the issue of one pre-deceased child (that

issue takes or splits the remaining half); or
3. You leave no issue but are survived by one parent (he/she gets the remaining half); or
4. You leave no issue but are survived by the issue of one parent (they either take or split the remaining half); or
5. You leave no issue but are survived by more than 1 parent (they split the remaining half).

c. If you have a surviving spouse, and any of the following are true, the surviving spouse gets one third of the estate:

1. You leave more than 1 living child; or
2. You leave one child living and the issue of a predeceased child; or
3. You leave issue of two or more predeceased children.

There are also issues here about how much the issue (descendants) of predeceased children should take — and state laws do differ on this point.

d. If you do not leave a surviving spouse, then your entire estate will pass to your heirs in the following priority:

1. To your issue (descendants);
2. If you have no surviving issue, then to your parents;
3. If you have no surviving issue or parents, then to the issue of your parents;
4. If you have no surviving issue or parents or issue of your parents, then to your grandparents, or their issue;
5. If you have none of the above, then to the surviving issue of your predeceased spouse, if any;
6. If you still have none of the above, then to your "next of kin" (any blood relative, in order of kinship);
7. If you still have none of the above, then to the parents of a predeceased spouse, if any;
8. If you still have none of the above, then your hard-earned property will escheat (be transferred) to the state.

Unfortunately, million of dollars in property every year escheats to the state in this way — because the decedent had no relatives or they cannot be found. *Do not let the state decide how your property will be given away — do the smart thing and establish a living trust and pour-over will as soon as you can.*

APPENDIX E
"ALL ABOUT LIVING TRUSTS"

One point I have repeated throughout this book is that everyone should have a Living Trust, rather than a will. The reason I have made this point so often is that a Living Trust will save your loved ones thousands (or even tens of thousands of dollars) in probate fees when you die and it gives you more control over the wealth-transfer process as well. In short, I see no downside to having a Living Trust control your estate plan, instead of a will.

To be more accurate, I should be saying everyone should have "a Living Trust and a pour-over will, rather than a bare will." The pour-over will is a simple document which "pours over" to your Trust any property not already named in the Living Trust when you die. It is a short document which states that any property you own when you die not already transferred to your Living Trust is thereby transferred to the Trust.

This way, if you accumulate property after setting up your Living Trust, your Living Trust still controls its disposition — so you save probate fees on this property as well.

While I have explained much of what a Living Trust is and what its chief benefits are, here I will outline, in bullet-point form, other facts about Living Trusts which I think are important for you to know.

- **The assets owned by your Living Trust will avoid the costs, delay, and lack of control of the probate process.**
As I have explained, the court's process of distributing assets according to a will is very expensive and time-consuming —while the court decides what to do with your assets. The costs average around 4% of your gross estate and the entire process can take two years or more. That means, if you die leaving $1 million worth of property in your will, your loved ones will be stuck with a $40,000 bill and won't be able to get their inheritances for months, even years. And all this can be avoided by using a Living Trust — because the *assets owned by the Trust automatically avoid the entire probate process*.

- **You keep control of the assets transferred to your Living Trust.**
When you transfer your assets to your Living Trust while you are alive, you

maintain 100% control over these assets — just as if you still owned them in your own name. For your car, stocks, bonds, bank accounts, home, or any other asset — the process of transferring an asset to your Living Trust is the same. If the asset has a registration or deed, change the name on such a document. If the asset is jewelry or artwork which has no official ownership record, use an assignment document to officially transfer ownership to your Living Trust.

These ownership changes will transfer the name of the registration or deed to "John Doe Revocable Living Trust" or "John Doe, Trustee of John Doe Revocable Living Trust," rather than "John Doe" as it now reads. As sole trustee of the Trust, you have unlimited power to buy, sell, mortgage, invest, etc. — just as you did before. Further, because the Trust is revocable, you can always change beneficiaries, remove or add assets, or even cancel your Trust entirely.

And remember — the transfer of assets to the Living Trust (called "funding the Trust") is a necessary activity. While it has no income tax ramifications at all (you are still treated as the owner for income tax purposes) it is crucial to gain the probate-saving benefits when you die.

■ You May Name Yourself Or Someone Else As Living Trust Trustee.

You need not name yourself as the trustee of your Living Trust, although most people do. You could name an adult child, another relative or close friend, or even a corporate trustee, like a local bank or trust company. However, if you do not like the way the outside trustee is handling the Trust, you always have the power to remove them — as the Grantor (creator) of the Trust.

■ When You Die, Your Successor Trustee Will Take Over.

If you are the trustee while you are alive, you will name, in your Living Trust, someone (or something like a corporate trustee) as the successor trustee. That person or entity will take over trustee duties when you die. If you have a third person trustee or co-trustee while you are alive, that person will complete trustee duties after you have died.

These duties involve collecting income or benefits due your estate, paying your remaining debts, making sure the proper tax returns are filed, and distributing your assets according to the Trust instructions. This person or entity acts like an executor for a will. However, unlike a will, actions under a Living Trust's directions are not subject to court interference.

■ You Decide When And How Your Beneficiaries Will Receive Their Inheritances.

Another significant advantage of a Living Trust over a will is that you decide when and how your beneficiaries get their inheritance, rather than the courts. Since the court is not involved, the successor trustee can distribute assets right after he/she/it concludes your final affairs. This can be weeks or even days.

If you choose, assets need not be distributed right away. Instead, you may direct that they stay in your Trust, managed by your individual or corporate trustee, until your beneficiaries reach the age(s) at which you want them to inherit.

■ The Successor Trustee Must Follow Your Living Trust's Instructions.

Your successor trustee (as well as your primary trustee if it is not you) is a fiduciary — that is a legal term meaning that he/she/it has a legal duty to follow the Living Trust instructions and to act in a reasonably prudent manner. He/she/it must treat the Living Trust as a binding legal contract, and must use "best efforts" to live up to the obligations of the contract. If your successor trustee mismanages the Trust by ignoring the instructions in your Living Trust, he/she/it could be legally liable.

APPENDIX F
"10 BLUNDERS OFFICERS OR DIRECTORS MUST AVOID" AND "2 WAYS THEY CAN PROTECT THEMSELVES"

Corporate officers and directors, as well as board members of charitable organizations, are extremely vulnerable to lawsuits. They can be held accountable for the acts of the organization and even the organization's employees. If you are a corporate or charitable officer or director, make certain you avoid the following ten mistakes. Each mistake makes it easier for a court to "pierce the corporate veil" and make you personally liable for acts and decisions involving the corporation/ charitable organization.

1. Failure to conduct regular meetings of the board of directors
2. Failure to conduct annual shareholder meetings
3. Failure to issue corporate stock or maintain a shareholder ledger
4. Failure to maintain corporate records
5. Failure to conduct the required initial organizational meeting
6. Failure to adopt the corporate by-laws
7. Failure to maintain proper accounting records
8. Failure to advertise and make known that the entity is operating as a corporation
9. Failure to acquire the proper state and local licenses in the name of the corporation.
10. Failure to file annual state and federal reporting forms

This list is certainly not complete — it only represents the more common mistakes directors and officers make which expose their personal finances to corporate creditors and lawsuits.

If you are a director or officer sued for the act of your corporation or charitable organization, you may be able to avoid liability if you can show you acted prudently; as a reasonable person would have acted under the circumstances. This means your decisions as officer or director must be made using diligence and due care. Even more, you must document how you came to these decisions — such as relying on outside experts like accountants or consultants, reviewing internal reports, or attending and voting at meetings. You must always act as if your decisions will later be questioned — have reasonable justifications for the actions you take and maintain proper records to prove your "prudent behavior."

Of course, the advice "act prudently" is too vague. Even the most reasonable decisions have been judged to be unreasonable by juries, who award millions of dollars to disgruntled shareholders. Therefore, you need to do more than act prudently and keep detailed records. You also need to take the following 2 steps:

1. Get Insurance and an Indemnification Agreement

An indemnification agreement is one whereby the corporation or charitable organization agrees to indemnify you (pay you back) for any losses you incur as a result of lawsuits stemming from your service as an officer or director. While this certainly is important — because it puts the financial burden on the organization rather than you — it is not foolproof. The central shortcoming of the indemnification agreement is that, if the organization itself experiences financial difficulty, it will have no funds with which to reimburse you. That is why you also need director's and officer's insurance.

You should have the organization purchase a liability insurance policy to protect you. Many insurance companies offer these types of policies, and they are used to shield the wealth of the directors and officers of practically all of today's Fortune 500 companies. These successful business leaders understand that in today's lawsuit-crazy world, to serve as an officer or director without insurance is foolish. You should demand such a policy in your organization as well.

2. Shield Your Personal Wealth

Insurance is never a solid enough protection to rely on solely. Every policy has numerous exclusions; any one of which can end up burning you in the end. Moreover, simply by having a large insurance policy, you encourage a lawsuit against you — because the insurance company is the ideal "Deep Pocket."

Also, as I have explained earlier, when you rely on your insurance carrier to protect you, your interests are no longer under your control. You may want to deny that you did anything wrong, yet your insurance company wants to make a large settlement, which makes it appear as if you are admitting your wrongdoing. Further, you can bet that your policy premiums will skyrocket after a successful suit against you. While this may not be an issue if you work for a large public company, if it is your small privately-held corporation, this can be a significant cost.

The better solution, which I hoped you have realized by now, is to *add an asset protection plan for your personal wealth to a moderate insurance policy coverage. This not only discourages lawsuits against you, but also provides an additional layer of security for your personal finances.* It will give you the sense of security you deserve — no matter what type of corporation or charitable organization you run.

Appendices

APPENDIX G
"BASIC ESTATE TAX SAVING TACTICS"

Estate taxes are a serious threat to the financial well-being of your loved ones after you are gone. The danger is that, to pay the tax bill, they will use up much of what they should inherit from you. And this is a real threat ... as the estate tax rate is so high — starting at 37% and quickly increasing to 55%. Do you want the government to take over half of what you have earned when you die — instead of leaving it to your family or other intended beneficiaries?

No matter how patriotic you are, I cannot imagine you would want to give the IRS any more than you have to. With that in mind, here are three basic tactics for saving estate taxes. Of course, as with any legal or tax issue, make sure you review your particular strategies with your asset protection and tax attorneys.

1. Make Annual Tax-Free Gifts To Reduce Your Taxes By Thousands

As mentioned earlier in the book, you can make annual gifts of up to $10,000 per person with no gift tax and without using any of your $600,000 lifetime gift tax/estate tax exclusion. Why not make gifts now to the people who will eventually receive your property after you die. If you do it in $10,000 increments (or $20,000 if you and your spouse jointly make the gifts), you can take out the IRS' share of the pie.

Thus, if you have 5 grandchildren who you plan to leave a total of $100,000 when you die, make gifts of $10,000 to each grandchild now over two years or gifts of $20,000 in one year (if you and your spouse make the gift). This achieves your objective of providing for your grandchildren and saves between $37,000 and $55,000 in estate taxes as well. If you were leaving $1,000,000, your tax savings would be over half a million dollars! Further, by using this strategy in conjunction with family limited partnerships, you can make such gifts and save estate taxes while keeping control of the gifted property while you are alive.

2. Extend Your $600,000 Exemption Into Multiple Exemptions By Using It Now

Gifts that exceed the $10,000 annual per person limit explained above can count toward your $600,000 estate tax exemption (which actually applies to both estate and gift taxes). Essentially, when you make a large gift, you can choose to pay the gift tax now or use up some of the $600,000 estate tax exemption now — so you have less available when you die.

This opportunity to use up a portion, or all, of your $600,000 exemption now allows you to save hundreds of thousands of dollars on estate taxes. This is because the $600,000 exemption is worth exactly that — $600,000 — if you use it when you die. However, if you use it now, by transferring assets which will likely appreciate over time, you can squeeze much more tax-saving value out of the $600,000.

For example, let's assume you have stock worth $600,000 today which you plan on leaving to your two daughters. And let's say when you die, in twenty years, those stocks will be worth $2 million dollars; a reasonable annual return, if reinvested. If you wait to leave it to them when you die, through your Living Trust, you will shield only $600,000 worth of the stock from estate taxes. The remainder, $1.4 million, would be subject to estate taxes, and between $500,000 and $800,000 worth of your estate would end up going to the IRS.

On the other hand, if you gave all $600,000 to your daughters today, the entire value of $2 million would be excluded from your estate when you died (assuming you die in twenty years). *You would save between $500,000 and $800,000 in estate taxes — and this extra value would go to your daughters!*

If you are concerned about making outright gifts at this point — because you do not want beneficiaries to have complete control of the gifts — explain this to your asset protection lawyer. He can set up a family limited partnership or a limited liability company, which can save taxes in this way while preventing beneficiaries from getting 100% control of their gifts until a future time.

3. Save Over $200,000 In Estate Taxes By Using an A-B Trust

Many married couples think the best way to provide for the surviving spouse is for the first to die to leave everything to him/her. *This a tragic financial blunder — it will usually cause you to pay hundreds of thousands of dollars in estate taxes — unnecessarily* (For this discussion, let us assume that you die first, your spouse second).

It is true that if you leave everything to a surviving spouse, you will pay nothing in estate taxes when you die. This is called the "unlimited marital deduction." However, after your spouse dies, the entire tax bill may be much larger than it needs to be.

This is because if you leave everything to your spouse, you make use of the unlimited marital deduction, but you make no use of the $600,000 exemption.

That is because you do not need the exemption. If all the property goes to your surviving spouse, the unlimited marital deduction covers it all anyway.

While this seems fine when you die, when your spouse dies, the IRS gets you back. At that point, your spouse's estate can only make use of her $600,000 exemption. That means everything over $600,000 will be subject to estate taxes — and you already know how high they are.

The better strategy is to set up an A-B Living Trust and fund it with your assets. Then, when you die, the Trust creates two separate Trusts — an "A" Trust for your surviving spouse, and a "B" Trust for you. The Trusts assets are similarly divided and poured into each Trust so that both $600,000 exemptions are utilized. An alternative scenario lets the income of the "B" trust assets to be used for the surviving spouse while he/she is alive. He/she can even receive the principal if needed for health, maintenance, education, or support.

Either arrangement lets you use both $600,000 exemptions — yours and your spouse's. *By using an A-B trust in this way, you can leave up to $1.2 million worth of savings and property tax-free — saving over $200,000 in estate taxes.* Again, it is important that the Trust be properly drafted to include viable A-B provisions and that the Trust be funded. Check with your asset protection attorney on this.

Appendices

APPENDIX H
"FINANCIAL ASSESSMENT WORKSHEETS"

The following appendix has two sections: a Lawsuit Risk Factor Analysis & an Asset Checklist.

Use the Lawsuit Risk Factor Analysis worksheets to analyze lawsuit dangers that are specific to your individual situation. Check off any lawsuit risks that apply to you in your medical practice or in any outside businesses that you may be involved in, as well as those risks that apply to your personal life. This should give you an accurate picture of the types of lawsuit dangers you face.

Use the Asset Checklist worksheets to make a list of your assets, like you would in any balance sheet. However, in these worksheets, we ask that you separate these assets into "safe" assets* (those that are not likely to create liability) and "dangerous" assets (those that are likely to create lawsuit problems). Also, please examine any titles or registrations to determine the type of ownership form applicable to each asset. This will give you a sense of which assets can be shielded by co-ownership protections, such as that of tenancy by the entirety.

Though the text has been copyrighted, we suggest you make copies of the Financial Assessment Worksheets for future use. You should complete these forms annually before meeting with your asset protection attorney to review your financial situation. Doing this will better prepare you for your discussions with your attorney and will save you money on legal fees.

*WARNING: Safe assets are really a misnomer because they are vulnerable to any lawsuits against you if you own them in your name.

The Doctor's Wealth Protection Guide

Financial Assessment Worksheets

Lawsuit Risk Factor Analysis

Professional Lawsuit Risks

1. **By Patients**

    ___ Medical malpractice lawsuit because of your behavior
    ___ Medical malpractice lawsuit because of the behavior of a partner
    ___ Medical malpractice lawsuit because of the behavior of an employee
    ___ Medical malpractice lawsuit because of the behavior of another doctor in the office space who appears to the patient to be a partner of yours
    ___ Sexual Harassment lawsuit by patient because of your behavior
    ___ Sexual Harassment lawsuit by patient because of the behavior of a partner
    ___ Sexual Harassment lawsuit by patient because of the behavior of an employee
    ___ Sexual Harassment lawsuit by patient because of the behavior of another doctor in the office space who appears to the patient to be a partner of yours
    ___ Negligence lawsuit by patient for injury occurring on office premises

2. **By Employees**

    ___ Age, race or other discrimination lawsuit by employee because of your behavior
    ___ Age, race or other discrimination lawsuit by employee because of the behavior of a partner
    ___ Age, race or other discrimination lawsuit by employee because of the behavior of an employee
    ___ Sexual Harassment lawsuit by employee because of your behavior
    ___ Sexual Harassment lawsuit by employee because of the behavior of a partner
    ___ Sexual Harassment lawsuit by employee because of the behavior of an employee
    ___ Negligence lawsuit by employee against you as trustee of pension fund
    ___ Negligence lawsuit by employee for injury occurring on office premises

Appendices

Financial Assessment Worksheets

Lawsuit Risk Factor Analysis

Professional Lawsuit Risks (continued)

3. **By Third Parties**

   ___ Negligence lawsuit by third party for injury occurring on office premises
   ___ Negligence lawsuit by third party because of your behavior (i.e., car accident)
   ___ Negligence lawsuit by third party because of the behavior of a partner
   ___ Negligence lawsuit by third party because of the behavior of an employee
   ___ Breach of contract lawsuit by third party because of your behavior
   ___ Breach of contract lawsuit by third party because of the conduct of the business/practice
   ___ Breach of contract lawsuit by third party because of the conduct of an employee
   ___ Breach of contract lawsuit by third party because of the conduct of a partner
   ___ Overdue debt of the business/practice
   ___ Overdue tax bill of the business/practice

TIP: You can effectively protect yourself against many of the above lawsuit risks by using professional corporations or associations. These will (1) shield your savings from lawsuits arising out of the conduct of partners or employees and (2) protect your personal wealth from the business-type lawsuits emerging from your practice.

The Doctor's Wealth Protection Guide

Financial Assessment Worksheets

Lawsuit Risk Factor Analysis

Lawsuit Risks Against Any Non-Medical Business

1. **By Customers**

   ___ Negligence lawsuit by customer for injury occurring on office premises
   ___ Breach of contract lawsuit by customer because of your behavior
   ___ Breach of contract lawsuit by customer because of the conduct of the business
   ___ Breach of contract lawsuit by customer because of the conduct of an employee
   ___ Breach of contract lawsuit by customer because of the conduct of a partner
   ___ Product liability action against business

2. **By Employees**

   ___ Age, race or other discrimination lawsuit by employee because of your behavior
   ___ Age, race or other discrimination lawsuit by employee because of the behavior of a partner
   ___ Age, race or other discrimination lawsuit by employee because of the behavior of an employee
   ___ Sexual Harassment lawsuit by employee because of your behavior
   ___ Sexual Harassment lawsuit by employee because of the behavior of a partner
   ___ Sexual Harassment lawsuit by employee because of the behavior of an employee
   ___ Wrongful termination lawsuit by employee because of your behavior
   ___ Wrongful termination lawsuit by employee because of the behavior of a partner
   ___ Wrongful termination lawsuit by employee because of the behavior of an employee
   ___ Negligence lawsuit by employee for injury occurring on office premises

Appendices

Financial Assessment Worksheets

Lawsuit Risk Factor Analysis

Lawsuit Risks Against Any Non-Medical Business (continued)

3. By Third Parties

___ Negligence lawsuit by third party for injury occurring on office premises
___ Negligence lawsuit by third party because of your behavior (i.e., car accident)
___ Negligence lawsuit by third party because of the behavior of a partner
___ Negligence lawsuit by third party because of the behavior of an employee
___ Overdue debt of the business
___ Products liability action against the business
___ Overdue tax bill of the business/practice

TIP: Family Limited Partnerships and Limited Liability Companies are the asset-protecting, tax saving entities of choice when dealing with the threats listed above. They are the best entities for protecting your savings when operating a non-professional business. They are also ideal vehicles for saving taxes.

The Doctor's Wealth Protection Guide

Financial Assessment Worksheets

<u>Lawsuit Risk Factor Analysis</u>

<u>Personal Lawsuit Risks</u>

1. **Because of Your Home**

    ___ Negligence lawsuit by guest for injury occurring at your home
    ___ Negligence lawsuit by guest of your children for injury occurring at your home
    ___ Negligence lawsuit by neighbor for injury occurring at your home
    ___ Breach of contract lawsuit because home sold with defects

2. **Because of Rental Property**

    ___ Negligence lawsuit by tenant for injury occurring at rental property
    ___ Negligence lawsuit by tenant's guest for injury occurring at rental property
    ___ Negligence lawsuit by guest of your children for injury occurring at rental property
    ___ Negligence lawsuit by neighbor for injury occurring at rental property
    ___ Breach of contract lawsuit because lease provisions violated

3. **Because of Cars, Boats, etc.**

    ___ Negligence lawsuit because of your use of a boat, car, plane, offroad vehicle, etc.
    ___ Negligence lawsuit against you as owner of a boat, car, plane, offroad vehicle, etc., whether or not your use caused injury

4. **Because of Overdue Debts**

    ___ Breach of contract lawsuit because of overdue personal debts
    ___ Breach of contract lawsuit because of overdue mortgage
    ___ Breach of contract lawsuit because of failed investments

TIP: Along with FLPs and LLCs, trusts and co-ownerships are most effective here. These will allow you to keep control of assets while sharing ownership of them with family members, so as to protect them from lawsuits and to save you taxes.

Financial Assessment Worksheets

Lawsuit Risk Factor Analysis

Other Personal Dangers

___ May disinherit loved ones because of hidden joint ownership
___ May have too large an estate tax bill because of poor estate planning
___ May lose privacy, time and probate fees due to lack of a living trust
___ May die with a will that has not been updated recently
___ Risks associated with an overdue tax bill
___ Risks associated with a costly divorce
___ Divorce of family members risks ownership of family assets
___ Loss of loved ones' savings to qualify for Medicaid

TIP: Living Trusts, Medicaid Trusts, and Pre-Marital Agreements are all appropriate asset protection devices to avoid the above risks.

The Doctor's Wealth Protection Guide

Financial Assessment Worksheets

Asset Checklist, Part I – "Safe" Assets[1]

ASSET	FAIR MARKET VALUE	EQUITY	OWNERSHIP FORM
Stocks			
Bonds			
Mutual Funds			
Life Insurance			
Artwork			
Jewelry			
Pension Funds			
IRAs or other retirement plan			
Certificates of Deposit (CDs)			
Savings Accounts			
Checking Accounts			
Safe Business Assets (inventory, accounts receivable, non-dangerous equipment)			
Other			
TOTAL		[2]	

[1] WARNING: The term "Safe Assets" is really a misnomer because these assets are vulnerable to any lawsuits against you if you own them in your name.

[2] Unless Otherwise shielded because of an ownership form, this equity value is at risk.

Appendices

Financial Assessment Worksheets

Asset Checklist, Part II – "Dangerous" Assets[3]

ASSET	FAIR MARKET VALUE	EQUITY	OWNERSHIP FORM
Home			
Other Real Estate			
Rental Property			
Cars			
Boats			
Other Vehicles			
Dangerous Business Property Owned in Your Name (cars, machinery, leases, real estate)			
Other			
TOTAL			

[3] These assets are dangerous and should be isolated from safe assets so that their potential liability problems do not endanger safe assets.

BIBLIOGRAPHY

Books

Brett K. Kates, *Keeping What's Yours: Proven Asset Protection Strategies for Everything from Handling Creditors to Becoming Legally Judgment-Proof* (Chicago: Enterprise Dearborn, 1994.

Mark Warda, *Simple Ways to Protect Yourself from Lawsuits* (Clearwater: Sphinx Publishing, 1996).

Robert J. Mintz and James J. Rubens, *Lawsuit Proof: Protecting Your Assets From Lawsuits and Claims* (San Juan Capistrano: LawTech Publishing, 1995).

Jay W. Mitton and Ginita Wall, *Cover Your Assets: Lawsuit Protection* (New York: Crown Trade Paperbacks, 1995).

Arnold S. Goldstein, *Asset Protection Secrets* (Deerfield Beach: Garrett Publishing, 1995).

Arnold S. Goldstein, *How To Settle With The IRS For Pennies On The Dollar* (Deerfield Beach: Garrett Publishing, 1994).

Peter Spero, *Asset Protection: Legal Planning and Strategies* (New York: Warren, Gorham & Lamont, 1994).

Walter Olson, *The Litigation Explosion* (New York: Truman Talley Books, 1991).

Andrew D. Westhem and Donald Jay Korn, *Protecting What's Yours: How to Safeguard Your Assets and Maintain Your Personal Wealth*, (New York: Birch Lane Press, 1995.

Papers Delivered at Meetings

Stanley W. Lamport, "Ethics and Attorney Liability Aspects of Asset Protection" (Presented at The Third Annual National Conference On Asset Protection Planning And Asset Protection Trusts, Newport Beach, Calif., June 1996).

Marc B. Hankin, "Asset Protection For The Elderly And Those Facing Institutionalization For Long Term" (Presented at The Third Annual National Conference On Asset Protection Planning And Asset Protection Trusts, Newport Beach, Calif., June 1996).

Darren Craig Stark, "Offshore Trusts From A Foreign Fiduciary's Perspective" (Presented at The Third Annual National Conference On Asset Protection Planning And Asset Protection Trusts, Newport Beach, Calif., June 1996).

Peter Spero, "Use Of Foreign Asset Protection Trusts" (Presented at The Third Annual National Conference On Asset Protection Planning And Asset Protection Trusts, Newport Beach, Calif., June 1996).

Peter Spero, "Choice Of Entities — Asset Protection — Tax and Legal Aspects of Limited Liability Companies, Limited Partnerships, and Corporations" (Presented at The Third Annual National Conference On Asset Protection Planning And Asset Protection Trusts, Newport Beach, Calif., June 1996).

Medical and General Periodicals

Marc Crane, "Could a malpractice suit wipe out your assets?," *Medical Economics* (July 6, 1992).

Robert D. Gillen, "Protecting Your Assets ... Before It's Too Late," *American Medical News* (June 10, 1996).

Kenneth Robbins, "Legal Liability Under Managed Care," Hawaii Medical Journal (April, 1995).

R. Stephen Trosty and Randy Hackney, "More or Less Liability For Physicians," Michigan Medicine (June, 1995).

Philip Hager, "Verdict Brings Donations to 'Hero' Cabbie," *Los Angeles Times* (February 17, 1992).

Mona Charen, "Abuses highlight need for reform," *The Detroit News* (January 19, 1995).

Steven Budiansky, Ted Gest, and David Fischer, "How lawyers abuse the law," *U.S. News and World Report* (January 30, 1995).

Christopher Cox, "Is public hostility to lawyers justified?," *Insight Magazine* (November 13, 1995).

Pamela Warrick, "The Convict Who Sued for a Cookie Qualified for this List," *The Sacramento Bee* (November 26, 1995).

Peter Garland, "Litigious world forces investors to rely on asset-protection trusts," *USA Today* (June 26, 1995).

Lynn Asinof, "Family Limited Partnerships Can Be Dysfunctional," *Wall Street Journal,* (April 26, 1996).

Kathy Kristof, "How to Protect Your Assets and Sleep at Night," *Los Angeles Times* (June 20, 1993).

Kathy Kristof, "Protecting Assets is Not Only for the Wealthy," *Los Angeles Times* (June 6, 1993).

David Burros, "Keeping Your Assets from Tempting Plaintiff's Attorneys," *American Medical News* (April 22, 1996).

Donald Jay Korn, "Out of Harm's Way," *Worth,* (April/May 1992).

Ronald Rudman, "Here's how to protect your assets before going to court," *Chicago Medicine* (August 7, 1991).

Geanne Rosenberg, "Your Survivor's Guide To Litigious Living: 7 Ways You Can Protect Your Assets Against Lawsuits," *Investor's Business Daily* (July, 24, 1995).

David Rees, "Put your trust in foreign havens to protect you wealth from suits," *Los Angeles Business Journal* (July 27, 1992).

Bibliography

William Barrett, "Ozzie and Harriet, L.P.," *Forbes* (June 21, 1993).

Graham Button, "Pulling up the drawbridge," Forbes (April, 27, 1992).

Margie Williams, "Violence and Sexual Harassment," *American Association of Hospital Nurses Journal* (February, 1996).

Ronald Rudman, "Painless Protection," *Financial Planning* (October 1989).

Roderick Smith, "Offshore Trusts: Testing times for wealth protectors," *The International* (December, 1990).

Gene Epstein, "An offshore trust can be the ultimate insurance policy for your assets," *Barron's* (August 7, 1995).

Carolyn Geer, "Prenuptial for business partners," *Forbes* (December 5, 1994).

Dale Buss, "Tax-Wise Ways to Pass Along a Family Business," *Business94* (August/September).

Anita Sharpe, "Prenuptial pacts shield businesses from an heir's ex," *Wall Street Journal*, (June 19, 1996).

Diane Glassman, "How to Protect Your Assets in a Divorce," *Success in Sight* (October, 1993).

Don Battle, "Avoid tax on retirement benefits for your ex-spouse with a QDRO," *Tax Reduction Reporter* (January 30, 1995).

Sue Shellenbarger, "With Elder Care Comes a Professional and Personal Crisis," *Wall Street Journal* (November 9, 1994).

Earl Gottschalk, "Taking Financial Steps for Terminally Ill," *Wall Street Journal* (June, 30, 1992).

David Karp, "How Can Physicians Reduce Their Malpractice Risks?," *Hospital Physician* (April, 1994).

Legal Periodicals

Howard Young, "Asset Protection Planning With The Use of Foreign Situs Trusts," *Michigan Bar Journal* (May, 1994).

Barry S. Engel, "Using Foreign Trusts For Asset Protection Planning," *Estate Planning* (July/August, 1993).

Stefan Tucker and Mary Ann Mancini, "Family Limited Partnerships and Asset Protection," *Journal of Real Estate Taxation* (Spring, 1996).

Jerome Friedlander, "A Limited Liability Company Checklist," *Federal Lawyer*, (March/April, 1995).

Richard Reuben, "Added Protection: Law Firms are Discovering that Limited Liability Business Structures can Shield them from Devastating Malpractice Awards and Double Taxation," *ABA Journal* (September, 1994).

Jonathan Macey, "The Limited Liability Company: Lessons for Corporate Law," *Washington University Law Quarterly* (Summer 1995).

Gideon Rothschild, "Establishing and Drafting Offshore Asset Protection Trusts," *Estate Planning* (February, 1996).

Larry Gibbs, "Asset and Tax Protection: The Foreign Trust As A Solution," *Trusts and Estates* (February, 1993).

Peter Spero, "How To Arrange A Client's Property for Asset Protection," *Estate Planning* (July/August, 1995).

Gail Gouskos, "Providing Peace of Mind For the Elderly Patient," *Trusts and Estates* (December, 1989).

Elizabeth McCroskey and Michael Gilfix, "Housing Options for the Elderly: Tax, Care, and other Issues," *Trusts and Estates* (July, 1992).

Gideon Rothschild, "Asset Preservation: Legal and Ethical Strategies," *New York Law Journal* (March 11, 1994).

James Fife and Verne Hosta, "The Family Limited Partnership," *Journal of Asset Protection* (November/December, 1995).

Peter Spero, "Fortifying Foreign Asset Protection Trusts," *Jounal of Asset Protection*, (November/December, 1995).

Government Reports

1. State Court Caseload Statistics, 1994, *State Justice Institute*, 1994.

2. Report of the Council on Competitiveness, delivered by Vice-President Dan Quayle (1988).

Non-Government Reports

1. *FACT BOOK: 1995 Property/Casualty Insurance Facts*, Insurance Information Institute, 1995.

2. *Asset Protection Strategies: How to plan for and survive the financial devastation of long-term nursing home care* (Alexandria: National Institute of Business Management, 1996.)

Legal Treatises

Witkin, *Summary of California Law*, Community Property, Sections 151 et. seq.
Witkin, *Summary of California Law*, Wills and Probate, Sections 130 et. seq.

Bibliography

Restatement (Third) Foreign Relations, Section 403
Restatement (Second) Conflict of Laws, Section 269-273

Statutes
1. New York statutes on prejudgment remedies: NY C.P.L.R. Sections 6201 et. seq.

2. Fraudulent Transfer Laws:
    a. The Uniform Fraudulent Conveyance Act (UFCA)
    b. The Uniform Fraudulent Transfer Act (UFTA)
    c. Federal Bankruptcy Code at Sections 540-548

3. Exemptions:
a. Federal Bankruptcy: 11 U.S.C. Section 522(d).
b. Federal Non-Bankruptcy:

50 U.S.C. Section 403	5 U.S.C. Section 8346	22 U.S.C. Section 4060
10 U.S.C. Section 1440	45 U.S.C. Section 231	42 U.S.C. Section 407
38 U.S.C. Section 3101	10 U.S.C. Section 1450	28 U.S.C. Section 376
33 U.S.C. Section 775	5 U.S.C. Section 8130	33 U.S.C. Section 916
42 U.S.C. Section 1717	10 U.S.C. Section 1035	15 U.S.C. Section 1673
25 U.S.C. Section 543	25 U.S.C. Section 545	38 U.S.C. Section 770
45 U.S.C. Section 352	46 U.S.C. Section 11110	46 U.S.C. Section 11111

b. State: See individual state exemption reports.

4. Limited Partnerships
    a. Uniform Limited Partnership Act (ULPA)
    b. Revised Uniform Limited Partnership Act (RULPA)
    c. I.R.C. sections 704, 731, 752

5. Corporations
    a. I.R.C. Sections 1361 et seq.

6. Foreign Asset Protection Trusts
    a. I.R.C. sections 706, 708, 2701

Cases

a. Fraudulent Transfers
    1. 66 A.D.2d 208
    2. 465 PA 558
    3. 549 A2d 151

b. Exemptions
    1. 112 S.Ct. 2242

GLOSSARY OF TERMS AND DEFINITIONS

Award:
The amount of money the plaintiff is entitled to take from the defendant as a result of the outcome of the lawsuit. Also called money damages, judgment, or recovery.

Burden of Proof:
Duty of a party to prove an allegation or issue in a case to avoid the issue being dismissed early, or to convince the trier of fact as to the truth of the claim.

Civil Lawsuit:
A lawsuit between two private parties, usually for money.

Commercially Reasonable Means:
What a reasonable person would use when trying to advertise, show, and sell an item.

Consideration:
Something of value given in return for a performance or a promise of performance by another, for the purpose of forming a contract.

Contingency fee:
Arrangement for paying a lawyer, only for plaintiffs. The lawyer gets a percentage of the recovery, if the lawsuit is successful. Usually, the fee is 30% of the recovery.

Creditor:
Someone who is owed money. The debt may be based on an agreement to pay or on a court order to pay.

Defendant:
The party who is being sued. The same term, defendant, is used for civil and criminal cases.

Estate Planning:
Planning for how your wealth will be distributed after your death.

Equity:
The current market value of any asset less any loan or mortgage; the cash value of an asset.

Exempt Assets:
Assets that are released from an obligation or duty to which others are subject.

Fair Market Value:
The price an item would sell for when a reasonable buyer and a reasonable seller are not pressed for time and can complete a series of negotiations.

Jurisdiction:
The power of a court to issue binding orders and judgments.

Net Estate:
The items you own at death, which are subject to the death tax, officially called the estate tax. Your net estate will consist of the following items, if any, owned by you at death; personal property, bank accounts, real estate, investment assets, IRA and other retirement benefits, and life insurance proceeds for which you have the incidents of ownership.

Non-Exempt Assets:
Assets that are released from an obligation or duty (tax) to which other assets are subject.

Plaintiff:
The party suing in the civil lawsuit, usually for money.

Probate:
The process by which the courts distribute property according to a will. This can take up to two years and cost tens of thousands of dollars.

Presumption:
A legal term relating to which side in the lawsuit has the burden of proof. Usually, a plaintiff has the burden of proof for the case she is bringing by the preponderance of the evidence; the legal standard in most civil cases. A presumption may shift the burden of proof, forcing the defendant, rather than the plaintiff, to prove a particular fact did or did not exist.

Punitive Damages:
Damages that are designed to punish the defendant. They are usually awarded when the defendant has acted maliciously or fraudulently. The award is also given to the plaintiff, along with compensatory damages which compensate the plaintiff for injuries.

Security Agreement:
A financing arrangement where the creditor has an interest in an asset owned by the debtor. This asset, called the collateral, backs up the debt. That is, if the debtor defaults on the debt, the creditor can take the collateral. Creditors who have security agreements are called secured creditors. Those who do not have such agreements are called unsecured creditors.

Statute:
A law enacted by the legislature. As opposed to law which is created by the courts when they decide cases, which is called case law.

INDEX

Accountants, 5
Age discrimination lawsuits, 174
Agreements,
    post-marital, 210-211
    pre-marital, 208-210
Annuities,
    exemption of, 57
Anti-alienation clauses,
    in irrevocable trusts, 139
    in Foreign asset protection trusts, 155
Antigua, 164
Architects, 5
Aruba, 164
Asset protection planning, 27-39
Attorneys,
    as lawsuit targets, 5
    hidden danger of bankruptcy attorneys, 229-230
    increased numbers of, 2
Attorney's Fees,
    billing practices, 20-21
    saving on fees during a divorce, 216-217
Bahamas, 164-165
Bank accounts,
    joint ownership of, 67
    vulnerability to IRS, 198
Bankruptcy, 219-229
Barbados, 164
Belize, 164
Bermuda, 164
Board members, *see* Directors and Officers
British Virgin Islands, 164
Businesses,
    assets of, 175-180
    best ways to structure, 173-191
    family, *see* Family-Owned Businesses
    finding cash for, 185-186
    forms of ownership, 173-175
    shielding with mortgages, 184

Caicos, 164
Cash value life insurance,
    protection of, 57
Cayman Islands, 164-165
"C" corporations, *see* Corporations
Chapter 7 bankruptcy, *see* Liquidating bankruptcy

Chapter 11 bankruptcy, *see* Reorganizations
Chapter 13 bankruptcy, *see* Reorganizations
Charging order,
    and family limited partnerships, 101-103
    and limited liability companies, 119-121
Charitable remainder trusts, 145
Children's trusts, 151
Closely-held insurance companies (CICs),
Cohabitation, 217
Contempt of court,
    impossibility defense, 155-156
Cook Islands, 164-165
Co-ownerships, *see* Joint Tenancy, Tenancy in Common or Tenancy By The Entirety
Costa Rica, 164
Credit,
    protecting during a divorce, 214-215
Cyprus, 164

Debts,
    dischargeable in bankruptcy, 225
    non-dischargeable, 225
Directors and Officers,
    actions they must take, A-15
    behaviors to avoid, A-15
Discretionary clause, 161
Divorce,
    generally, 205-219
    in community property states, 206-207
    in equitable distribution states, 206-207

ERISA, 58
Estate taxes,
    using family limited partnerships to save, 110-111
    using limited liability companies to save, 125-128

Family limited partnerships,
    in general, 93-110
    asset protection benefits, 93-108
Family-owned businesses,
    greatest threats to, 187-188
Foreign asset protection trusts, 149-166
Fraudulent conveyances, *see* Fraudulent transfers
Fraudulent transfers, 39-49

General partnerships,
    in general, 94
    liability of partners, 96-97
Gibraltar, 164
Grenada, 164
Guernsey, 164

Homestead laws,
    in general, 52-53
    using laws for maximum protection, 55

Insured mutual fund managed plans (IMFMPs), 257-259
Income tax,
    saving with family limited partnerships, 112-114
Incorporation, *see* Corporations
Inflation, 271
Insurance company ownership,
    closely held companies (CICs), 170-171, 261-270
    tax and asset protection benefits of, 263-268
Insurance trusts, *see* Irrevocable insurance trusts
IRS,
    in general, 191-203
    assets it cannot take, 193
    offers in compromise, 196
    rights to lien, levy and seize, 192-193
    shielding property from, 198
Irrevocable trusts,
    in general, 137-139
    important clauses, 140-141
Irrevocable Life Insurance trusts, 141-143
Isle of Man, 164

Joint ownership,
    in general, 63-69
    avoiding probate with, 71-74
    compared to living trust, 74-75
    creditor risks of, 67-69
Joint tenancy, *see* Joint ownership

Keogh plans, 58

Labuan, 164
Landlords and liability, A-1
Lawsuits,
    odds of being sued, 2
    the lawsuit process, 15-25
Lawyers *see* Attorneys
Leases,
    use of to protect business assets, 184
Liechtenstein, 164
Lenders,
    using friendly lenders, 184
Life insurance, *see* Insurance
Life insurance trust, *see* Irrevocable life insurance trust
Limited liability companies,
    in general, 115-132
    Nevis LLC, 168-170
Limited partnerships, *see* Family limited partnerships
Living trusts,
    avoiding probate, A-11
    compared to joint tenancy, 71
    other benefits, A-11
Loving trusts, *see* Living trusts
Luxembourg, 164

Madeira, 164
Malpractice insurance,
    failures in protecting against lawsuits, 8-10
Malta, 164
Marriage, *see* Pre-marital agreements, Divorce
Mauritius, 164
Medicaid,
    in general, 233-245
    countable assets, 250-253
Medical practice,
    asset not to own, 185
    best ways to run, 179-183
    legal forms to avoid, 174
Minor's trust, *see* Irrevocable trusts, Children's trust
Monaco, 164
Montserrat, 164
Mortgages,
    use of friendly mortgages, 184
    debt shields vs. the IRS, 199

Nauru, 164
Nevada,
    incorporating in, 90-91
Niue, 164
Netherland Antilles, 164
Nevis,
    in general 164-165,
    LLCs 168-170
Nursing home care, *see* Medicaid

Offshore banking, *see* Foreign asset protection trusts,
Offshore financial centers, 164
Offshore trusts, *see* Foreign asset protection trusts,
Officers, *see* Directors and officers

Panama, 164
Partnerships, *see* Limited partnerships and General partnerships
Paychecks, *see* Wages
Pensions, *see also* ERISA, Keogh, and Individual retirement accounts (IRAs)
    protection of, 58-59
Post-marital agreements, 221
Pour-over wills, *see* Wills
Practice, *see* Medical practice
Pre-marital agreements, 208-210
Probate,
    avoiding through joint ownership, 69-70
    avoiding through living trusts, 70
    process explained, 70
Professional corporations, 86-87
Property, *see also* Real property
    types of ownership, 63-65

Qualified Domestic Relations Order (QDRO), 215

Real estate,
    business/practice ownership of, 180-181
    and limited liability companies, 121
Real estate developers, as lawsuit targets, 5
Rental property owners, as lawsuit targets, 5
Revocable trusts, *see also* Living trusts

"S" corporations, 87
Self-defense, asset protection as form of, 30
Small business owners, as lawsuit targets, 5, 7, 174
Seychelles, 164
Sexual harassment lawsuits, 7, 175
Sole proprietorships, 174
Spendthrift clauses,
    domestic trusts, 138
Spouses, *see* Post marital agreements and Divorce
Switzerland, 164

Taxes, *see also* Income taxes, Estate taxes, IRS
Tenancy by the entirety,
    in general, 65
    availability in states, 65
    creditor protection of, 71-72
Tenancy in common,
    in general, 65
    dangers of, 65
Trusts, *see also* Irrevocable trusts, Revocable trusts, Foreign asset protection trusts, Living trusts
    in general, 134-147
Turks, 174

Uniform fraudulent conveyance act (UFCA), 40
Uniform fraudulent transfer act (UFTA), 40
Uniform limited partnership act (ULPA), 99

Vanuatu, 164
VEBAs, 281-282
Virgin Islands, *see* British Virgin Islands

Wages,
    state protection of, 56
    federal protection of, 56
Wills,
    pour-over will and living trust, A-11
Wrongful termination lawsuits, 174

Are You Interested in Having a Great Speaker Address Your Hospital or Medical Society?

Guardian's authors spend a great deal of their time addressing physician groups across the country on a variety of risk management and asset protection topics. If you book one of our speakers, we can make the CME books available to the attendees either at a discount or for free! The seminar topics include:

- Risks in the New Healthcare Delivery System
- Protecting Your Practice, Property and Savings from Lawsuits and Other Creditors
- Protecting Your Investments from Inflation, Bad Investments, and Stock Market Crashes
- How to Protect Yourself with Offshore Asset Protection
- Using Captive Insurance Companies for Risk Management and Tax Reduction

These speakers have appeared on numerous television and radio programs including NBC's Today Show and CNBC. They have also addressed conferences of the International College of Surgeons (ICS), the Society of Gynecologic Oncologists, the American Association of Physicians of Indian Origin (AAPI), and the UCLA Medical Center, to name a few.

These authors are often compensated by pharmaceutical firms, so they may be available to your organization at no cost to you or your society!

Call us to receive more information on Guardian's speakers and their availability.

1-800-554-7233

GUARDIAN PUBLISHING

Phone Orders
Call 1-800-554-7233
Fax 24 hours: 1-888-317-9896

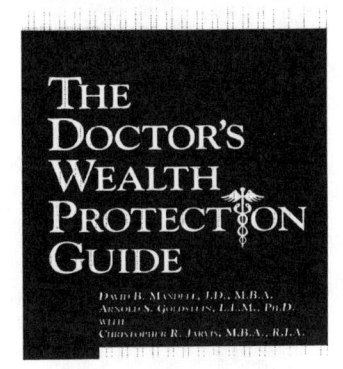

The Doctor's Wealth Protection Guide

...shows doctors how to protectect their practice, property and savings from lawsuits, taxes, bad investments, inflation, bankruptcy, divorce, and other creditor threats. Endorsed by the medical associations of Florida, Texas, Fairfield County (CT). This is a complete guide to domestic and offshore asset protection tools, tax saving vehicles, captive insurance companies, and little-known investment strategies from top money managers. Written by two leading asset protection and estate planning attorneys and a registered investment advisor, this is a must have for physicians concerned with building and protecting their practice and family wealth. $30.00

The Doctor's Wealth Protection Program

...is a three-part audio cassette program containing: **Offshore Solutions©** – a 90 minute lecture on domestic and international asset protection with Dr. Arnold S. Goldstein; **The Doctor's Asset Protection Forum©** – a 40 minute case study analysis on asset protection with attorney David B. Mandell, JD, MBA; **The Doctor's Financial Forum©** – a 40 minute Q&A session with investment expert Christopher R. Jarvis, MBA, RIA, where he offers financial solutions to typical physician tax, investment, benefit, and retirement problems. $20.00

Risk Management for the Practicing Physician
CME Monograph 5.5 Hours Category I Credit

...nationally accredited for 5.5 hours of Category I continuing medical education (CME) credits in risk management. Cowritten by a practicing physician and an attorney, this 75-page monograph includes chapters on: providing care in today's malpractice environment, liability and the doctor-patient relationship, managing diagnosis-related liability, minimizing risks of miscommunication, managing high risk communication areas, managing the dangers of drug therapy, nonmedical liability risks for the practicing physician, and liability in the new health care delivery system. $59.95

Send orders to:
Guardian Publishing LLC
269 S. Beverly Drive Suite 810
Beverly Hils, CA 90212

Qty	Title	Price	Total
	Doctor's Wealth Protection Guide	$30.00	
	Doctor's Wealth Protection Program Audio	$20.00	
	Risk Management CME Monograph	$59.95	

Name: _____
Address: _____
City: _____ St: _____ Zip: _____
Phone: ( ) _____
Payment Method: ___ Check to Guardian Publishing
___ MC ___ Visa ___ AMEX ___ Discover

Card No.: _____ Exp. Date ___/___
Signature: _____

Subtotal	
CA residents add 8.25% sales tax	
S&H: $5 per piece	
TOTAL	

JARVIS & MANDELL LLC
INTEGRATED PLANNING SOLUTIONS

Are You Ready to Build & Protect Your Practice & Family Wealth?

We provide integrated planning solutions for our clients.
We will create a customized plan for you that may include:

Asset Protection
Risk Management
Estate Planning
Retirement Planning
Captive Insurance Companies
Offshore Asset Protection
Investment Planning
Tax Planning
Insurance
Annuities

For your free consultation, please contact Guardian Publishing and one of our representatives will arrange your FREE 20-minute consult with the author of your choice.

1-888-317-9895

Call and Receive a FREE 20-Minute Consultation with the Authors!